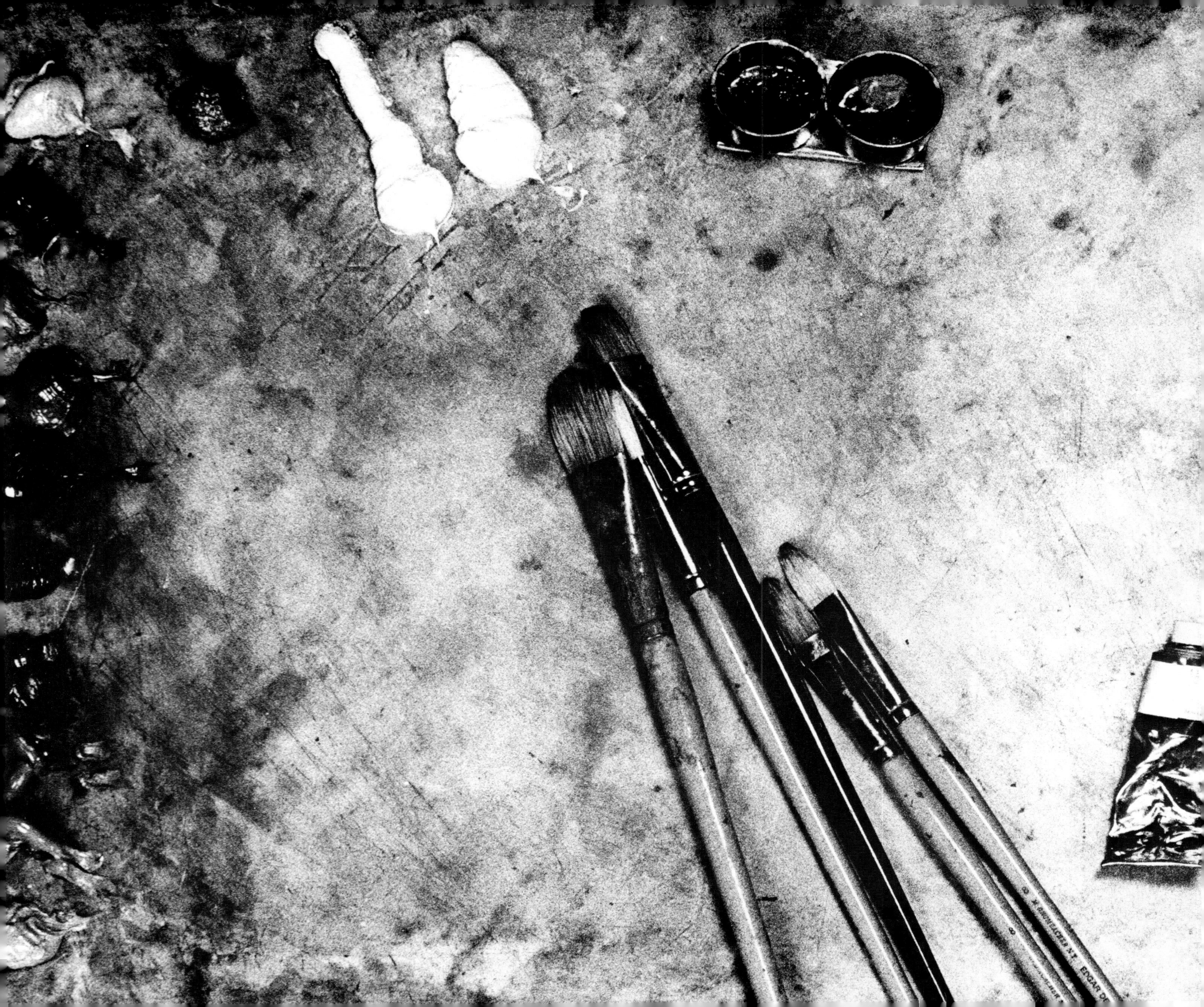

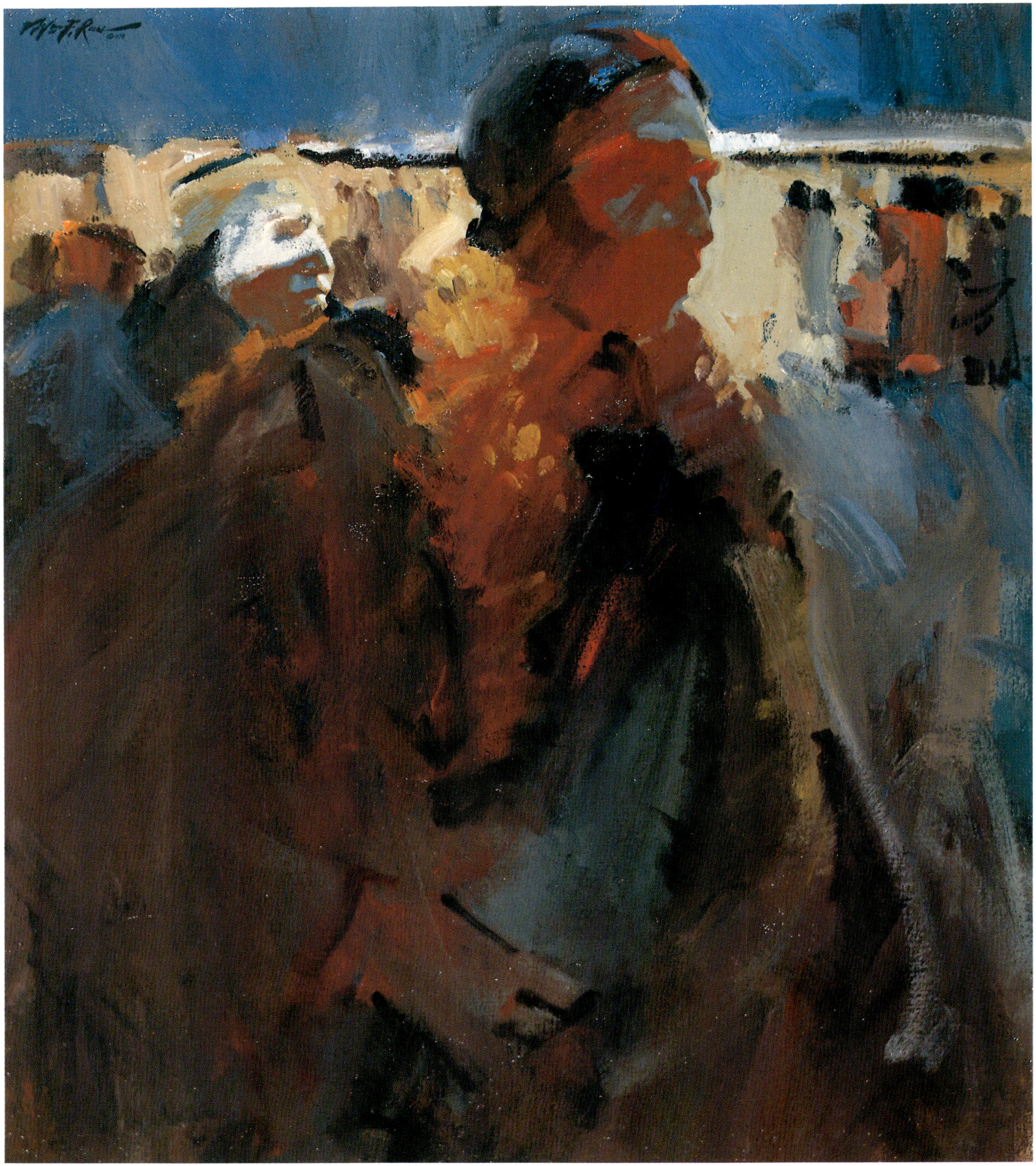

*Echoes Answer Drums*
Oil, 36x30″
Collection of Seattle University and Gene E. Lynn Family

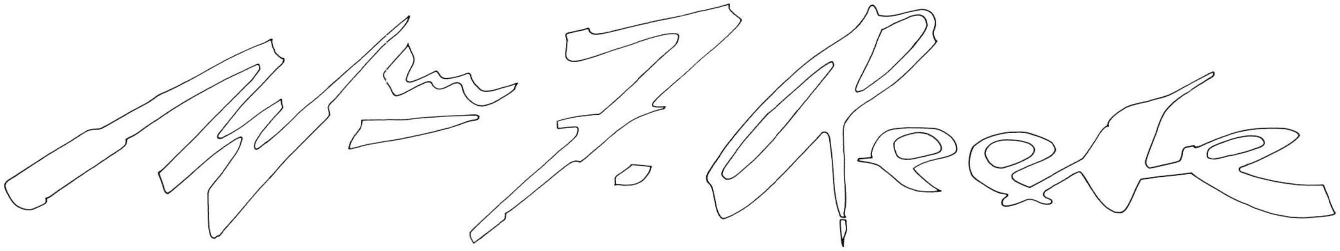

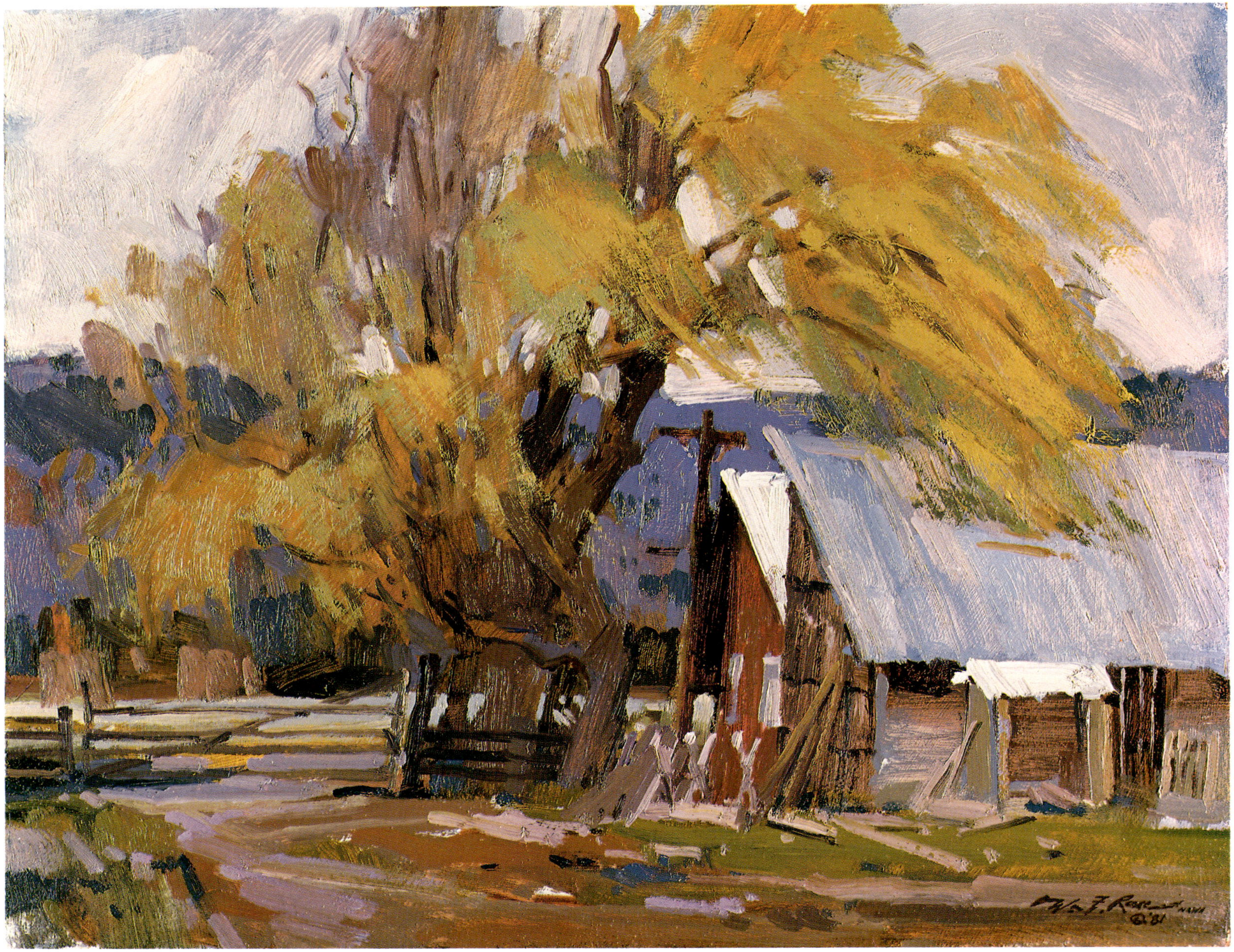

*Winds of March*
Oil, 16x20″
Collection of the
Charles and Emma Frye Art Museum
Seattle, Washington

# Wm. F. Reese

by Mary N. Balcomb

*Foreword by Wilson Hurley*
*Introduction by Mrs. Walser Greathouse*

BLUE RAVEN PUBLISHING

WILLIAM F. REESE
First Edition



First published in 1984 in the United States by the
Blue Raven Publishing, P.O. Box 5641,
Bellevue, Washington 98006

Library of Congress Cataloging in Publication Data
Balcomb, Mary N.
Wm. F. Reese.

Bibliography: p.
Includes index.
1. Reese, William F., 1938-
2. Artists — United States — Biography.
I. Reese, William F., 1938-
II. Title.
N6537.R34B35 1984 759.13 [B] 83-72443
ISBN 0-916029-00-X
ISBN 0-916029-01-8 (lim. ed.)



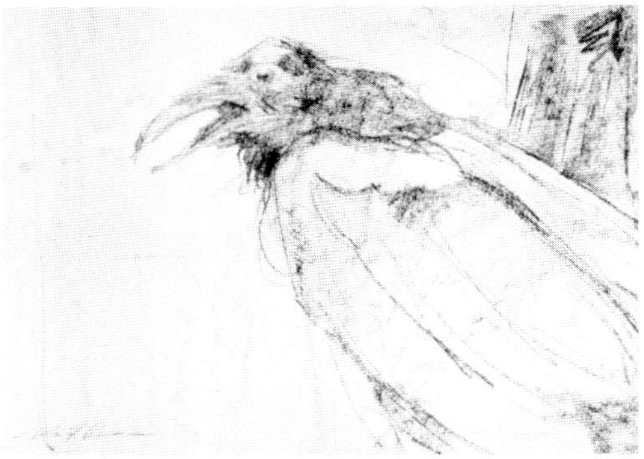

*To Fran,*

*For her empathy toward human nature and for her dedication to the arts.* — *MNB*

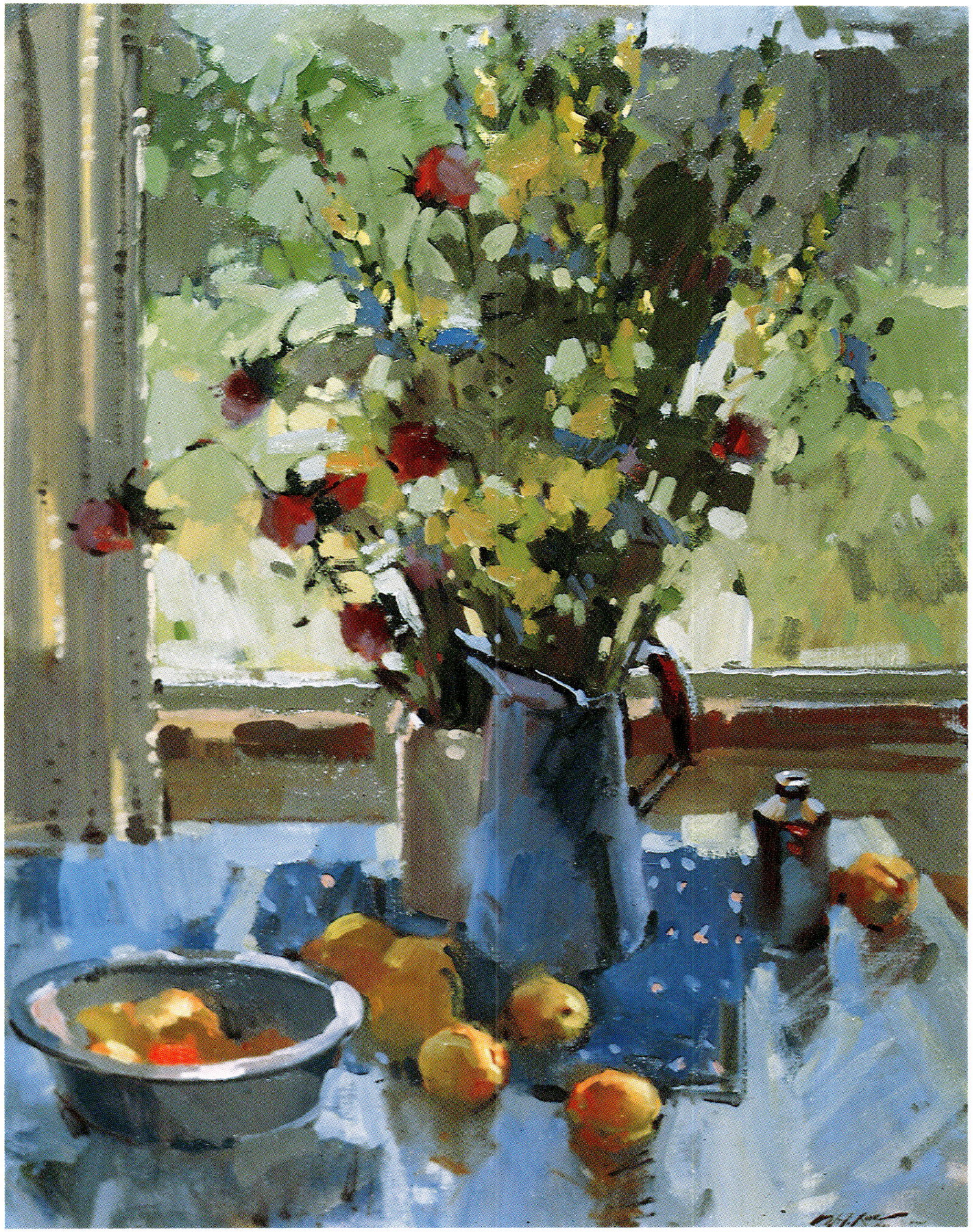

*Thistles and Wild Flowers*
Oil, 40x30″
Collection of
Safeco Insurance Co.

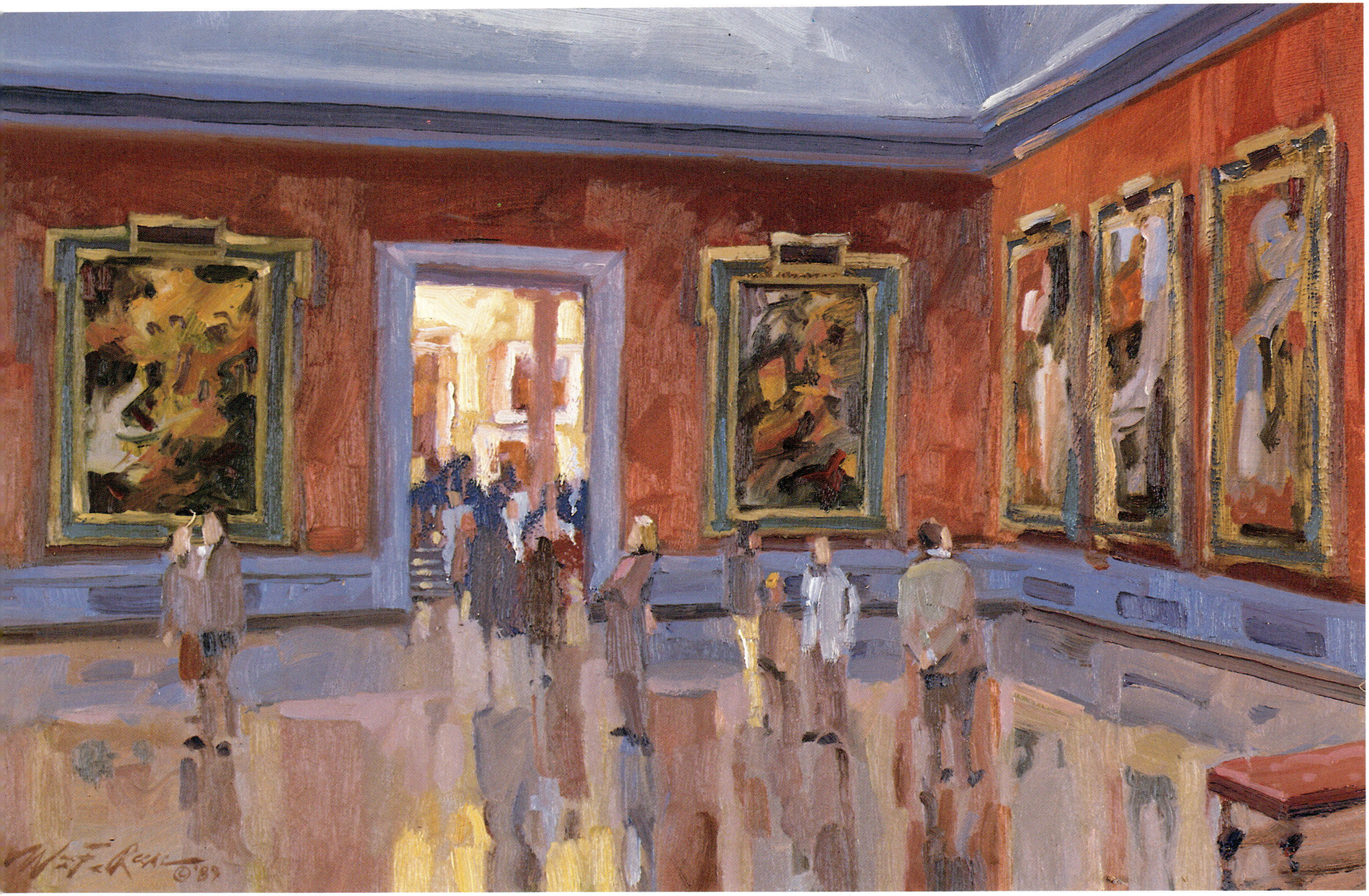

*Afternoon with Rubens*
Oil, 8x12″

*It is my philosophy that a work of art is nothing more or less than the sharing of a feeling or experience. This must be done on a very personal level to be fine art. I've found the greatest satisfaction, as far as my own work is concerned, in the reflection of my own surroundings and interests.*

*William F. Reese*

# CONTENTS

# PAINTINGS



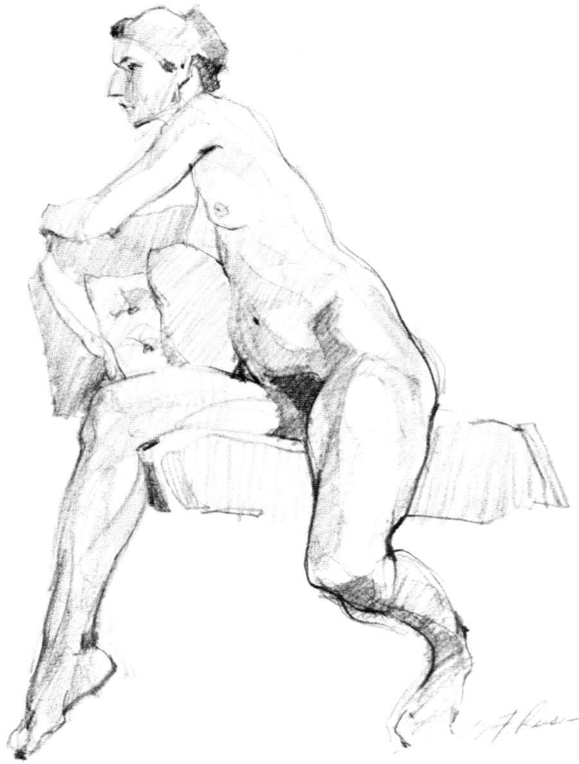

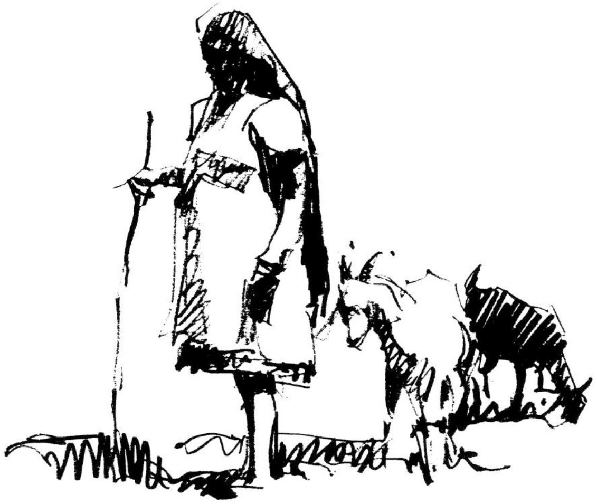



# FOREWORD

What is a painting?

It is certainly different from talking or writing. As you read these words your mind takes and stores each symbol, and as you complete sentences and paragraphs you can comprehend the whole idea and store the concept away. The same happens when we listen to music or go to the movies. In every instance we dedicate a certain amount of time to storing bits of information in succession toward the time when we can understand the whole.

It is astonishing to realize that paintings are not at all like that. The entire painting and its message come to us at once.

Forty percent of our central nervous system is involved in the processing of visual information. We are built to be able to look at something and size it up, comprehend it, in seconds. So when we come to consider painting as an art form we are exploring a system that is instantaneous, and a person who paints must be able to put down on canvas an image, an illusion, that will create this instant response from the viewer.

I doubt if anyone is able to catalogue what shapes, colors or relationships are necessary to evoke emotions when a picture is viewed. As nearly as I can tell, a painter has to carry those emotions in his heart when he starts his work or he will have no chance of communicating them in the painting. In addition to his feeling, he has to develop the technical ability to create his illusion for you.

A painting, to be fine art, must be successful in creating an illusion, but it also must give an emotional message. Your feelings, in the instant of seeing, must be different from those you had before you saw the painting.

A painting is a form of intellectual and emotional entertainment that can be received instantly and without effort. A good painting can be a joy and an enrichment to all who see it and can repeat its gift to each of us every time we care to look.

This is a heartwarming account of Bill Reese's life and his philosophy. We take it in a word, a sentence, and a paragraph at a time. To lead us into his life with words is also an art. But the real Bill Reese will show on the faces of his paintings, painted freshly, charged with enthusiasm, the emotion bursting through in his color, giving us a part of his experience in life. This is the basic purpose of fine art. By sharing these experiences with him we live not only our own lives but part of his, and that part of his that he has given us is beautiful.

— Wilson Hurley

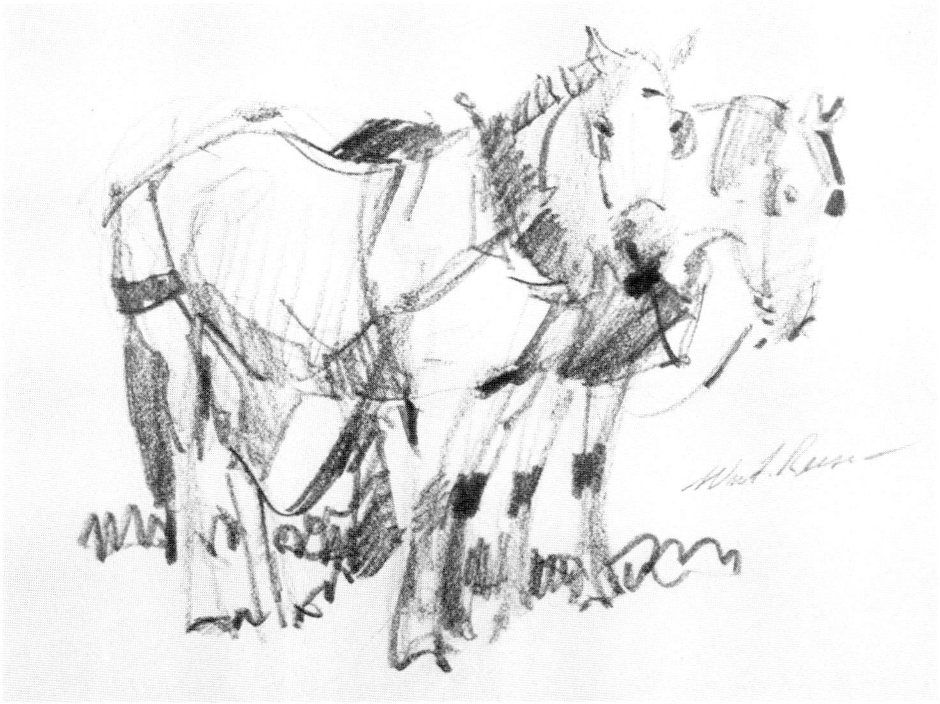

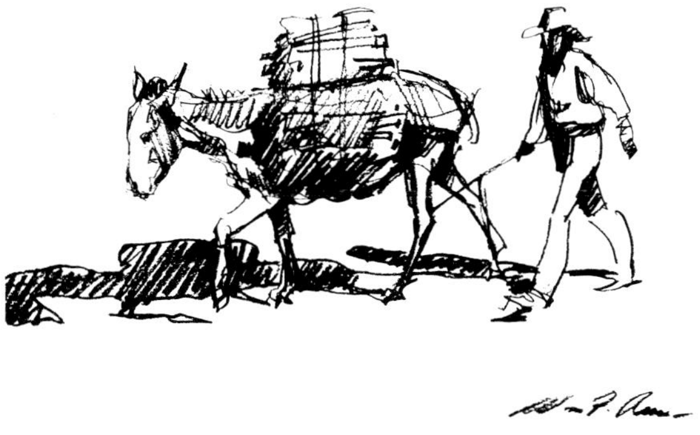

# PREFACE

*When I read about artists and their works I am not as a rule interested in what is said about their works, but I am keen to know of the personalities of the artists themselves. If I want to know about a picture I go to see it or I get a reproduction. I find it is usually not at all like the writer's description. Pictures explain themselves. They are their own best describers.*[1] — *Robert Henri*

These sentiments express my thoughts exactly. At the onset of the writing of this manuscript, I was more interested in presenting the "in-betweens," the life and philosophies that dealt with in-between the paintings and drawings, rather than in a text written exclusively about the works. However, at the beginning of our discussions and interviews, Bill was somewhat skeptical — "I don't know if anyone would find my life or what I have to say all that interesting."

In the decade of enjoying a quietly evolving friendship with him and his wife, Fran, of gaining a progressively stronger admiration for his work, and in observing his remarkable progress and their strong team effort, it became more and more obvious that their philosophies about living are also his philosophies about art. There is much others can learn.

Bill's attitude toward life — his friendships, his capacity for enjoyment, his habits — color his art. Conversations with him made me realize how inextricably his life and art are intertwined; the existence of one without the other would be unthinkable. Both are practiced with verve, enthusiasm, honesty, and dedication which overflow and fire the aspirations of others. Therefore, what he has to say, how he thinks, how he works, how he lives — what makes him tick — seemed of far greater importance than a mere word description of his paintings on my part.

It seemed important, too, to reveal some of the details, the good and the bad experiences, so that once again we are awakened to the fact that artists are human beings — not strange creatures with strange requirements, put on earth for the entertainment of humankind, but mortals of high intelligence; ones who perhaps march to a different drummer, yet have the same basic needs and desires of all others of their species. They also must cope with food costs, clothing, shelter, and survival; and in addition, they must maintain their sensitivities and acuities to be able to transform thoughts and ideas, to interpret the intangibles, into visual form. Often they must pursue their creative courses in the face of adversity, against derision or popular thought, in order to give us a new meaning or a new way of looking at things — to enable us to see things which we ordinarily take for granted or do not see at all.

*To paint is to love again, live again, see again. It's only when we look with eyes of love that we see as the painter sees. His is a love, moreover, which is free of possessiveness. What the painter sees he is duty bound to share. Usually he makes us see and feel what ordinarily we ignore or are immune to. His manner of approaching the world tells us in effect that nothing is vile or hideous, nothing is stale, flat, and unpalatable unless it be our own power of vision.*[2]

— *Henry Miller*

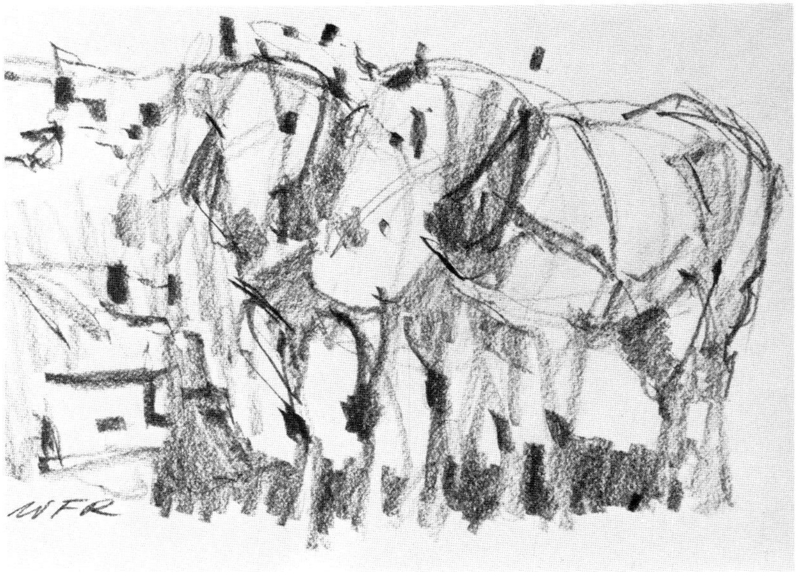

Acknowledgements:

Questionnaires sent to Reese's colleagues and former students, along with personal interviews, produced a rich lode of information, insights gleaned from several time spans and many perspectives. Those acquaintances and close friends alike, men and women, artists of national reputations, immediately spoke of his commitment to his work, his versatile talent, his integrity as a person, his strength of personality, and of the high standards he holds for himself and expects from other artists.

It was like Christmas to receive the replies and comments, "gifts" eagerly awaited and much appreciated, for I knew what some of their schedules were. Several artists even responded enroute to foreign countries, while others replied from their painting destinations away from their studios, and still others took the time to write in the midst of preparations for scheduled shows or other work commitments. I am deeply grateful to them. A special thanks should go to:

Tony Angell, Sergei Bongart, Harley Brown, Reynold Brown, Robert Cavanaugh, Harold Craig, Patricia Crain, Jo Anne Doyle, Mel Fillerup, Stan Galli, Del Gish, Kay Greathouse, Wilson Hurley, Chuck Lawton, Charlene and Brill Lee, Lois Lord, Gene Lynn, Brian and Gwen McKay, Alden Metcalf, Alfred and Elma Milotte, Fred Oldfield, Lloyd Powell, Joe Rhodes, Joanne Salkin, Wilfred Schoenberg, Conrad Schwiering, Catherine Shepard, Lowell Ellsworth Smith, Tucker Smith — and to Della Gregory for offering her class notes — to the Reese family for their cooperation, assistance, and good humor — and to Dennis Fahlen, Chris Spivey, Tom Gorton, Robert Balcomb, Doris Vinnedge, Margaret Reese and Joanne Metcalf for their valuable help.

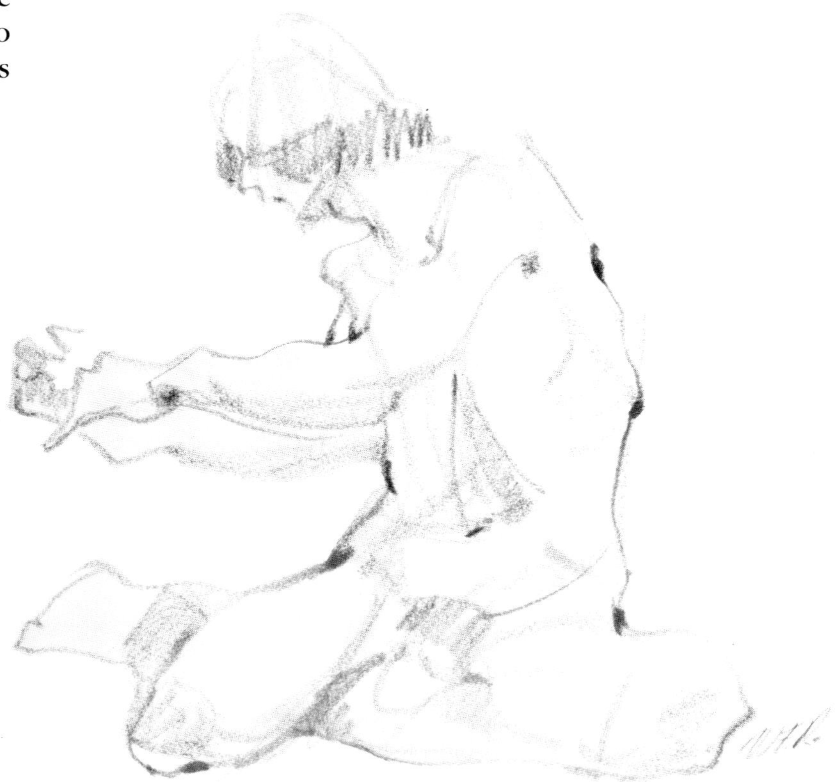

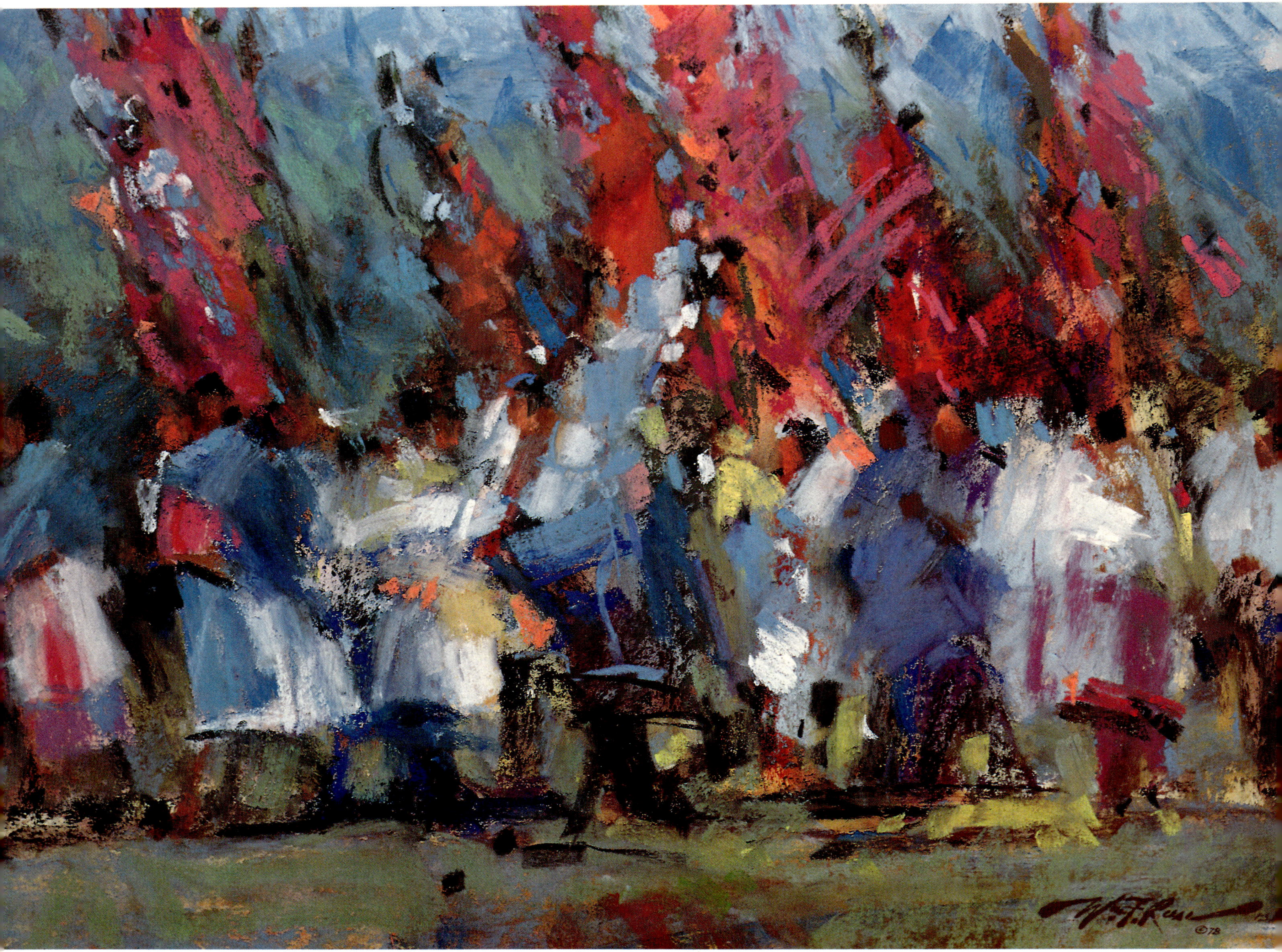

# INTRODUCTION

Good, strong color, excellent draftsmanship, uncluttered composition, and appealing subject matter — these are the qualities in a Reese painting.

I first became acquainted with Bill's work when we had the West Coast Oil Show here at the Frye in 1967. Subsequently, I went to an exhibition in Tacoma and saw a wonderful oil, the head of a man, "Taos Indian," and decided on the spot to buy it for the Frye Collection. That was the first Reese in our accession. Now we have six.

I admire the versatility and high quality of his work. I admire the man. His generosity to others, his perpetual study, and his dedication to art are an inspiration for all. He has enough confidence in himself to take risks and to challenge the unknowns, which coincides with my sense of gamble, with my philosophy: If you lose it, brush yourself off, get up, and try again.

Mrs. Walser Greathouse
Director
Frye Art Museum, Seattle

*Mexican Memories:*
*Mother's Day Procession*
Pastel, 14½x20½''
Collection of Karen A. Bender

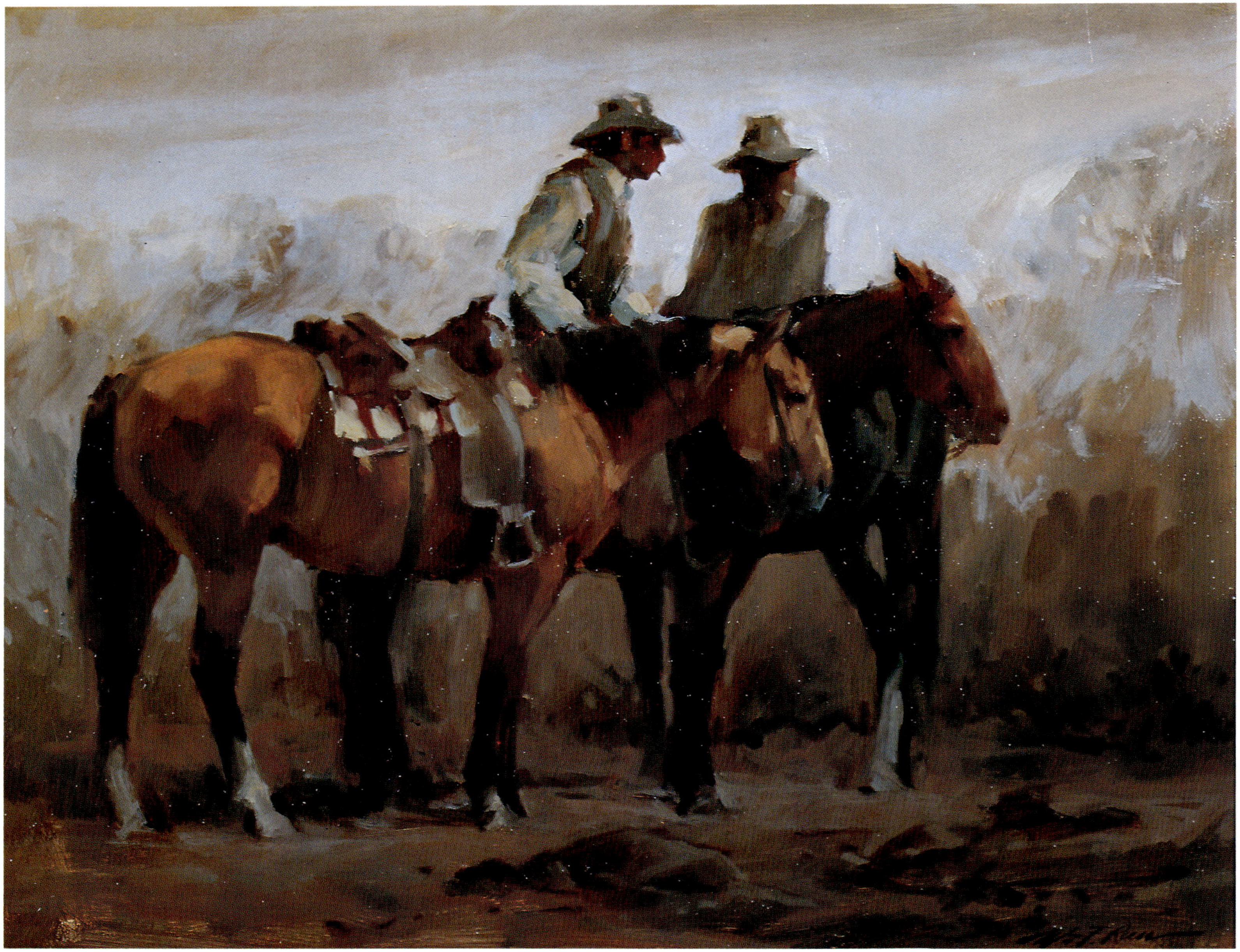

*Rest Stop*
Oil, 12x16''
Collection of
Robert M. Johnson, M.D.

# Art and Living

*"Beauty is no material thing. Beauty cannot be copied. Beauty is the sensation of pleasure on the mind of the seer."* — Robert Henri

*XXII*

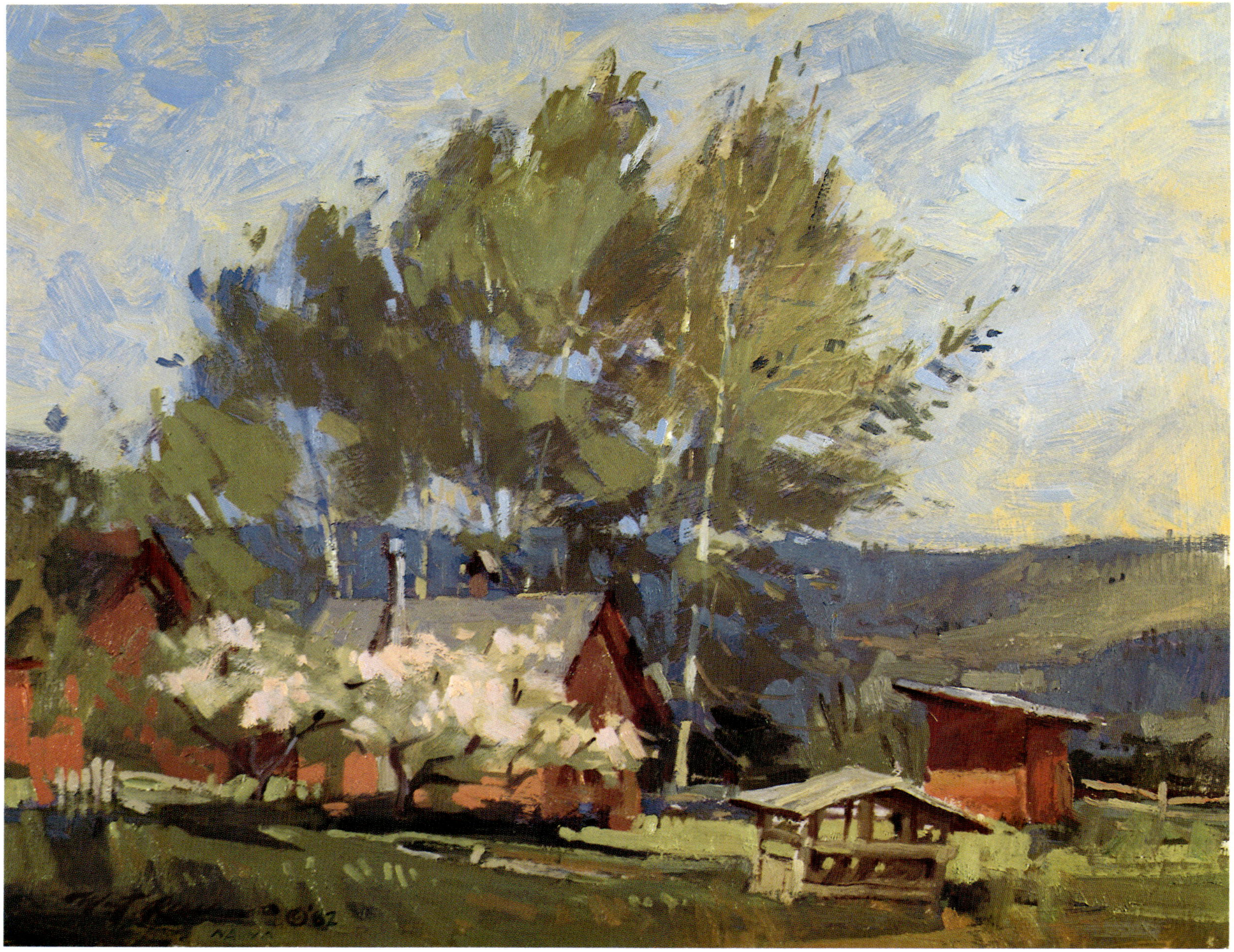

*Apple Blossom Time*
Oil, 16x20''

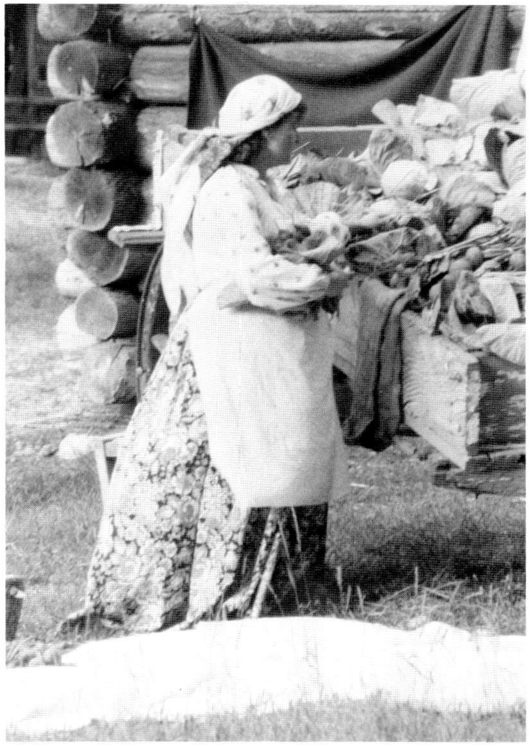

# 1 *Cabbages and Things*

"Give me four dozen."

"Do you realize how many four dozen is?" asked the vendor, his mouth gaping in disbelief.

"Almost fifty, isn't it!"

"Ya, I know how many that is — waddya gonna do with fifty cabbages — did you ever have fifty cabbages before?" Then he saw the amused look on Bill Reese's face and realized that it wasn't really any of his business how many the man wanted. "Okay. I'll get 'em for you." But as he opened his order book his face still bore a look of amazement. "Okay," he went on, "you can pick 'em up Tuesday. I'll have 'em all cleaned up so they'll look nice. You gotta van or somethin' — that's a lot of cabbages!"

"Yes, I'll bring a van," Bill replied and quickly added, *"Don't clean them.* I want them just like those over there. I want all the outer leaves left on — don't touch them!" A newly opened crate of cabbages sat on the floor, still packed, the contents hadn't been prepared for display. The heads had large, flowery leaves which gave them beautiful, undulating, lace-like fringed collars — perfect for Reese, wilted leaves and all.

"This must really be some kind of nut. He don't even want 'em cleaned up. Well, it's his dough. I'll gettim a hunnert cabbages if he wants." He turned to Bill, "Anything else?"

"Beets. Give us six dozen large beets with tops."

Pre-conditioned by the cabbage order, the merchant quietly finished the rest of the sales ticket. He did it with a nonchalance, yet his expression betrayed his continued astonishment as the two agreed on a sum of $35.00 for the lot — uncleaned cabbages and beets with everything left on. On Tuesday they loaded up the van, and the Reeses headed east of the mountains to their farm.

The farm is nestled in the meadowlands and forests adjacent to the foothills of Washington's Cascade Mountains, surrounded by spectacular scenery. Snow-capped peaks rise high above lush evergreens in the distance, while poplars, cottonwoods, quaking aspen, and willows sweep the pasturelands below. A hand-hewn weather-beaten log barn with a high, open loft, a small red-shingled house, and a dozen or so derelict buildings reflect a once active farm life. Now, many of them have become useful again, this time in a totally different way. They serve art and artists. The old board shelters with their rusted tin roofs and disparate angles have become props and prop houses, providing endless subject matter for paintings.

Fran and Bill Reese had dreamed for years of a place where they could keep animals, go for quiet, unhurried walks, breathe fresh country air, and have plenty of space for studios and workshops and storage for all their "raw" materials.

That morning as they, with friend Dave Powell, drove through Snoqualmie Pass, surrounded by their unusual cargo, they were excited and felt moments of incredulity. Was it true? Were they actually going to have their own workshop? Or, were they having a dream, one that would be rudely interrupted by an alarm or the telephone? Fran glanced back at the mountain of cabbages. No, it was real all right!

After some months of preparations and planning, they had invited twenty artists to participate in the first workshop. The spaces filled quickly, the participants due to arrive the next day. Bill had developed the format for the seven-day session based on his experiences with other workshops and on his own development as an artist. He wanted something different. "Most workshops are conducted in a typical class room or art school studio — you've got the subject and you stand in front of it. You stand around your easel and you paint and you paint until you're sick of it. You're bored. The subject or still life isn't all that exciting. You lose interest, and you think: I have to paint this and then I can go home. So I wanted to build challenge and excitement into the classes: the kind of excitement of coming around the corner and seeing something so inspiring that you can hardly wait to start painting — something challenging enough to rouse and stretch the mind and stimulate the imagination. I've found with myself that I do my best work when I am able to stretch or paint beyond myself."

*Dad's Onions*
Watercolor, 21x29″
Private Collection

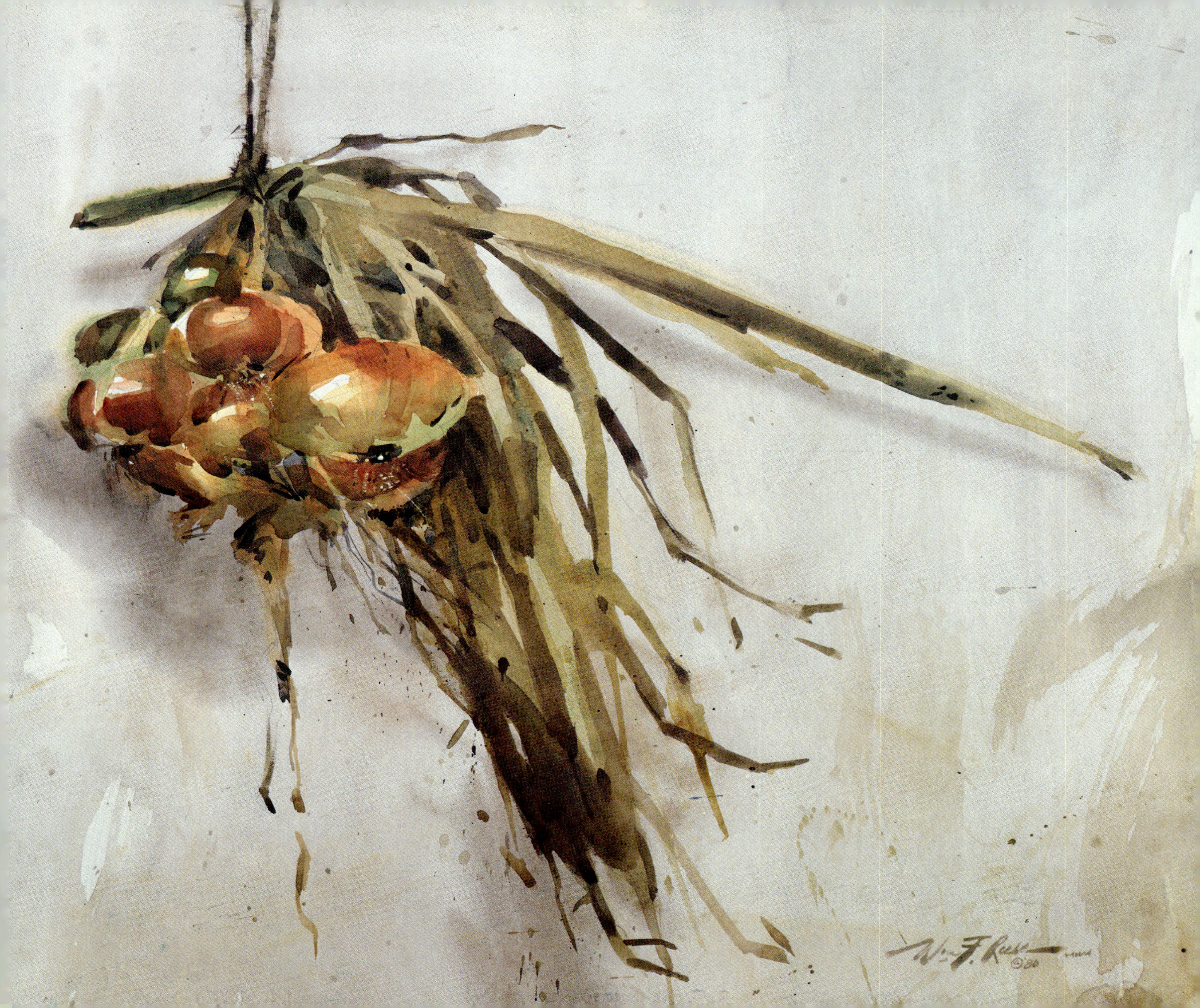
Wm F. Reese
©'80

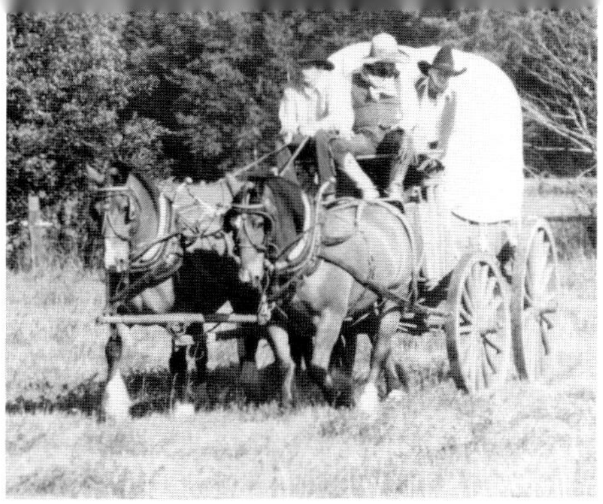

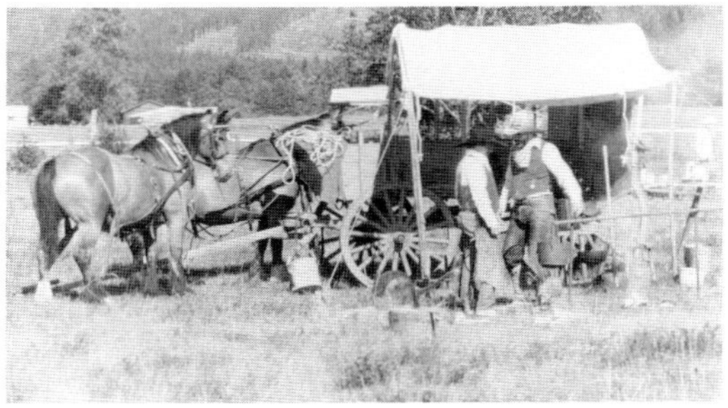

They had planned their workshop for a time when the weather was generally good so that they could work outdoors. With the help of their son Dean and of artist-friends Harold Craig and Powell, Reese spent hours cutting and stripping saplings and building and arranging the set-ups.

"I wanted them to be life-size still lifes that people could move in and out of and around and actually be part of," Reese said. "The first one we built was an Indian camp with a tepee. But, we didn't just build the tepee and say: 'Okay, you make up the rest.' We built meat-drying racks and used all kinds of accoutrements: parfleches, medicine bundles, lance cases, saddles, cooking pots, a raven hanging from the lodge pole (for medicine) — we tried to make it look just as authentic as we could.

"We took an old two-wheeled cart and made what they called a Red River cart, the type used in Canada. Of course, theirs had wagon wheels made by hand and were much bigger than ours, but the shapes were right and we added racks so ours looked like the real thing, too.

"When the people arrived, all they saw was the bare tepee which

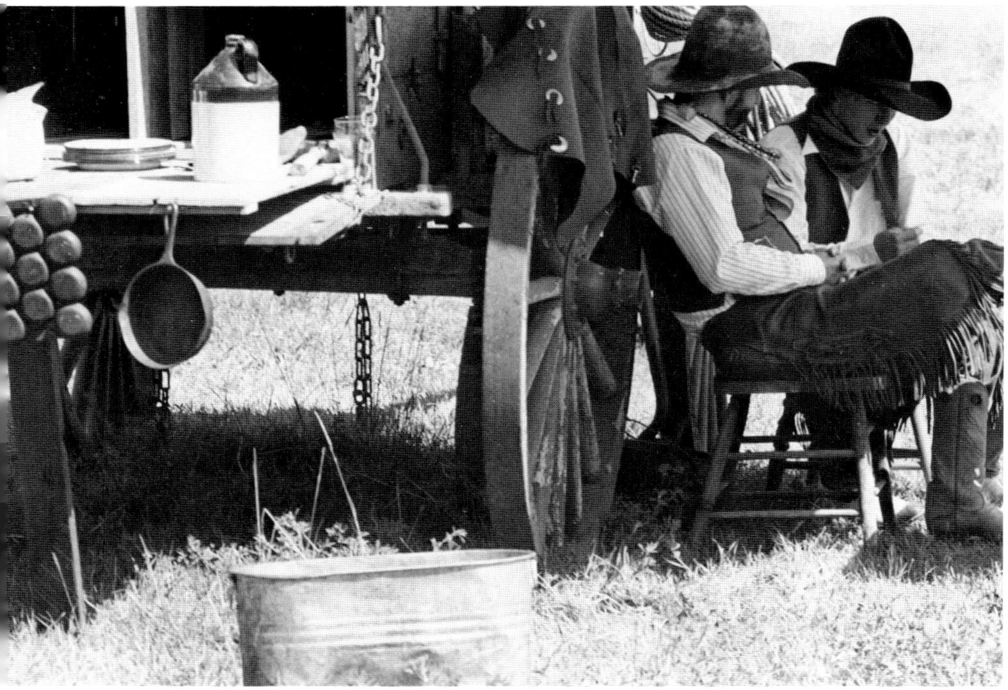

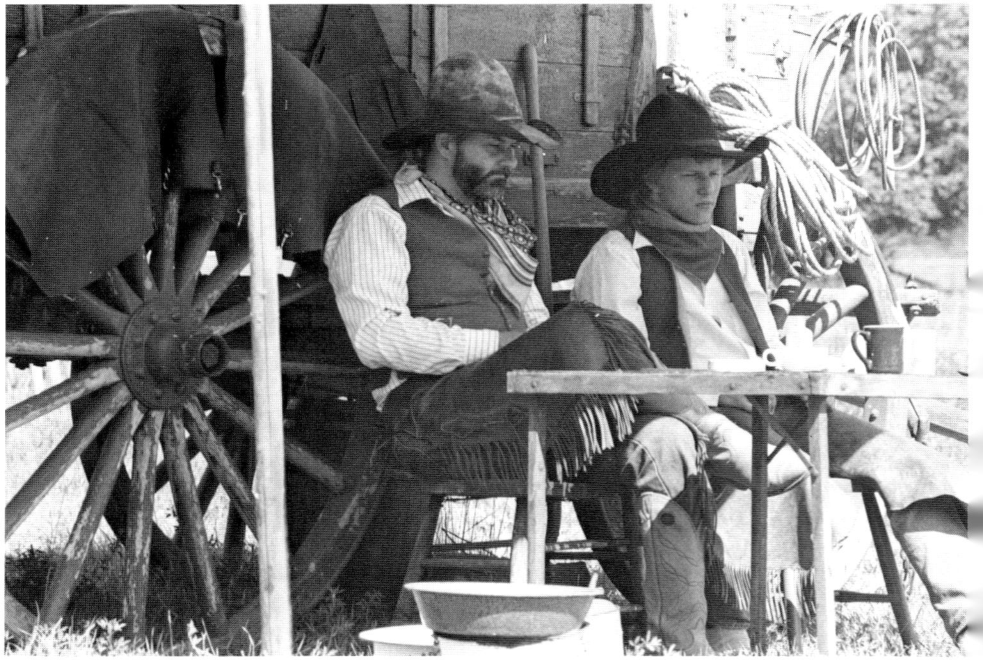

didn't command special notice, especially with all the flurry of arrival; and I purposefully gave them a first assignment elsewhere — to paint other things around the farm that appealed to them, just to get the feel of the place and to settle down from their traveling — we all have to go through a certain adjustment period in any new situation.

"The second morning, hours before the group was due to arrive again (they stayed in town or in their RVs in a camp ground), we started 'dressing the Christmas tree.' We wheeled out the Red River cart, put up a fire tripod with a black pot and built a fire — and we had a travois, old buffalo robes, including a buffalo-calf robe for the door of the tepee, and all the other trappings that made it look as if someone lived there.

"When everyone had arrived, we took them to the location of the tepee. And, when they saw all this and smoke coming out through the smoke flaps, the excitement hit them! Just the day before, it was an empty shell — and now it looked as if someone had actually moved in and just set up camp. It was a surprise. It really excited them."

Before they started to paint, Reese talked about some of the prob-

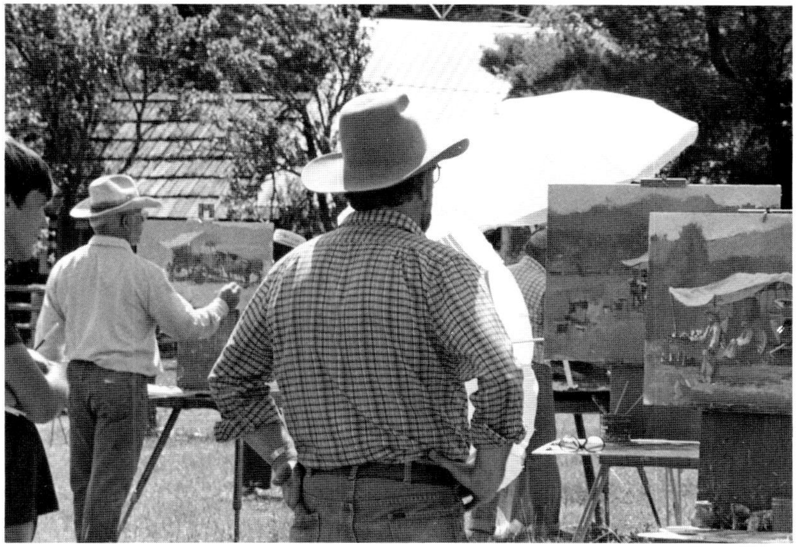

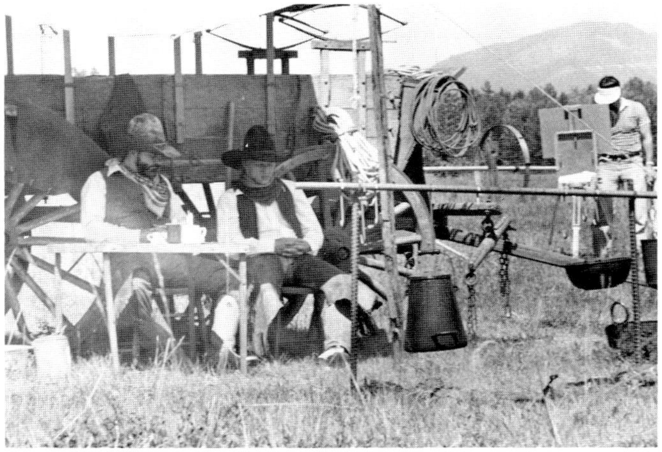

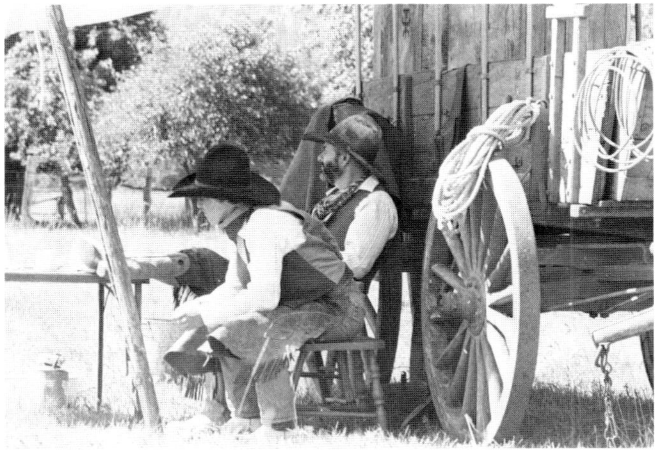

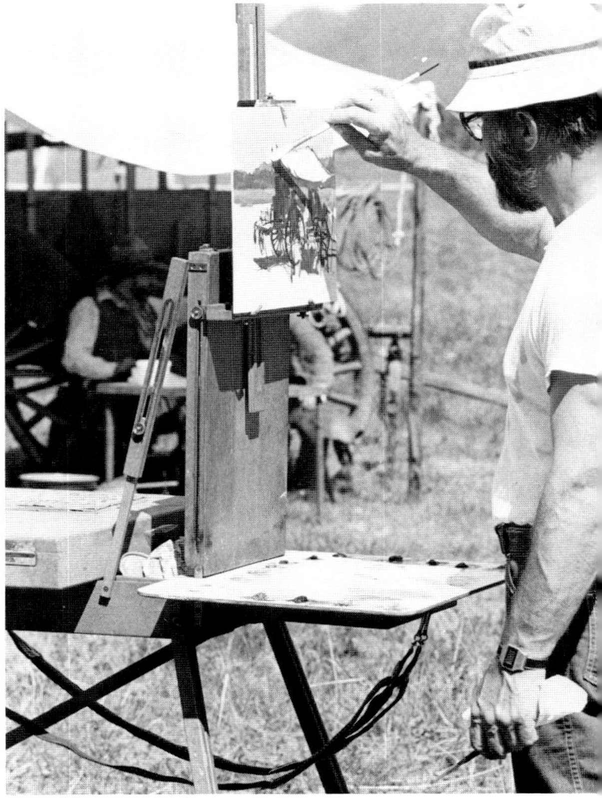

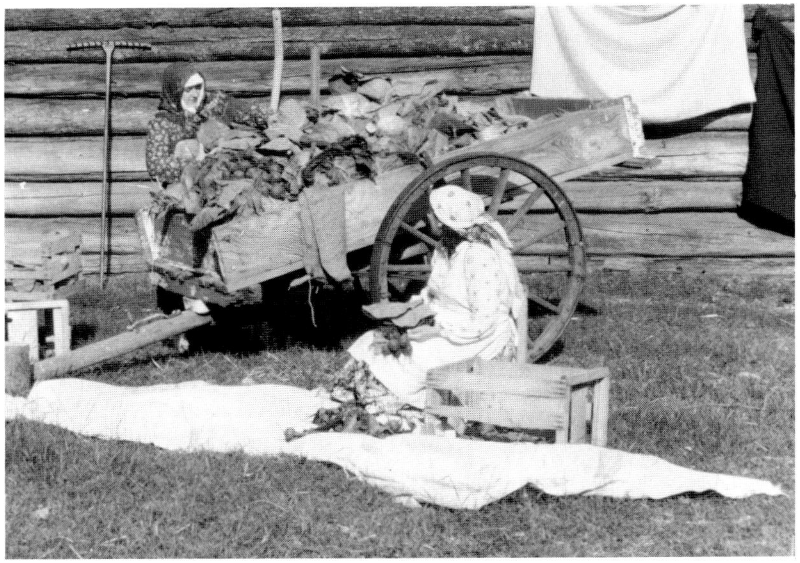

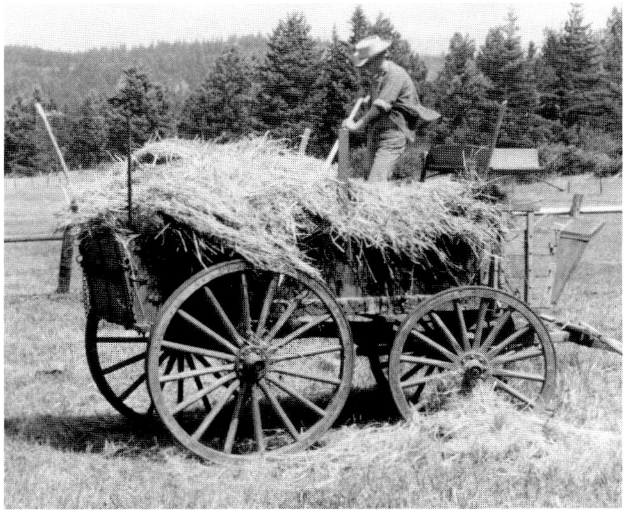

lems of painting the white canvas of the tepee in sunlight: how the values and colors change with the directions and planes, what the light looks like coming through the smoke flaps, and the effect it was going to have on the quality of light as it hit various objects on its way to the ground.

"As I was talking, Dave came out of the house. We had dressed him up as a Blackfoot warrior; his face was all painted with vermilion and yellow, a black stripe down the nose, and a blue chin, with white accents — really kind of startling at first — and he wore a black wig. He was holding a black-powder musket at arm's length. I didn't even finish what I was saying when I nodded my head and Dave let 'er go! He let out a war whoop like you wouldn't believe, and he blasted the musket for emphasis... those people whirled around not knowing what to expect next. There was the surprise element again, the excitement. That's what art is all about: *Excitement*."

Powell lives and paints in Santa Fe. He is also a free-lance set-and-prop man for Hollywood studios and goes on location as the assignments require. His expertise with props and wardrobe was invaluable for Reese's workshop. He came so well supplied that his sagging van would do only 35 mph for the entire 1,500 miles.

The second set-up, prepared two mornings later, was located next to the old log barn. Again, the "tree was trimmed" early, before anyone arrived for class.

"We had been inspired by the log barn to do a Russian scene because it looked Russian. We took the rack off the 2-wheeled cart and turned it into a Russian cart. And, finally we used the cabbages! We filled the cart with them. It was a still life all by itself and was absolutely beautiful. We had old scythes and rakes and blankets hanging on the barn wall. We laid an old tarp, a kind of directional piece, in the foreground for compositional design; and we had crates with beets, as well as empty boxes, stacked around for additional shapes and forms. It was a complete painting just the way it was.

"The people were kept at the front gate, completely away from the set-up. At the right moment I signaled to them to come and then took them around the buildings to the back. After the previous experience with Dave, they didn't know what to expect. They didn't know what

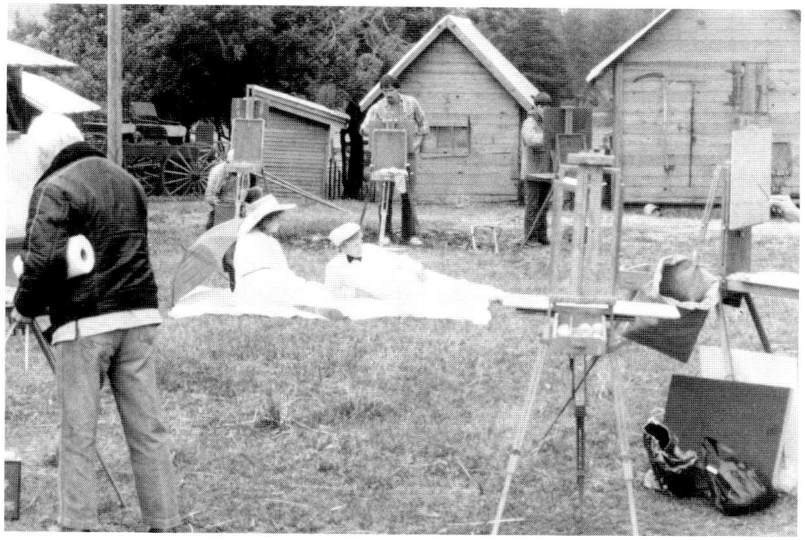

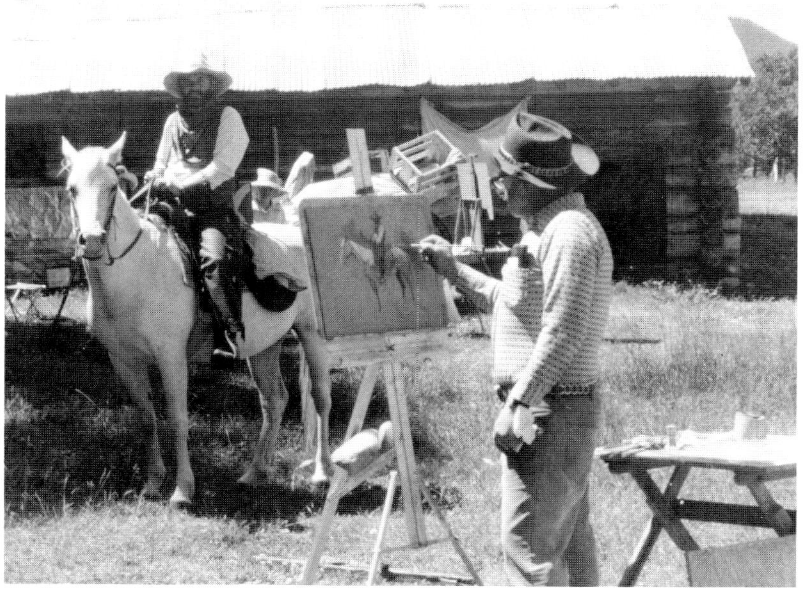



was around the corner. So the anticipation and excitement were already building and when they saw the new set-up, the impact was so great that they all started talking at once and then they started running to get their paints! Then, as they were setting up their easels and squeezing out paints, Dave went into the house again and brought out Fran and Janie [Powell] who were dressed as Russian peasant girls in long print dresses, with babushkas on their heads. They walked onto the set like no one else was there, and the people went crazy. It was really exciting, even when you knew what was going to happen."

The mornings, usually two, were spent painting each set-up. "Reese pushes us very hard," Alessandra Bitelli, a watercolorist from Turin, Italy, recounted of a subsequent workshop. "He pushes hard but only because we like it. The whole experience is frustrating, stimulating, interesting, and tremendously inspiring all at the same time — and beyond that, much of the subject matter is legendary — we see cowboys, horses, chuck wagons and so on only in the movies; yet, here they all are!"

Reese agreed to the intensity of the morning work-outs, "This kind of extreme concentration, exertion, pushing, and stretching is exhausting and makes you feel somewhat drained; and for that reason I felt we needed a change of pace for the afternoons: simpler problems, moving subjects, something that would make us paint faster. We could paint them more casually. More sketchily. In a more relaxing way." Reese paints along with the other participants, most of whom are practicing professionals or advanced students.

"Just painting with him has improved my brushwork and deepened my understanding of the elements which make up the composition and bring a painting together. His new way of letting each student fight out his problems is a good way to teach; then if you work yourself into such a hole that you can't get out, he is available."[3]

Even the singular models of the afternoon were costumed: a young woman in a long prairie dress and white apron, accompanied by her white dog, hung clothes; a good friend of Reese (whom he teasingly calls a "closet cowboy") dressed as a 1920-30's cowboy, in a complete outfit with leather chaps, rode his horse and posed; and on another occasion, a 4-H neighbor girl came with her horse and buggy.

"After three hours of this kind of pace, we stopped for the day and I showed them slides of Old Masters' paintings, selected because they were germane to what we had been working on. They were able to see how Sorolla and others handled sunlight on white objects, on horses' coats, for example, and some of the approaches the Old Masters used. Beyond showing possible solutions, the other reason for showing the slides was to boost their morale — the intense painting kind of wears them down and then you try to pick them up again, gradually, with a different pace — and then you inspire them with the slides so that they are sent home on a new high.

"For years I had felt the need for a workshop for the advanced painter, the practicing professional — something beyond the posed model, the still life sitting on a table, and the landscape chosen only to accommodate large groups. I wanted a workshop with involved, exciting set-ups and fun situations and elements that dealt with the whys and wheres of art more than with the mechanics of painting."

The workshops were anything but ordinary. One evening, using the mare from his pasture, Reese lectured on the anatomy of horses, and of animals in general, accompanying his words by drawing the skeleton in soft blue chalk directly on the mare's side (she seemed to enjoy the attention). Participants learned, too, that they are able to paint in practically all kinds of weather. Many had never painted outdoors nor had ever attempted the type of subject matter set before them; constantly changing light made them work faster and forced them to become more decisive and bold. There was never anything dull or boring — never the feeling of having to *endure* it, to wait to finish so that they could go home.

It was as if one had been dropped into the middle of another country, or another culture or era — right in the center of the subject itself! The Russian scene, for example, was quite authentic, not only in the immediate location but for 360-degrees around. The background was right. The building and the whole environment looked as if they were located in the Russian hinterlands. It was not a stage flat or false front, good only to the edge of the frame — it was full-round, real. And you were *in* it.

*Charritos*
Oil, 20x30″
Private Collection

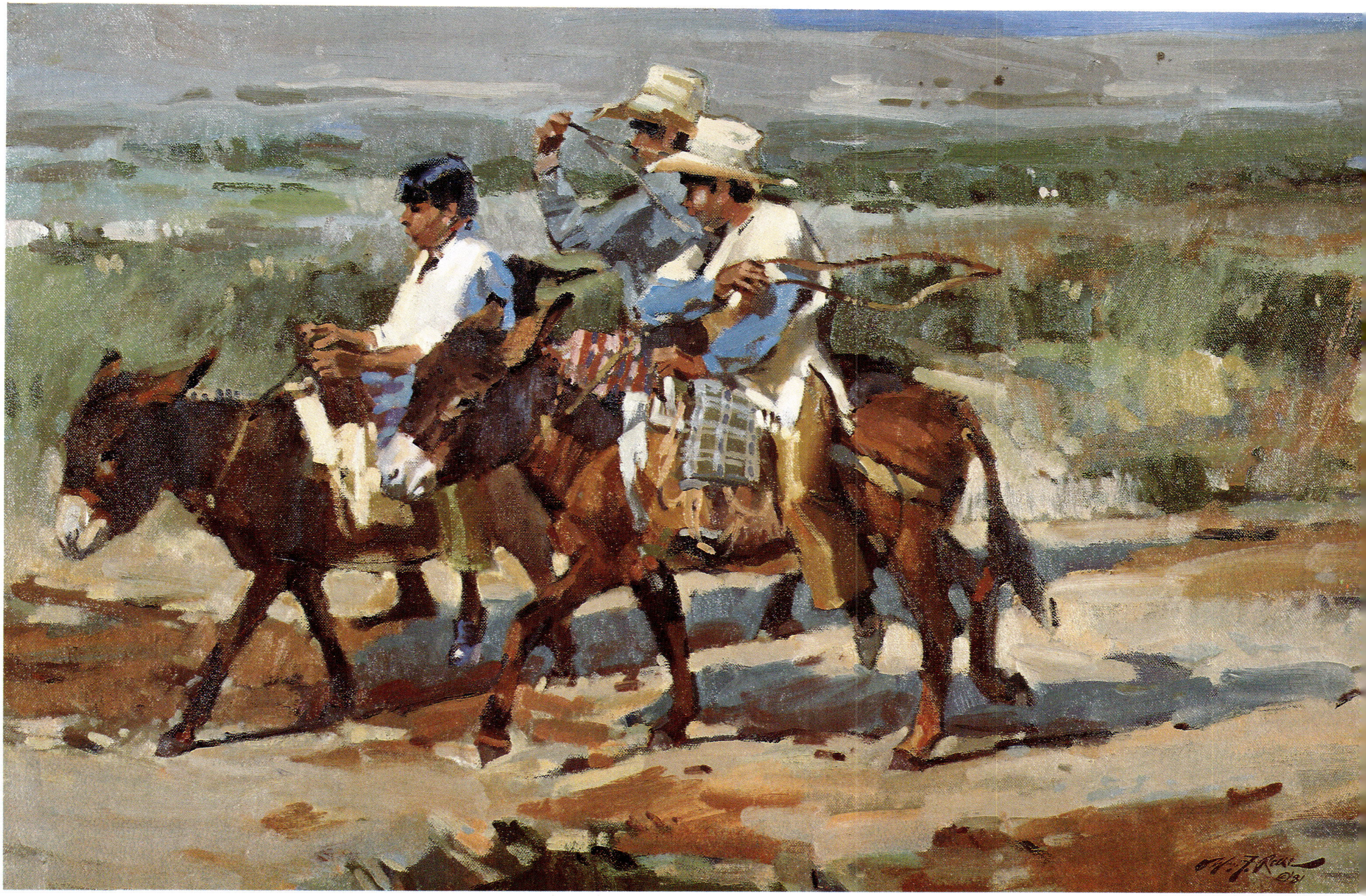

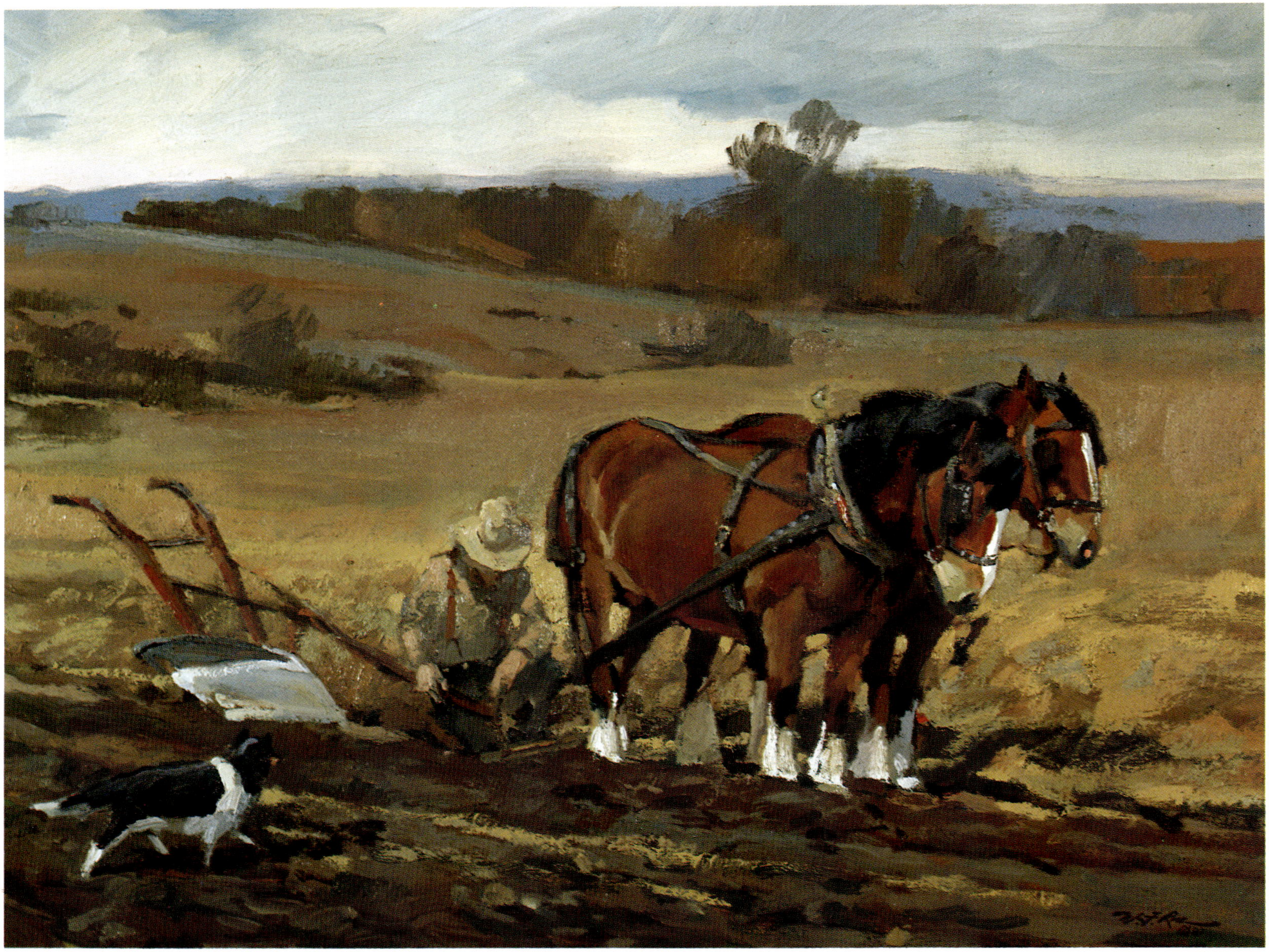

*Spring Plowing*
Oil, 18x24″

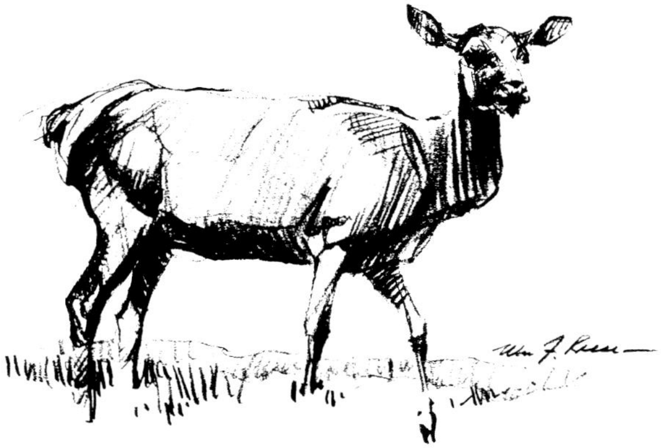

# 2 *Shaping Up*

"What does your son do?"

"He's an artist."

"Yes, but what does he do for a living?"

"He is an artist — he paints pictures."

"*All day long?* You mean, he gets *paid* for painting pictures? Ge-e-ez, that's rough!"

Margaret Reese said that is a typical dialogue and reaction about her oldest son's profession.

Born in Pierre, South Dakota, to Margaret and Harold Reese, Bill is the oldest of five children. The family moved to Seattle when Bill was two, and a few years later settled on an apple ranch in Cashmere, Washington.

"We didn't know anything about apple ranching and weren't sure we wanted to," Margaret recalled, "but my father said it was a good deal, and we bought it. The first year it rained so much that the whole crop molded. The second year brought unusual temperatures that were 30° below and froze most of the trees. There was nothing to do but bulldoze them to the ground and start over."

It was a devastating experience for them. Nature had wiped out their livelihood right from the beginning and for a number of years to come. Apple trees take from eight to twelve years to start bearing a respectable crop, to say nothing of the expense and hard physical labor involved in preparing a new orchard. In the meantime, father Reese had to seek employment elsewhere to support his family and to be able to bring their orchards back to life. Despite the blows dealt in those first years, the ranch was of great benefit for the children. They had fresh air, plenty of wholesome food from their own garden, and opportunities to explore their world.

"Considering the economy of the area, our children didn't actually realize how well off they were," Mrs. Reese said. "We raised our own

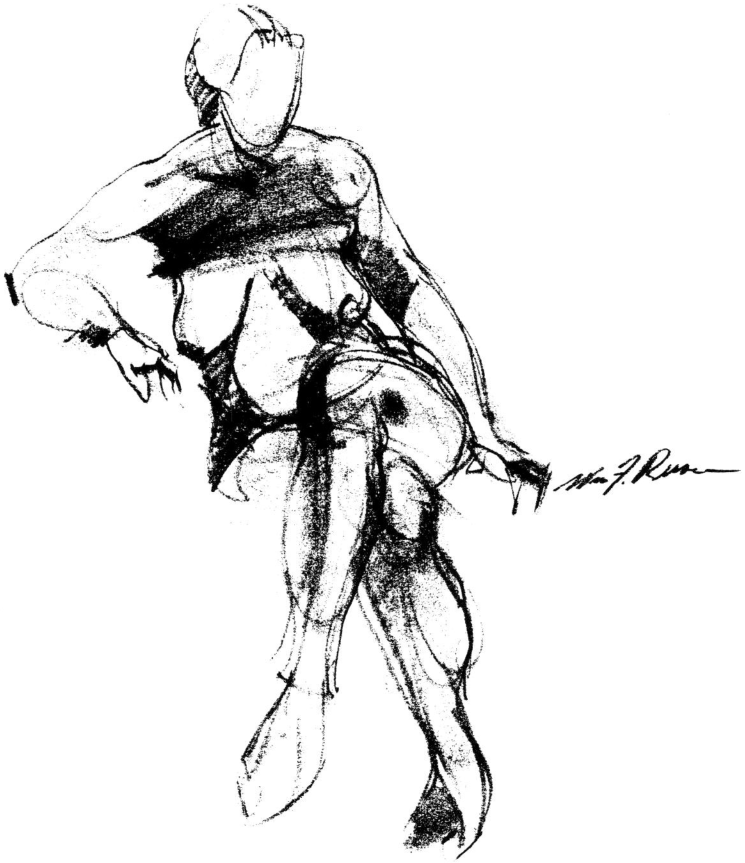

beef cattle so we had almost unlimited access to good meat, roasts, and other choice cuts; but the children being children, they fussed and wailed: 'Steak again-n-n — why can't we have hotdogs like the other kids get?'"

Responsibility for cattle and horses during those early years created a sense of self-responsibility within the children as well as a love and appreciation for animals. The two older boys shared a saddle horse, playing pony express whenever time allowed; and, active in 4-H, they were instrumental in organizing the Chelan County Fair. They built booths for the other exhibitors and maintained one of their own. One year Bill raised a registered Hereford, lovingly named "Miss Cashmere," for the fair; and the following year his charge was a steer, a prize-winner ultimately purchased by the Pioneer Fruit Growers Association. The winnings from this venture went into a college fund.

With spring, as soon as the snow had melted, playtime and hobbies became a luxury, taking low priority to pruning trees, cutting firewood (from the prunings), and building apple boxes. With autumn came apple picking and final preparations for the fair. And so it went, year by year.

Younger brother Tom recalled the Federal Government's offer, during a particularly poor economic year, for financial assistance to the apple growers if they agreed to cut all their prunings to a certain length for mulch. It was a wonderful idea. The boys got busy with the "loppers" and spent every spare minute for several months cutting fourteen acres of prunings, happy in the thought that they would be able to help their parents financially. "When at last the task was finished, we called the government inspector to see our accomplishment and to sign approval. He came with his ruler and measured the cut lengths at random; but soon he said, 'No. Sorry,' and wouldn't approve our work. We had mistakenly cut all the pieces two inches longer than the specified six inches! We were fit to be tied. We'd worked so long and so hard for nothing; and as difficult as it was, we just had to forget about it — they wouldn't break their rules and we weren't able physically or mentally to retrace our steps and cut two inches from every twig on the farm. It all seems really incredible now."

During conversations with the other two brothers and their sister, the three reminisced about Bill's painted cars, how Tom and Bill always seemed to "tinker" with cars, cutting the tops off, chopping and channeling them so that the bodies were low-slung with tiny windows. One was a five-window coupe. First they dismantled it, then reassembled it, and then painted all the visible parts. Bill decorated the body with pin-striping and designed a huge, showy flame for the hood. Bonnie grinned, "they couldn't get the car to run, but it was gorgeous to look at."

It is interesting to note that all five Reeses, similar yet diverse, had the same upbringing and advantages — each was loved and cared for by the same parents who instilled in them responsibility, stability, wholesomeness, and a fine sense of humor — all are highly successful in their own fields — but of the five, one became a painter. Why? What circumstances, beyond a specific combination of genes, ignited and fueled Bill's creative path? "We all did the normal kid things, Bill included," they agreed, "but he was different. We were all more interested in camping, sports, music, and other recreational activities, while Bill was always drawing. He used to sit in church drawing designs from the stained glass windows — possibly he didn't even hear the sermons, but he sure got a lot of sketching done. *Art* was his recreation."

*"Charm is everything in art — if there is no charm there is no art; and what sort of charm can there be when one sees only drudgery on the canvas."*
*— Ilya Repin*

Mrs. Reese talked of an early enterprise, a circus, conceived by the two older children, using the family's apple storage shed as the "Big Top," for which Bill painted a sign (his first), "Reese's Circus." They built cages and pens for the wild animals and printed handbills to promote the event, distributing them to neighboring children. The admission fee was to be one penny per head; but soon they had to abandon the charge in order to get patrons to enter the Big Top. That idea met with great favor — well, what did it matter if it wasn't a financial success!

It had been a super day for the kids, seemingly perfect until the family sat down for the evening meal, when they discovered that their little girl was missing! It was most unusual — she never wandered off by herself, at least not without notice. They called and called, but Bonnie simply wasn't in the house or in the immediate vicinity. A

*"Paint beyond yourself — beyond your ability."*

moment of alarm setting in, the family scattered in several directions to search for her. Then one of the boys remembered the Big Top and ran to the apple shed. As he approached, he could hear sobbing inside; there, in an isolated, locked cage, he found a most unhappy little girl. The Reese Circus managers, lacking real tigers, elephants, and lions, had rounded up their pets and cajoled the three younger children into substituting for the wild beasts. In the hubbub of events, they had totally forgotten to release the "tiger."

When asked about his early exposure to art, Bill credits his grandmother in giving him his first art book, a text used in the South Dakota public schools, *Drawing Made Easy* by Charles Lederer.

"I practically lived with it night and day," Reese recalled. "From it I learned perspective drawing, the color spectrum, and just a lot of good solid, basic information." The book is now coverless and worn thin.

"My great uncle carved heads out of potatoes, cabbage stocks, and other vegetables, and he used squirrels' teeth and chicken spurs for the teeth. Also, my dad used to draw horses' heads for me (he'd done some cowboying in his younger days and he had a special feeling for horses). And, he showed me a little bit about painting with a Prang watercolor set. That was the closest I had ever come to being exposed to art. I'd never even seen a painting hung on a wall — people just didn't own paintings in Cashmere, that I knew of.

"The only other art I came in contact with was the covers of *The Saturday Evening Post* and the paintings in the *National Geographic*; also, I saw Willis Carey's collection of Indian artifacts and became hooked on them. I didn't realize then what treasures they were, I just knew I liked them and somehow they were linked to my desire to paint. I had no idea at that time either how much art has to do with everything we have: soup can labels, cereal boxes, our clothing, furniture, cars, the houses we live in, all were designed by someone.

"My biggest treat was to go into town and buy house painter's oils in tubes. One tube at a time was all I could afford. Then, when I was thirteen, my folks gave me a set of artist's oils, in a nice oak box which I still have. I think my father would have liked for me to become a veterinarian or a cattleman, but he never insisted on it; and when he finally realized that I wanted to be an artist, he seemed to be all for it. Neither parent ever discouraged us about what we wanted to do — at least they never expressed their fears or displeasures, if they had any, about our choices. My father always said, 'Be yourself.' "

About the time Bill was twelve, the apple trees were bearing well enough to require additional help during harvesting. One of the pickers hired was a commercial artist. Instead of going into town on his days-off like the rest of the crew, he stayed at home and worked on his art. He drew for Bill, and they drew together. The young boy was so inspired that he drew pictures on all the shiplap siding on the bunkhouse walls. This picture gallery in itself was not as much of a concern to the Reeses as the man's influences on their son.

"If the man was a commercial artist, why wasn't he working at his profession?" they puzzled. "Why was he picking apples? And if he can't make a living at his art, perhaps he shouldn't be filling the boy's head with ideas about it." Even though they thought they were firm in their beliefs about wanting the children to pursue their own directions, they were apprehensive about a career in art. It was precarious at best. They worried, but they remained silent.

Just after high school and between the college years, Bill worked in the cold-storage section of an apple warehouse in Cashmere, stacking boxes. The storage-and-packing house was separated from the receiving-and-sorting facility by a city street, but the two were connected by an underground conveyor belt. Apples, sorted into categories according to size, were sent on the conveyor to the other side to be packed and boxed in appropriate boxes labeled: "88's", "100's", and so on, making them easily identifiable when orders had to be filled. On occasion the conveyor broke down, sometimes for lengthy intervals. As it was a bore to just sit and wait for repairs to be made, Bill took out his pencils and drew cartoons, horses, and grotesque faces on one box after another.

Some weeks later he received a call summoning him to the offices across the street. His boss, Sim Smith, wanted to see him.

*"Uh oh, I've been fired,"* Bill said to himself. *"Nobody ever gets called to the office from here for any other reason — but what did I do wrong?"*

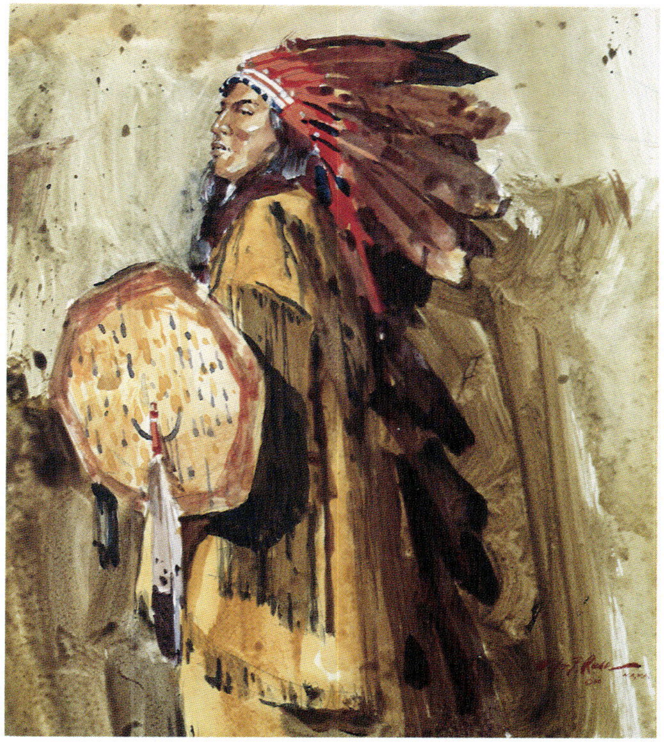

*Great Uncle's Shield, Comanche*
Watercolor, 10½x9½″
Collection of Michael Lyonais

As he entered, Sim looked him in the eye and then asked, "Are you the one who's been drawing on the apple boxes?"

*"So that's the problem. He's going to fire me because of the drawings,"* and then Bill admitted aloud, "Yes, — I'm the one."

With that, Sim grinned and said, "Here — here's some fan mail for you." The letter was from Germany (Washington apples are shipped the world over). It said, "The apples were great, but the drawings on the boxes were even better!"

Career choices in high school resulted in hours of introspection, and while Bill loved the art classes and did well in them, he knew art was just for fun, something to do in one's spare time. It wasn't a *real* job, nothing to be taken seriously like engineering or medicine or law. By trying to conform to society's ideas of worthy professions versus the frills, the boy vacillated from one choice to another until he finally decided to go into veterinary medicine; however, when his art teacher heard about it, "She hit the ceiling." Doris Stocking insisted that he reconsider and major in art instead. She continued to encourage him, giving him such confidence that he began to think more seriously about it.

"Perhaps I do have enough talent and maybe I can eventually make a living at it," he conceded. And, maybe he could become good enough to paint *Post* covers, too. "After all, *somebody* painted them, and that sure seemed like a mighty good job to me." Miss Stocking's reassurances and encouragement paid off when her student, now happy and confident with his new decision, enrolled in the art program at Washington State University.

"It's funny how things work out," Reese says in retrospect. "One person, like my high school teacher, can encourage you and build your confidence so much that you are inspired and want to continue; and then another discourages you and you drop out — like at WSU, where my adviser, who was also my lettering instructor, gave me an ultimatum: 'Drop out, or change your major,' because I couldn't letter. Well, I wasn't about to change my major, and of course the ultimatum only made me mad — I was determined to show him — that kind of experience makes you work harder and you go beyond all expectations." That experience, with its attendant sense of

*The Wild Ones*
Oil, 16x20″
Collection of
Thelma R. Carter

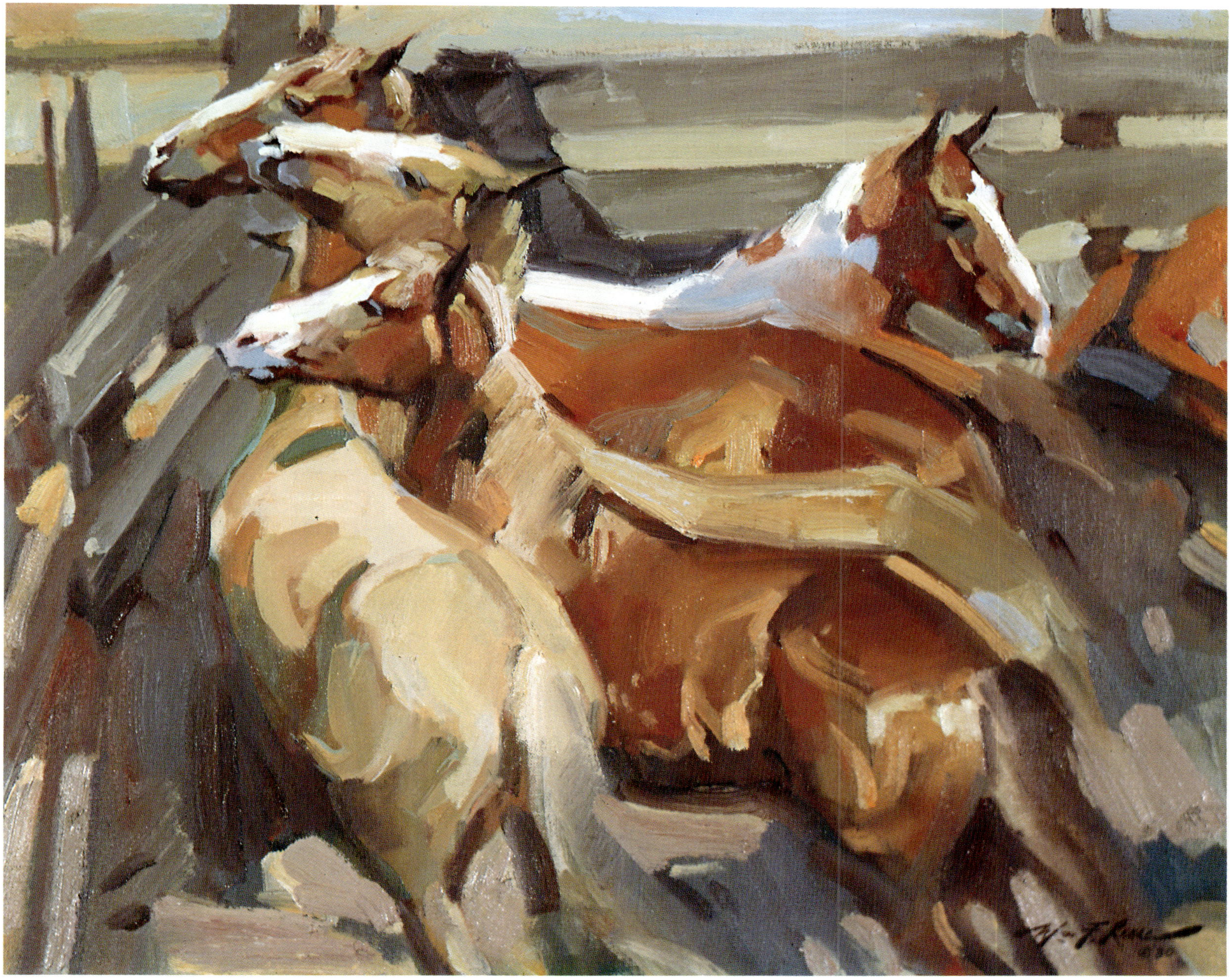

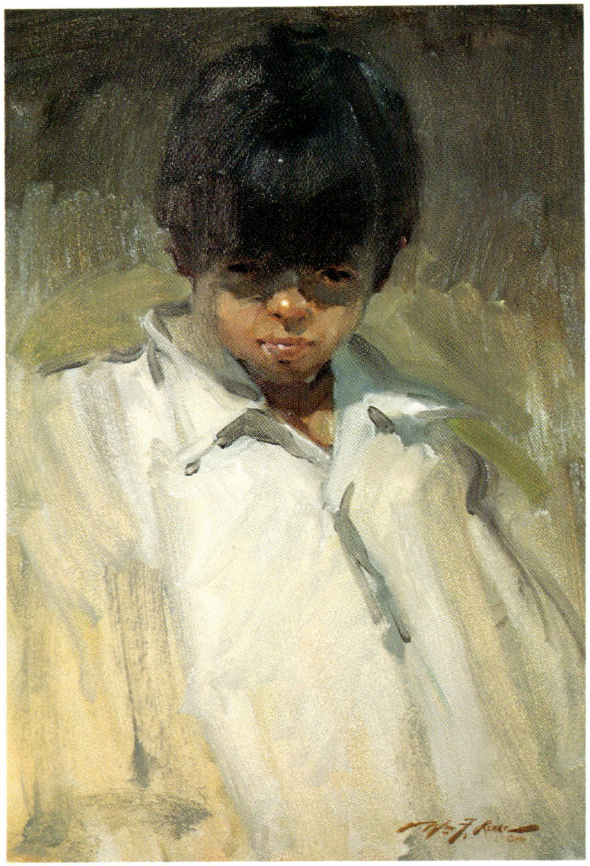

*El Muchacho*
Oil, 24x16″
Collection of
Dr. & Mrs. Lance Brigham

failure or inadequacy, actually helped him; but at the time it was a crushing blow.

"But, what if it had happened the other way around? If I'd gotten the discouragement, the blow, first? Maybe I really would have gone into veterinary medicine."

Out of college and out of funds. What direction next? He went back home and almost immediately found a job, first as an oiler for heavy equipment and then as a cement dispatcher on the Rocky Reach Dam project over the Columbia River in Wenatchee, not far from Cashmere. The dam being constructed of concrete, its multiple segments required a variety of cement mixes; and it was Reese's job to dispatch loads of the proper mix to wherever they were needed.

"It was a good job for a young fellow in those days. It paid well and was steady," his mother reflected, "but he didn't stay long before he quit and went to work for a sign company for *nothing!* My father was really upset with us for allowing Bill to do it. He kept telling Bill to go into something 'worthwhile.'"

However, Bill knew that he wanted to remain in the arts, and he wasn't going to take the rejection from the University lying down. He wanted to get on with it — but as a dispatcher he couldn't. He had to erase the deficiency in lettering. But where? How? He seemed to have had a resourcefulness, a reservoir of know-how or ingenuity, early in life, as evidenced by the circus venture, the leadership in 4-H, the teaching of leathercraft at summer camp; and now, once again, from these reserves came an idea: to offer to work in a sign shop for free in exchange for being taught the art of lettering. He went to a local shop and presented his scheme to the owner, who liked the proposition and put Bill to work — digging post holes! However, eventually Bill was allowed to start his training in lettering.

Determined, motivated, he quickly became proficient, developing a good script with a fast, steady hand. Seeing his progress, a friend in another city told many of his friends about Bill's abilities, adding a hoax by telling them that Bill worked for Von Dutch, *the* big car striper in L.A.

"Bill is coming to visit me on his vacation from L.A.," he lied. "If you want your car striped, you'd better arrange with me now." He

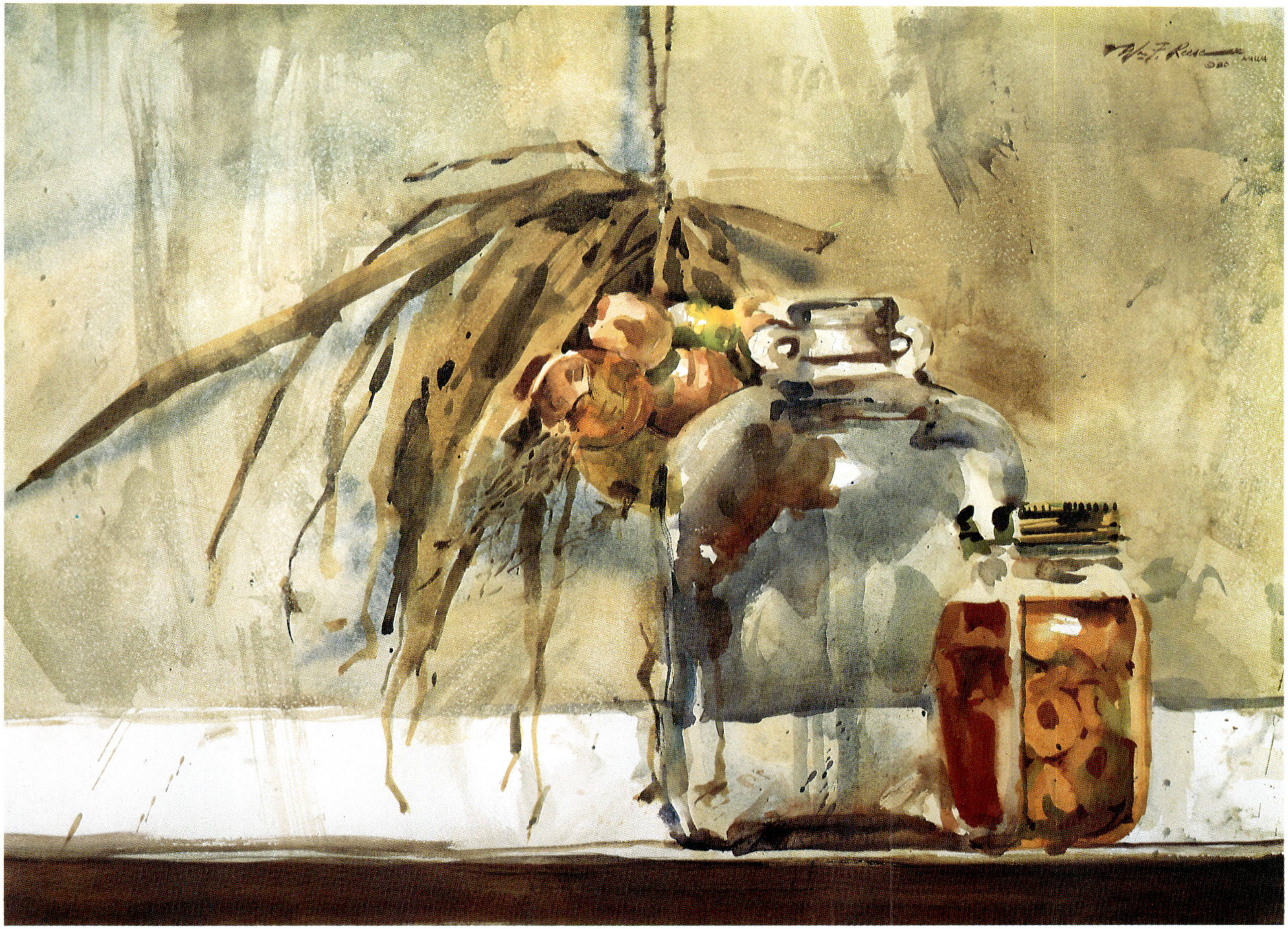

*Fall Harvest*
Watercolor, 21x29"

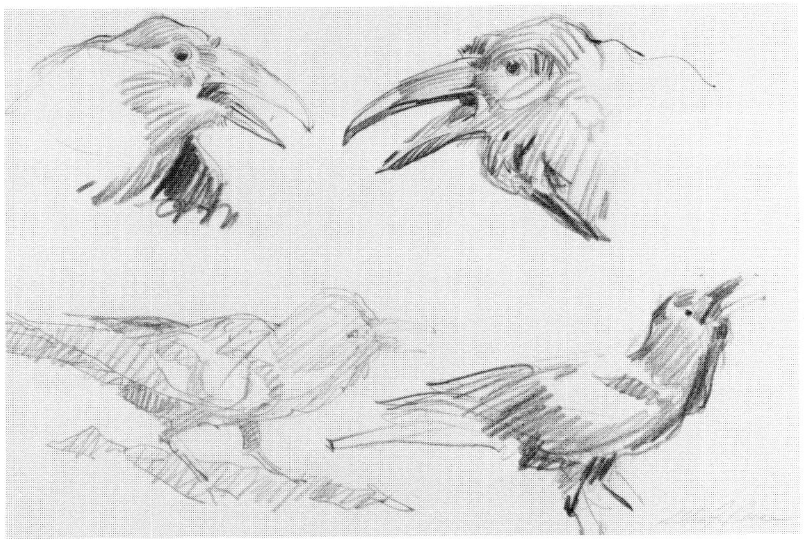

even gave his pitch to all the young car owners at a drive-in he and Reese later frequented. He was an excellent salesman, quickly selling Bill's talents, so that soon long lines of cars waited to enter the drive-in's parking lot, their owners eager to have the cars personalized. Bill deftly painted asymmetrical designs in brilliant colors on the dashboards, names on the doors, ugly faces, and stripes, right there on the spot. On the third night, the owner of the drive-in realized what was going on and asked the painter and his solicitor to leave.

"They're just blocking my driveway and lot," he complained of the cars. "By the time they pay you guys for painting, they don't have any money for hamburgers."

Pockets bulging with money, the two left with obvious disappointment, their brilliant scheme nipped in the bud. The pace of custom-work on demand and the excitement of instant money made readjustment to the ordinary activities difficult even after such a short time; and Bill, feeling that the sign shop had lost its challenge, decided to leave Cashmere for the "big time." He and a friend boarded a bus for Seattle armed with seven dollars, two return tickets, high aspirations, and a large supply of self-confidence. "I think we figured we had enough money to last one day," Reese recalled.

They reasoned that if they lived frugally they could make it through until the second day when one of them was bound to have a job. To stretch their money, they naively chose a flea-bag room in a run-down old building for $1.50 per night for two. The smell in the room was so foul they had to open all the windows and go down to the street to wait until the place aired out. As they leaned back against the building, a pimp hustled over to show them his portfolio of girls; but when he had finished showing the pictures and explaining the rates, Bill told him that they didn't have any money. Bug-eyed by such abundance and beauty, Bill's friend jabbed him hard, "Trade him your coat!"

"I was wearing a Jimmy Dean jacket, a popular item at the time and I could have gotten a good price for it — but I wasn't interested," Bill grinned.

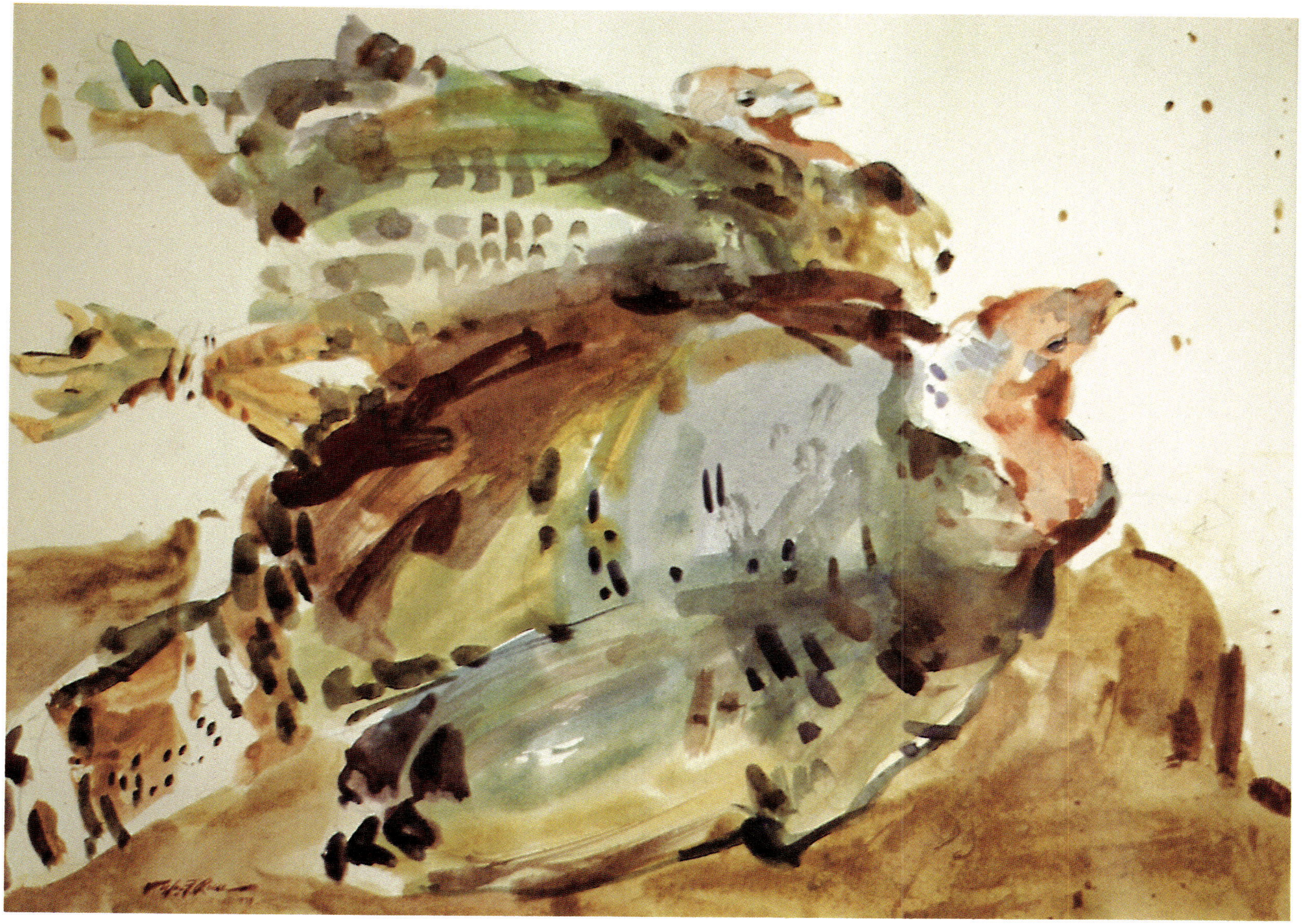

*Tied and Ready For Market*
Watercolor, 10½x14½''
Collection of
Mr. and Mrs. Ben Stahl

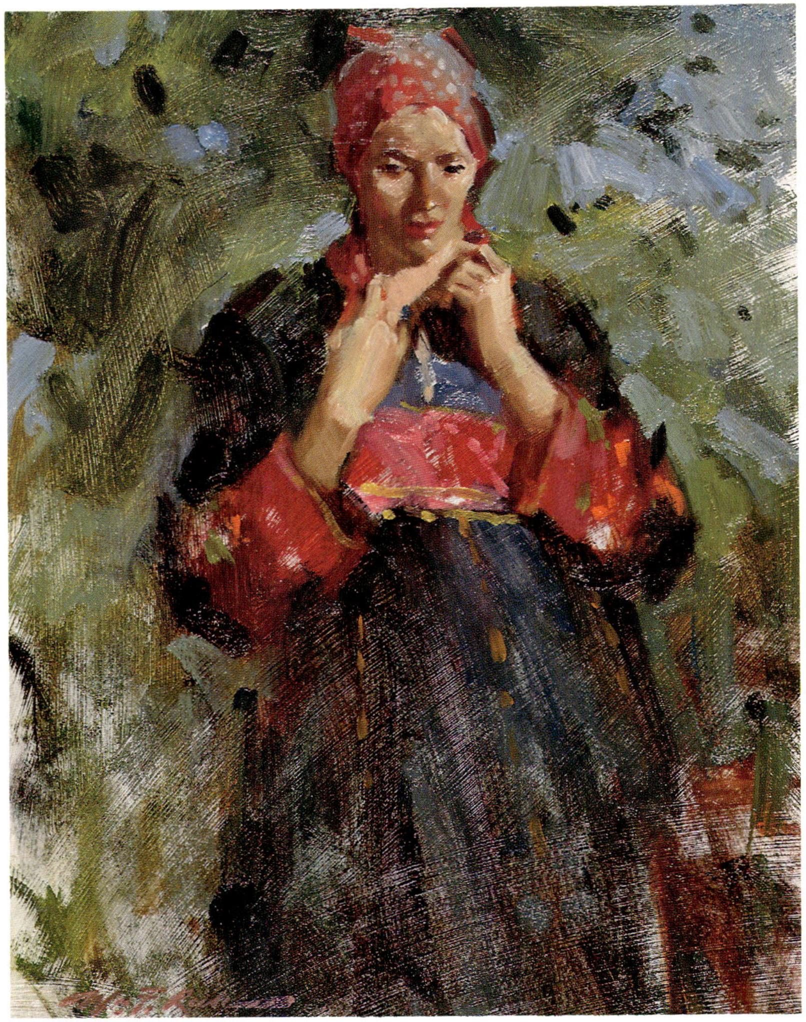

*Brenda's New Dress*
Oil, 16x12″
Private Collection

"The next day I did find a job — that is, I was hired until they found out I didn't belong to a union. They told me to go to the union hall to get a card; in turn, the union people told me they wouldn't give me a card because there weren't any jobs available. I insisted that I had a job, they didn't believe me, saying I had to have a contract to show them — and the others wouldn't give me a contract until they were sure I could get a union card. It was ridiculous. A Catch-22.

"Finally I convinced them, first the sign shop and then the union. The job lasted three months until the work ran out. I remember I was laid off on a Friday and on Saturday morning I took a bus to Eugene, Oregon, hoping to find a job through a friend who worked in a sign shop there. The timing was good; a sign shop hired me that afternoon for higher wages than I had been getting in Seattle.

"I had met Fran in Wenatchee the summer before and we had fallen in love, but my jobs hadn't paid enough to support us; and now, with a job that paid $2.75 per hour, we figured we could afford to get married — and did. Even though the pay from this shop was double, we soon found out it still wasn't quite enough to make ends meet. Not only that, we had to chase the shop owner half of the time to get our money on pay day. He was hardly ever there. Sometimes he'd be gone for two and three weeks at a time. We all kept a lookout for him so that when he did appear, we went into his office together; and we literally had to threaten him before he paid us. Then it was a footrace to get the checks cashed. Quite often one of us was left out — we ran out of people who would cash his check. It was time to move on.

"I went to work in the best sign shop in Eugene — maybe the best in the whole state — and for more money, but it was for the orneriest man I've ever come across. He was just terrible. He would yell at you and call you names." One time he called Bill a liar, one of the few things the generally amiable young fellow refused to tolerate. Seeing red, Bill hurled himself across the work table, knocking over cans of paint and scattering brushes in all directions, and landed squarely on his boss. "Liar, liar," kept ringing in Bill's ears. Fortunately (for Bill) several employees managed to separate them and things settled down, at least temporarily, until the next crisis. But he never called Bill a liar again.

"He was so ugly in disposition; for example, he would hire eight people on a Monday morning," Bill recollected, "but by noon half were gone and by Friday every one of them had left. The man had a knack for degrading people and inciting them to violence. Because I knew I could learn a great deal from him, I was determined to stay one year and kept sticking it out. Very quickly I was the only one left in the shop who knew where anything was, so I became shop foreman — by default!

"In the year I worked for him, which was a record, he hired and fired fifty-five different people. That's over one new one a week. I saw a grown man, 45-years old, a journeyman, leave in tears. Some wouldn't even come back for their checks.

"The first month that I was in that shop, I had to sleep in a chair because I developed asthma so bad that I couldn't breathe lying down. Not only that, but every morning I would eat breakfast and then go into the bathroom and throw it all up. Then I'd brush my teeth and go off to work. I did that every single day. One morning, a year later, I went through the same routine and when I finished throwing up I said, 'What the hell am I going through this for?'

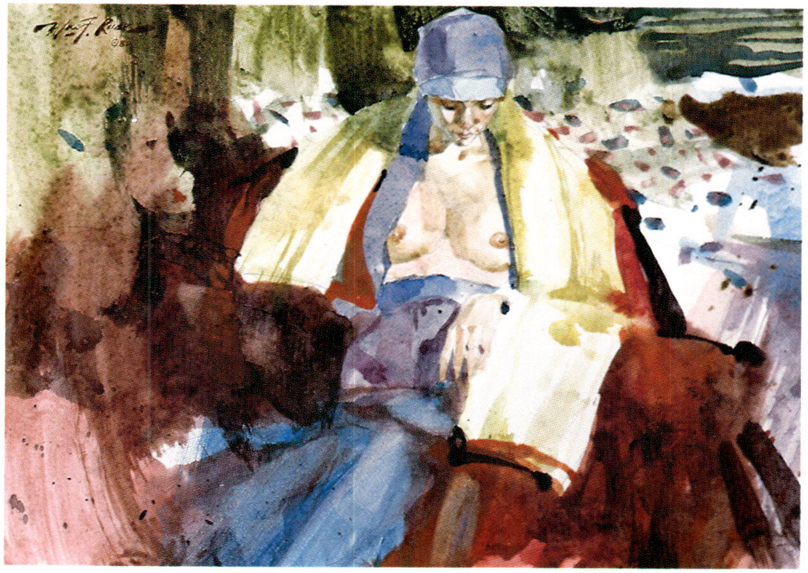

*Burgundy Robe*
Watercolor, 7x9½″
Collection of
Mr. & Mrs. Thomas C. Reese

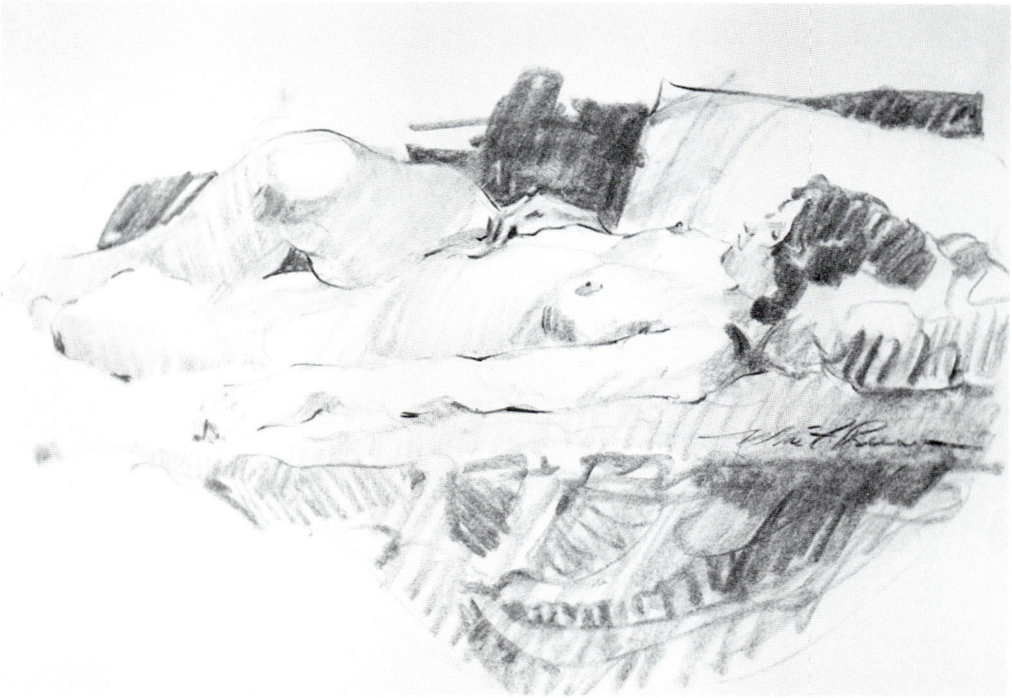

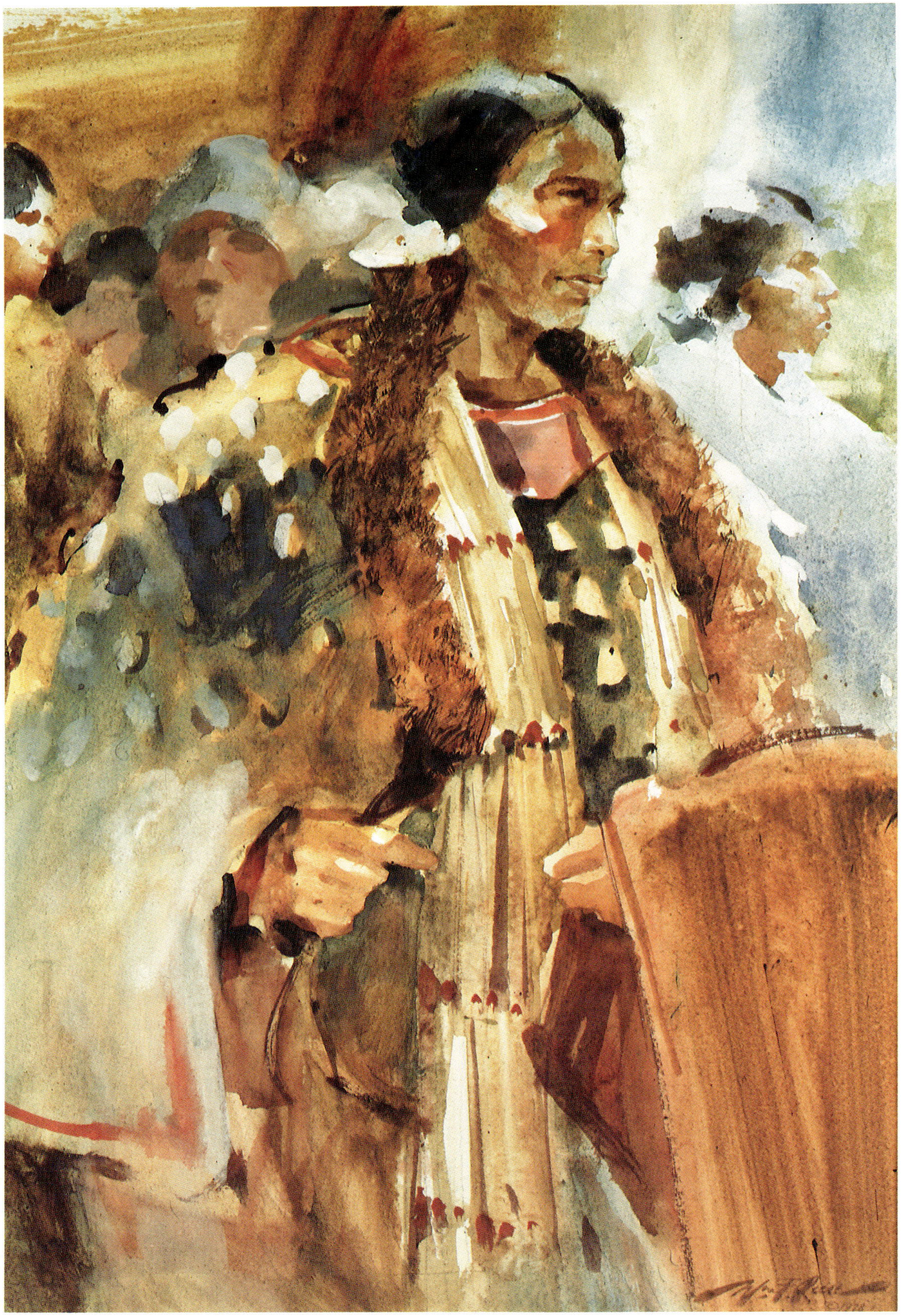

*Umatilla Dancers*
Watercolor, 28½x19½″
Collection of
Col. & Mrs. Tom Coblentz

*Dreams of Glory*
Watercolor, 22½x24½″
Collection of Gene E. Lynn

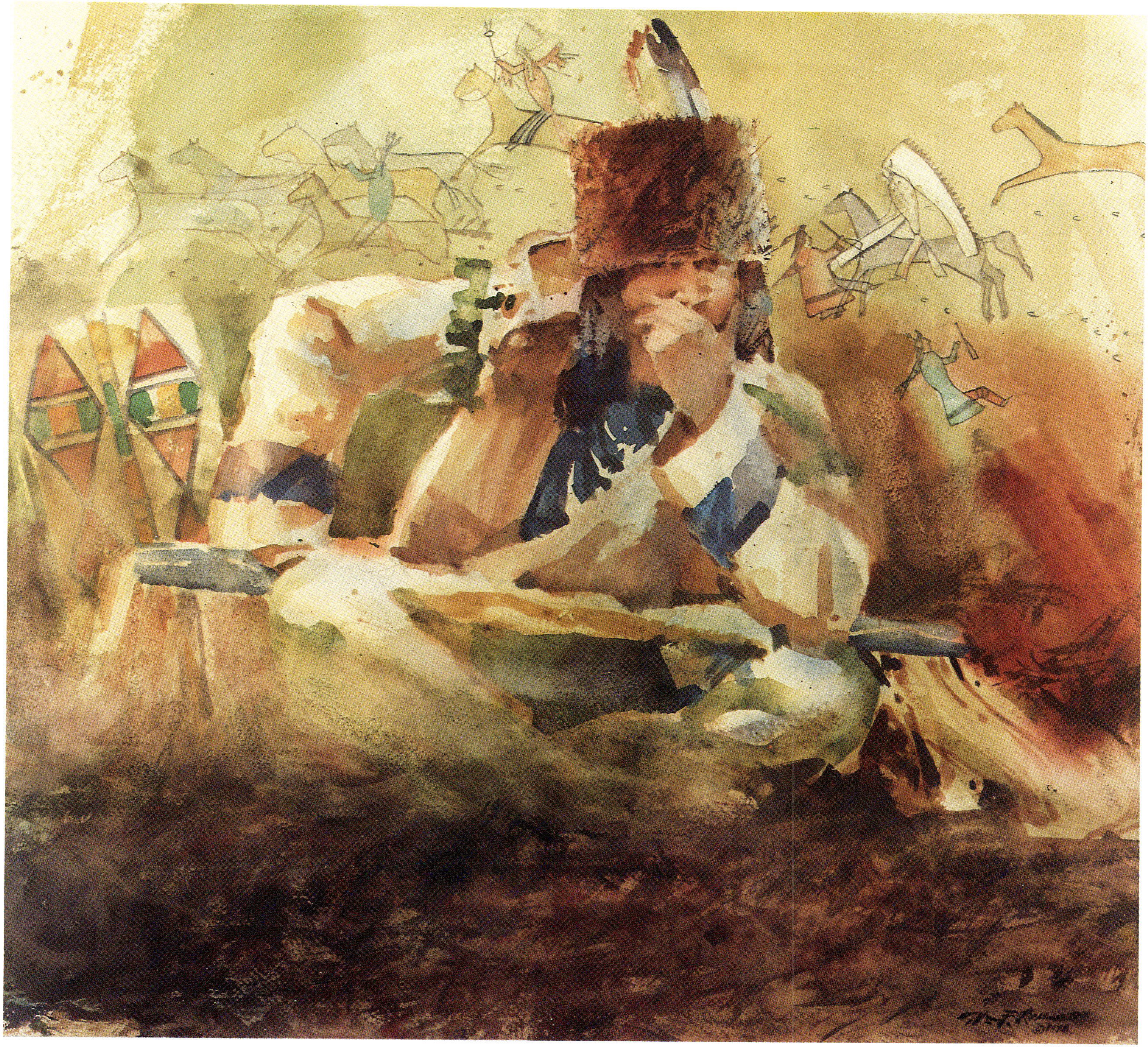

"I asked Fran to call him up to tell him that I was sick, then we went downtown to the newstand and bought the *L.A. Times* to check the classified ads. I had never in my life seen an ad for a sign painter, but there it was! A small ad by the Anaheim Sign Company advertising for a sign painter.

"I called them right away. The man's immediate response was 'No, you sound too young to me. How old are you?'

"Twenty-three."

" 'No, you're too young.'

"Now wait a minute! Where do you get off . . . you want somebody young but yet you want him to have fifty years' experience. What's my age got to do with whether I can do the job or not?" By that time, especially after working a year for the ornery boss, Reese felt that he was a pretty good sign painter; and fast, because that was one of the stipulations: "You had to be fast and you had to be good." In fact, to build up their speed and to take the monotony out of their projects, Reese and his co-workers constantly raced one another.

"In most of my career, I've hardly met anyone who could letter as fast because of those almost daily contests."

Confident that he was capable of handling practically any situation in a sign shop, Reese continued to state his case: " 'All I want is a try-out. You don't have to guarantee me anything. Just give me a try.' I knew that that was all anybody would get anyway — and if you can't do the work, they'll fire you — so I was 'forewarned,' but I knew that I could do the work and wouldn't really be risking anything.

"He was surprised that I was that sure of myself — that I would travel a thousand miles just for a try-out. He said, 'O.K. Come on.' "

Reese proved himself and stayed for a year. He was never able to work more than two or three years in any one shop because once the challenges ceased to exist he became bored. At Anaheim, he learned all he could and it was time to find a new challenge again, which came from the next employment for an outdoor advertising company, a shop specializing in pictorial billboards and highway bulletins.

What a variety! Pictures of people, home furnishings, modes of transportation, beverages — it was wonderful. Color, layouts,

*Shelly*
Oil, 13¾x11¾
Private Collection

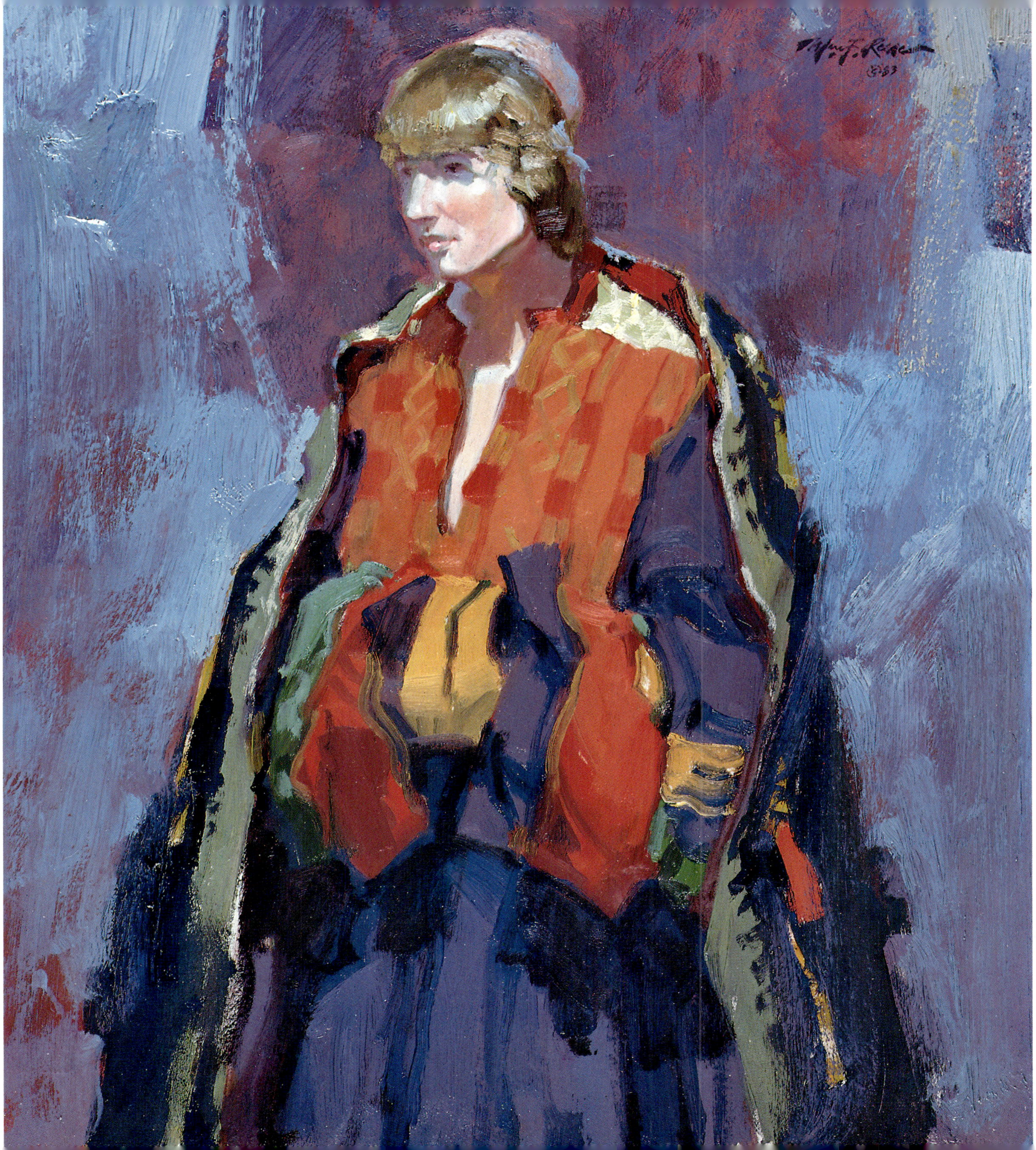

drawing, lettering, gold leafing — all added to Reese's knowledge and interests. He thought he had really found his niche and decided to further enhance his career by taking a class in pictorial art from a sign painter at Los Angeles Trade Tech. By so doing he also fulfilled a union requirement for a second Journeyman's card as a "picture painter."

"That old guy taught me a lot about painting, the application of paint, how to move it. When you paint billboards that are 48 feet wide by 14 feet high, you have to move a lot of paint around and you have to paint very direct."

They did a mammoth amount of color work at the plant for national accounts, including the numerous billboards. These were painted from photographs provided by the advertising agencies who dreamed up the ideas for their accounts. The photos were projected onto large sheets of paper attached to a wall. Then the images were copied with charcoal; however, they were always distorted because it is impossible to enlarge a photograph in this manner to such vast proportions without distortion. Reese corrected the drawings, which were then traced and perforated with an electric pounce, a tool similar to a tailor's tracing wheel. (The alternating current activated a stylus which struck a metal plate beneath the drawing, burning holes as it moved. Then the perforated drawing was affixed to the wood surface of the billboard, and the perforations were traced with a bag of charcoal, thus creating a dotted-line-drawing underneath.) Once the paper was removed, the fragile drawing was traced again with an indelible pencil to prolong the life of the lines (indelible lead "bleeds" through paint and continues to provide guidelines for the painter. If any evidence remains when the work is finished, the sun quickly bleaches it out).

On many occasions, the charcoal images were somehow lost in the early stages. Because of his ability, Reese's job was to redraw them freehand, giving him a distinct advantage over the others in not having to rely on patterns or outlines. With no more than a preliminary plan, he was able to paint any object, face, or figure, and consequently the work advanced more rapidly.

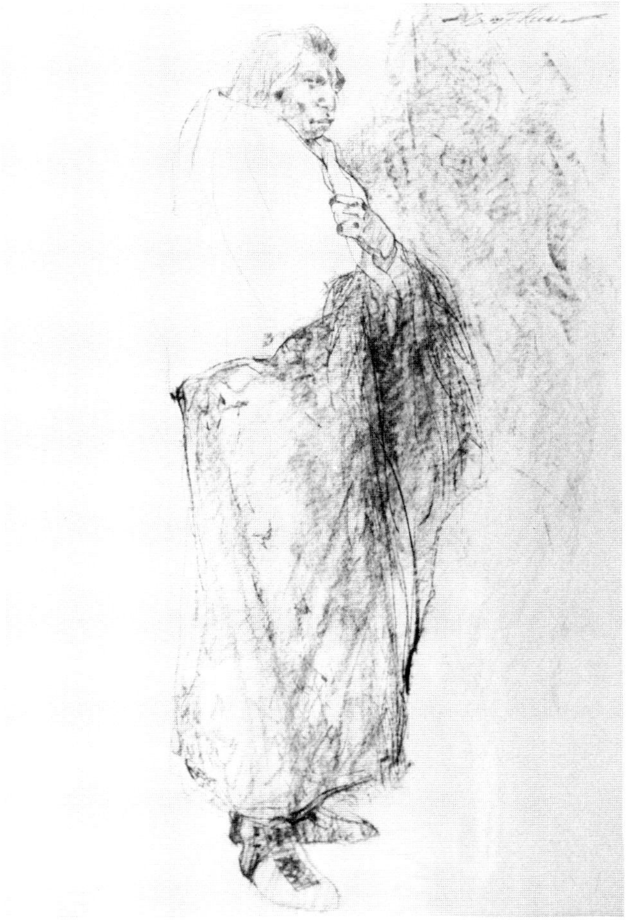

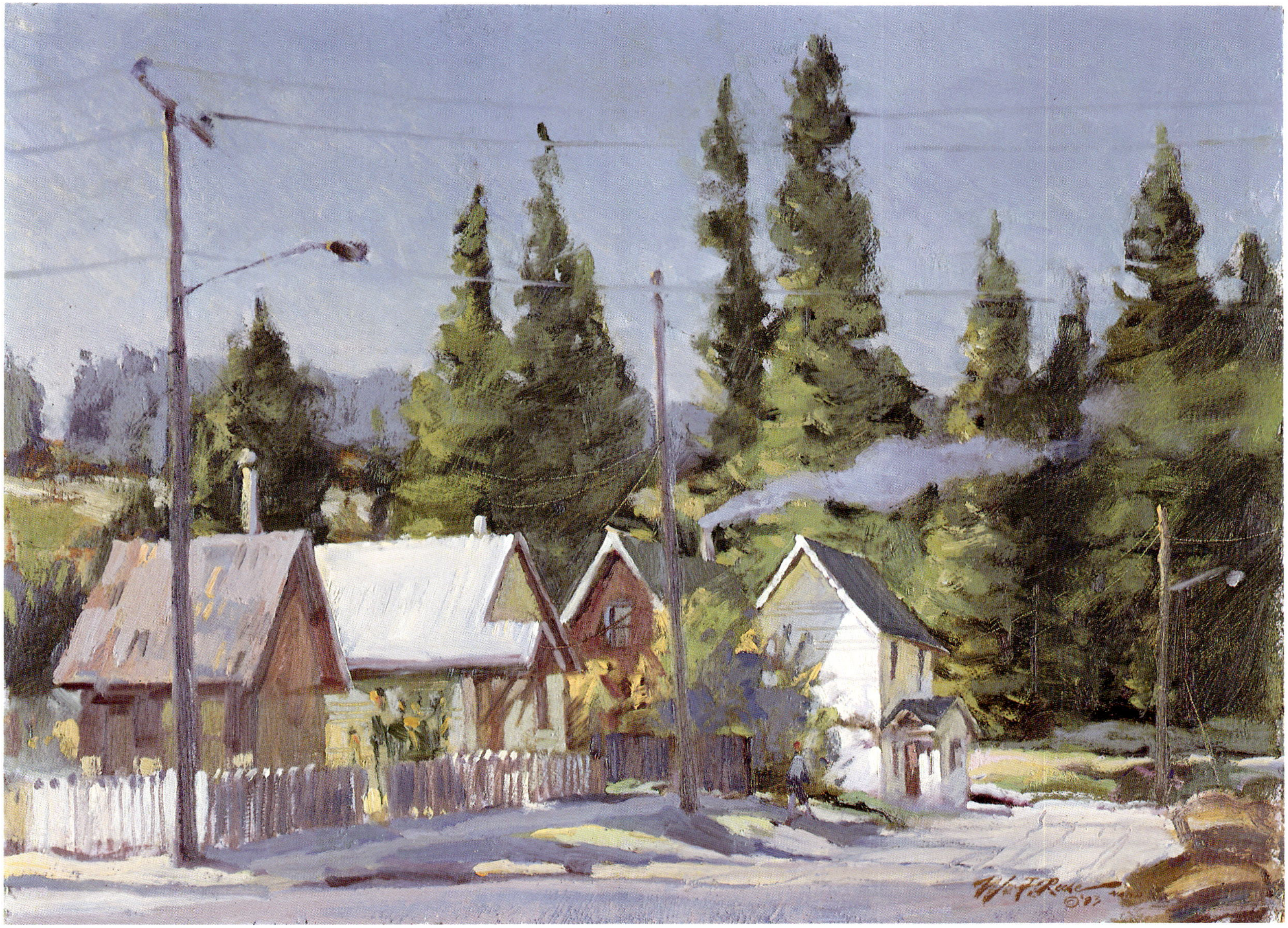

*Fall in Roslyn*
Oil, 12x16″

This was a significant period in Reese's life, for up to this point he had thought seriously of making sign painting his life's work. He took pride in what he did. Yet, even though he enjoyed it, the yearning to paint for his own pleasure and self-expression always haunted him until, despite his rigorous six-and seven-day-a-week work schedule, something motivated him to enroll at Art Center.

"I didn't have the time or money to attend Art Center full time so I had to be content with night school, three and four nights a week, always choosing a drawing class; but when I did have a spare evening, I sat in on some of the other classes, too. I learned a lot from Reynold Brown, for one, by sitting quietly, observing.

"Of all the drawing teachers I ever had, I admired Paul Souza the most. I took his class over and over again — it was the same class, but he never taught it the same way twice — I have to credit him for the best drawing instruction I ever had.

"It was through this experience that I knew I didn't want to be a sign painter for the rest of my life. I wanted to be an artist. I wanted to paint to please myself."

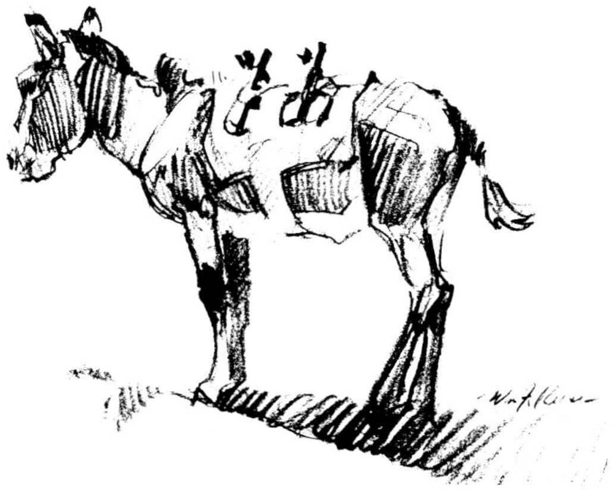

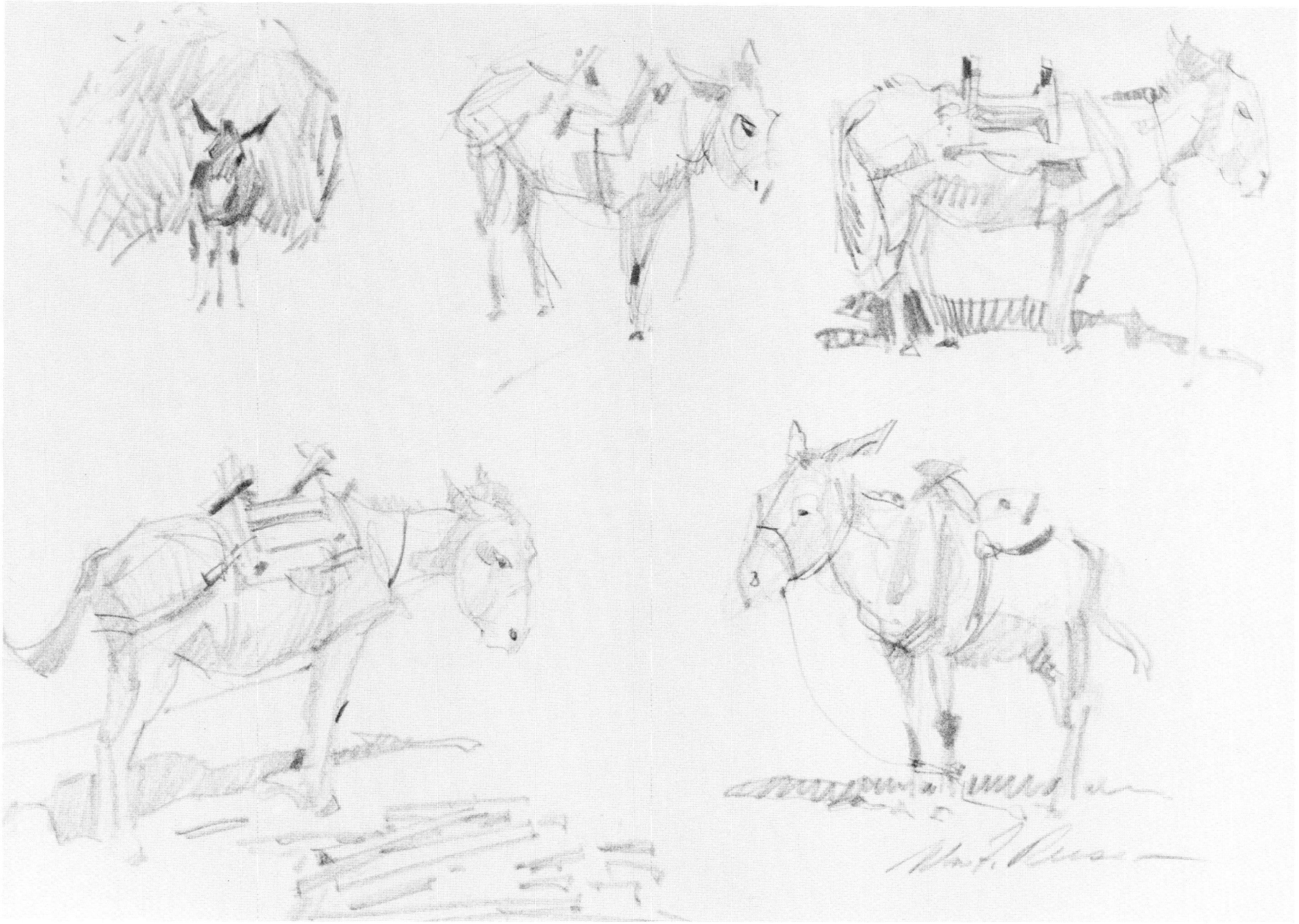

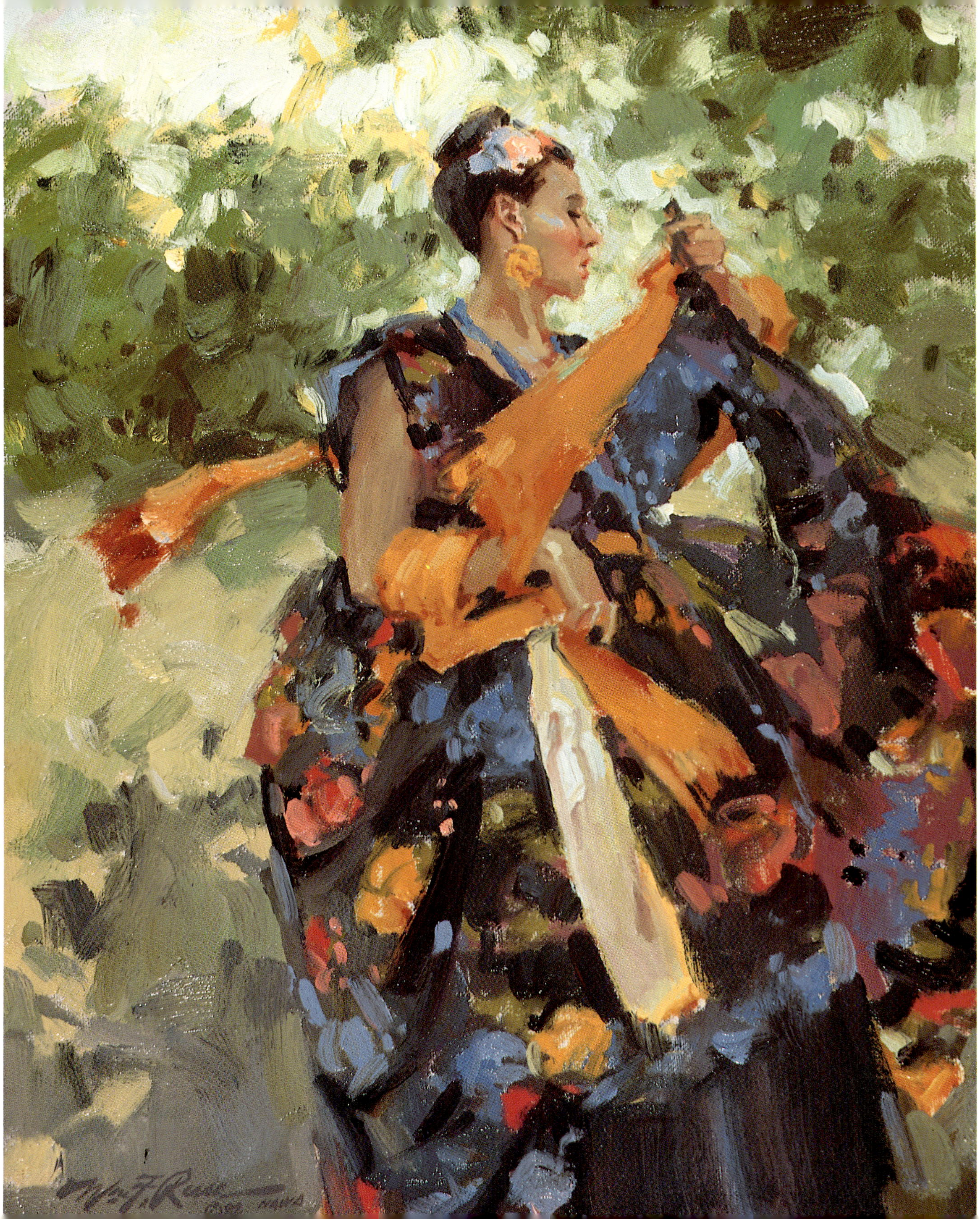

*La Danzarina*
Oil, 16x12″
Private Collection

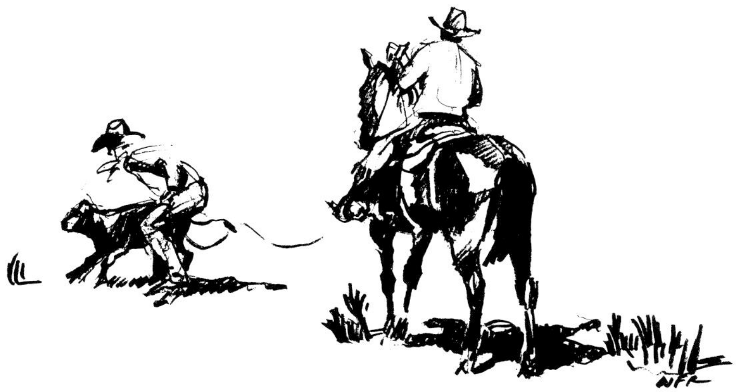

# 3 *Going After What You Want*

"Not to win is not a sin. But not to try is a tragedy."[4]

After a decade or so at the sign shops and easel painting at night, Reese realized that a career in painting was what he wanted. How was he to do it? How could he paint full time and yet support his family? That was the crux of the matter. Many circumstances had brought Reese to this point, a combination of experiences: from the perceptive high school teacher to an unyielding art professor, and even to the ornery little crank in the Oregon sign shop — as from the bulletin plant to Souza — all had contributed to shaping the artist. Even the negatives were changed into positives by Reese himself, perhaps by some strong, irrepressible guiding light from within.

Obviously, now with a clear-cut goal, the first step was to save enough money to finance it. The young couple drew up a budget, settling on a need of $4,000 to see them through the first year of their venture. This was their money goal. With this money, Bill could quit his job and paint full time, although by now they had two babies, Dean and Shelly, and their financial responsibilities were greater than ever; but they were determined, putting aside everything not needed for necessities. It was exciting to see the fund grow as they checked off the weeks and months, and waited for the big day. Two years went by — the savings had grown to $3,500, putting them in the home stretch, when suddenly their whole plan was shattered. The usually robust young father became deathly ill. His evasive symptoms baffled doctors, making treatment impossible while his condition continued to deteriorate daily. On the tenth day his fever rose alarmingly and his skin had a definite greenish cast, and the surgeons knew they must act immediately — another day, even a few hours, might be too late. Exploratory surgery revealed a ruptured appendix. Peritonitis and gangrene had already set in, and Reese's life literally dangled by a thread.

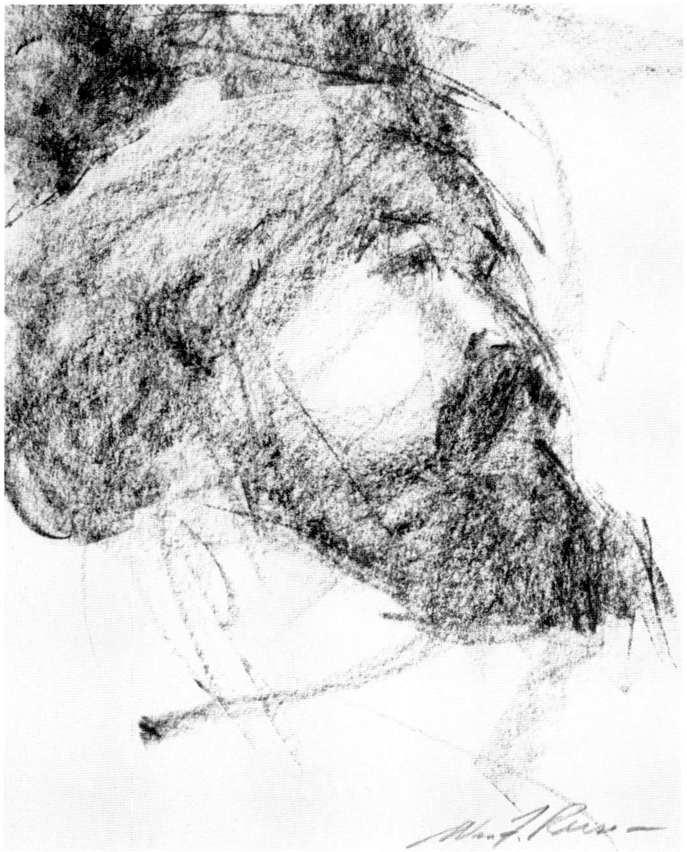

"At the time, I knew I was close, but I didn't *think* about death and dying, or the fear of dying. I was so upset that I would never know if I could make it as a painter — I would never see my kids grow up — that is what really bothered me. I just couldn't stand the thought of it; that's what really made my heart ache.

"As I lay there all churned-up inside, worried and upset, I decided that if I lived, I would never again *wish* I had tried something. I vowed that if there was something I wanted to do, I'd do it and live with the consequences. I'd rather do that than live with the thought 'I *could* have done this — or I *should* have done that — if *only* I had had the nerve . . . .' Just do it if you really want it and don't worry about it — somehow it will work out."

Through some miracle the crisis finally passed, but because of the complications Reese had a lengthy recuperation, giving him plenty of time to reflect on the recent events, to rejoice in his extension of life, and to reaffirm his vows for the future. It was a personal renaissance, but along with the sweet came the bitter as his elation was slowly eroded by their rapidly dwindling savings. He and Fran kept reminding themselves that money was only a material object, more readily replaced than health. Two months later, with new strength and vigor, Bill returned to the sign shop and started the savings program anew. This time they reduced their money goal to just enough to tide them through nine months. The amount grew surprisingly fast, in a little over a year, enabling Bill to quit his job.

"The guys I worked with told me I was crazy. I had a steady job for the rest of my life, and I was throwing it away. Well, the stint in the hospital made me realize that staying with the steady job for the rest of my days scared me more than starving or being broke — I was more afraid of the sure thing than I was of the danger of the unknown — of going hungry. Or dying and not knowing."

Fran supported his decision fully. She said they were accustomed to living without frills, and the lack of material things would be of little consequence. It was the concern and pity of well-meaning people that became the difficult things to cope with.

"Some women felt sorry for me having a jobless husband around all day, but I insisted that he did have a job, at home, painting. It wasn't as if he was going to be sitting on the kitchen counter all day, every day, wanting to eat all the time! People just don't realize that painting is a full-time job, just like being a doctor, or a lawyer, or a clerk in a store. They think it's some kind of play. A leisure-time activity, not requiring serious study or effort."

Bill continued, "Knowing whether I could paint or not became such an important question. *I had to know the answer.* In reasoning it out I asked myself: 'What's the worst thing that's going to happen from quitting a steady job?' Not making money. But, I'm going to have the greatest nine months of my life — then I'll go back to earn more. I knew that within a year we could save enough to do that again. The alternative would be to wait until I was 65 and retired — and hope I'd live two years after that to paint.

"No, the best plan was to paint for nine months *now* and then work every other year at a job until my paintings started to sell. Eventually they were bound to sell, somewhere along the way. Also, I knew I could teach one or two days a week, and anything extra like that would extend my nine months that much more."

Bill began to paint. The freedom to do as he pleased, when he pleased, and how he pleased was sheer heaven; no longer was there a time clock to punch (even if a job had taken only fifteen minutes, the time had to be accounted for, and the clock had to be punched). Now, no time clock, no schedule. The freedom proved to be rather heady.

"Painting for fun, even though that was my dream, was a hard thing for me to adjust to. The Puritan work ethic had made its mark. As a remedy, every morning after breakfast, I took an apple or pear or other fruit that Fran kept in the refrigerator just for that purpose, and I painted a small still life. I'd have a whole stack of 8″x10″ masonite panels ready to go. I painted these studies of two or three pieces of fruit every day without fail. It worked as a warm-up, and it gave me a finished product — something I accomplished and could see daily — something I could go to the market place with and sell for twenty-five or thirty dollars.

*"Painting is a way to transfer a thought too big or too personal to be put into words."*

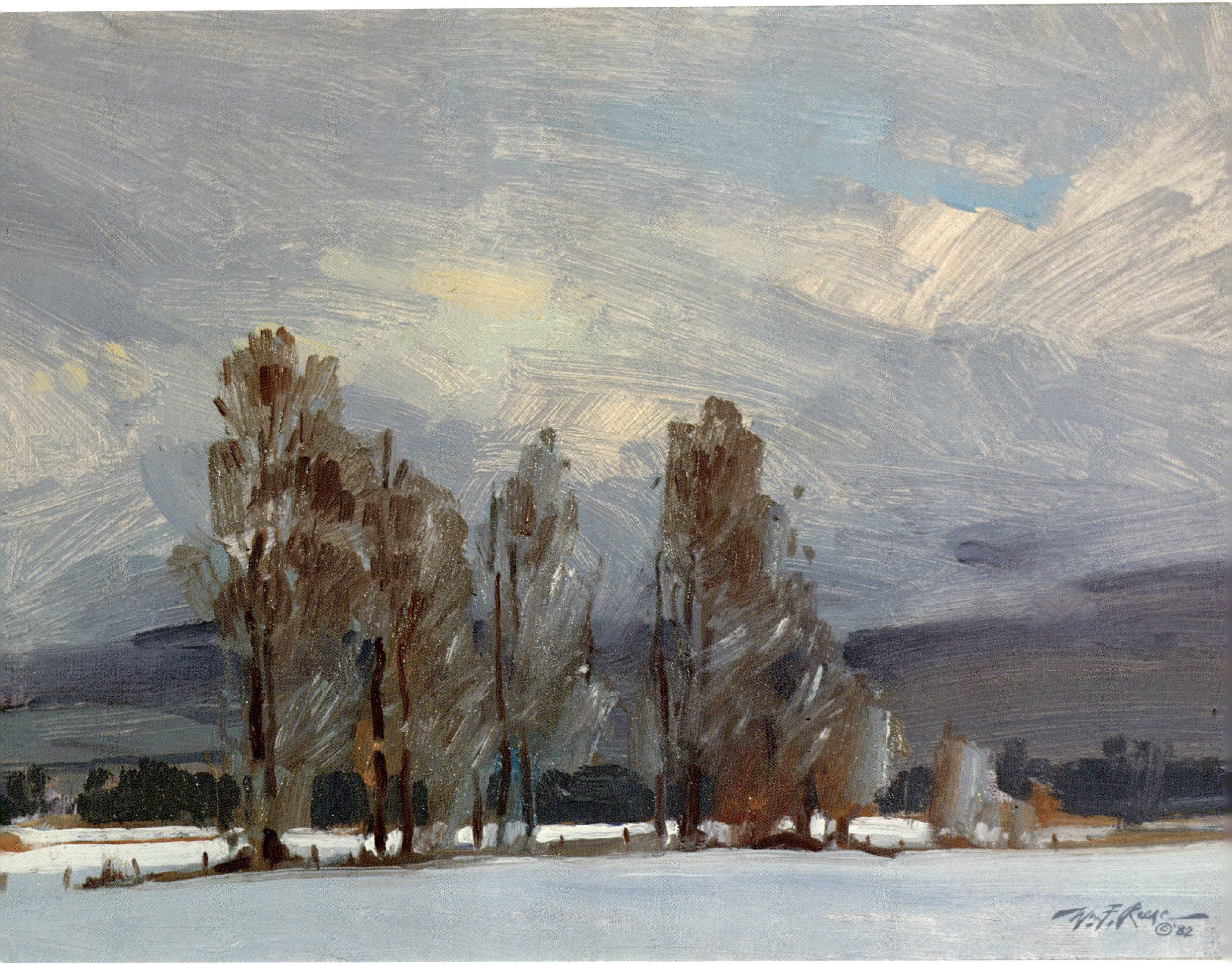

"Those were my pot-boilers! Every artist has to have his pot boilers, something that will earn his bread and butter. However, my studies were never really done for that purpose alone. They were more to satisfy my psychological needs, because once I had completed my still life I was mentally free for the rest of the day. The most important thing to a painter is *freedom.* One must be free to study, to daydream, to think, and to wonder about the world. This is seemingly frivolous and non-productive, at least in the direct or immediate sense, but extremely important to the work of an artist. In the transitional stage between a lifetime of productive labor and the life of an artist, I needed the one-hour exercise every morning to ease my conscience, then I could sit and read, or dream or go out into the country to sketch — or I could do nothing — I had already 'picked my hundred boxes.' Also, that hour served as a point from which to start the day."

Reese painted with fervor, as if it were his last day. By selling a painting now and then and teaching classes, he and Fran managed to stretch their nine months further and further; yet they knew they were reaching the point where Bill was going to have to go back to the sign shop.

One evening they received a call from Gene Lynn, a friend of Bill's dad, whom they had met some years back. Gene had worked for a housing development, the same project Bill's dad worked for. Sr. Reese said he had a tremendous respect for that young fellow, "Gene's a world-beater. He's going to make it and he's going to make it big. I don't know how he's going to do it, but he's got ideas and he's a winner."

"Of course my dad told him all about me and he seemed very interested in what I did — I was still painting signs in Los Angeles at the time. Now, four or five years later, we had moved back to Washington. Gene was an entrepreneur/developer with his own construction company, building his own nursing homes; and he had hired both my father and my brother to work for him. They had just finished a nursing home in Juanita and were preparing for an open-house. Gene was out there planting flowers and pushing bark around,

*Against the Blue*
Oil, 12x16″

just like his own employees, and he asked my brother if I had any paintings that he could borrow for the Opening.

"When he called, I said, 'Sure.' He wanted to come to the house that evening at 7:00 to see them. Another young couple had previously arranged to come at 7:30 to look at a painting, too. I hoped the timing would work. As it turned out, Gene was late and the other two were early. I was showing them the painting in the back part of the studio when the doorbell rang. I excused myself to let Gene in. As he entered the studio, his eyes already examining the painting closest to him, he asked, 'How much is that?'

"$150."

"I'll take it. And, I'll take that one and that one . . . ."

"By the time he was finished, and he hadn't even stopped walking yet, he was headed for the back studio, where the young couple waited, to look for more. They saw him come through the doorway and they almost shouted, 'Get him out of here. He's not going to get this one!' They had their knees and arms wrapped around the painting that they had come to see.

"Well, Gene convinced them to buy, and he bought a couple more himself. I was adding up the figures in my head — that was $1,350 worth of paintings sold in one night, for cash — that was more money than I'd seen in my life!

"Gene told me the next day as I was delivering the paintings that I shouldn't go back to sign painting; I should continue to paint full time."

"What I'd like you to do," he said, "is to go home and figure out what you need to live on each month and I'll give it to you. I want to be a patron."

"I thought, 'Oh, God. I've died and gone to heaven.'

"What a fantastic offer. How many times does something like this happen in one's lifetime — even in ten lifetimes?" Bill started home. Mind racing, buoyant, exhilarated, he couldn't get there fast enough in his excitement. He and Fran talked excitedly and impetuously and planned a champagne celebration.

*Copper Still Life*
Oil, 30x40"

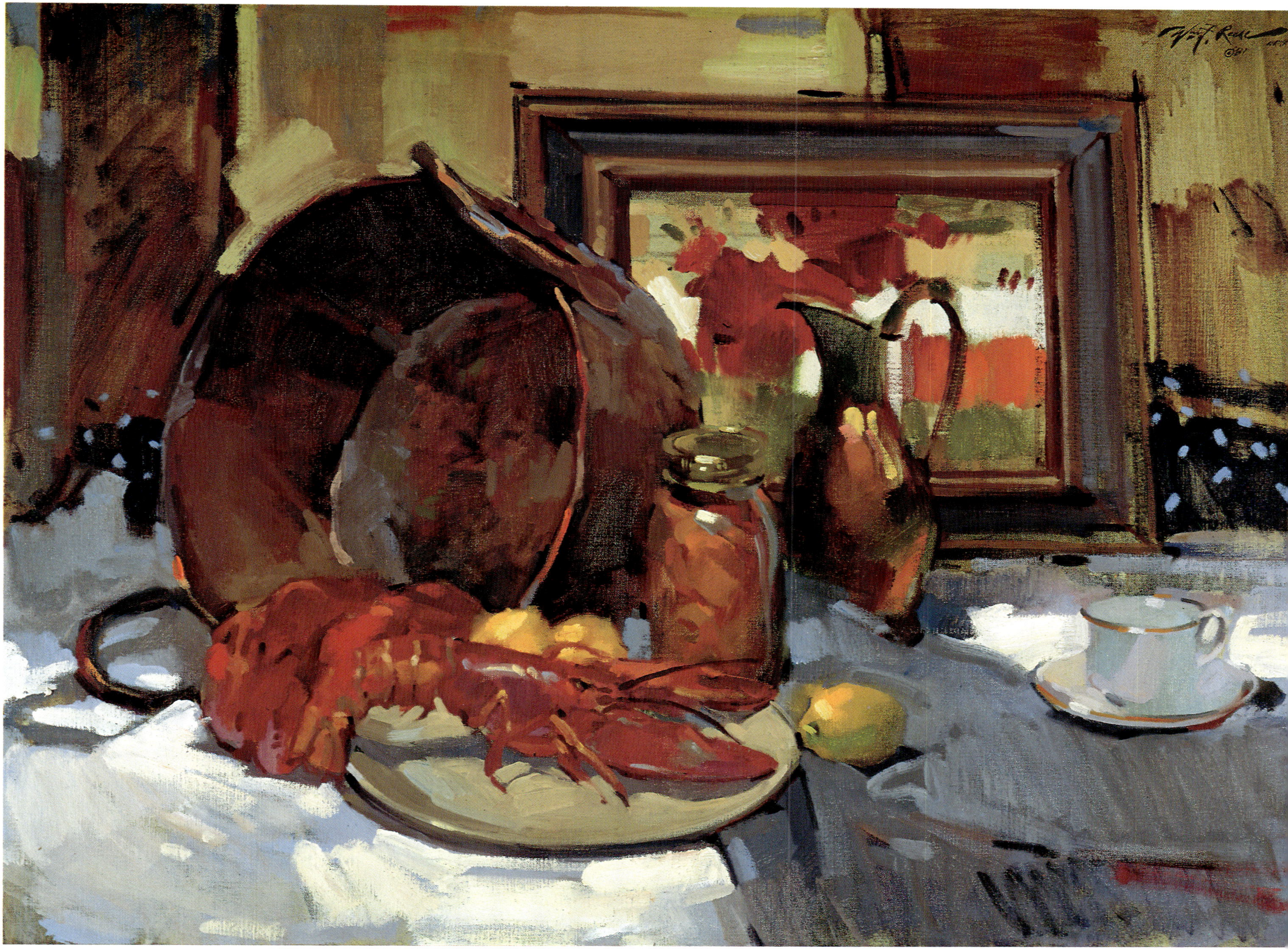

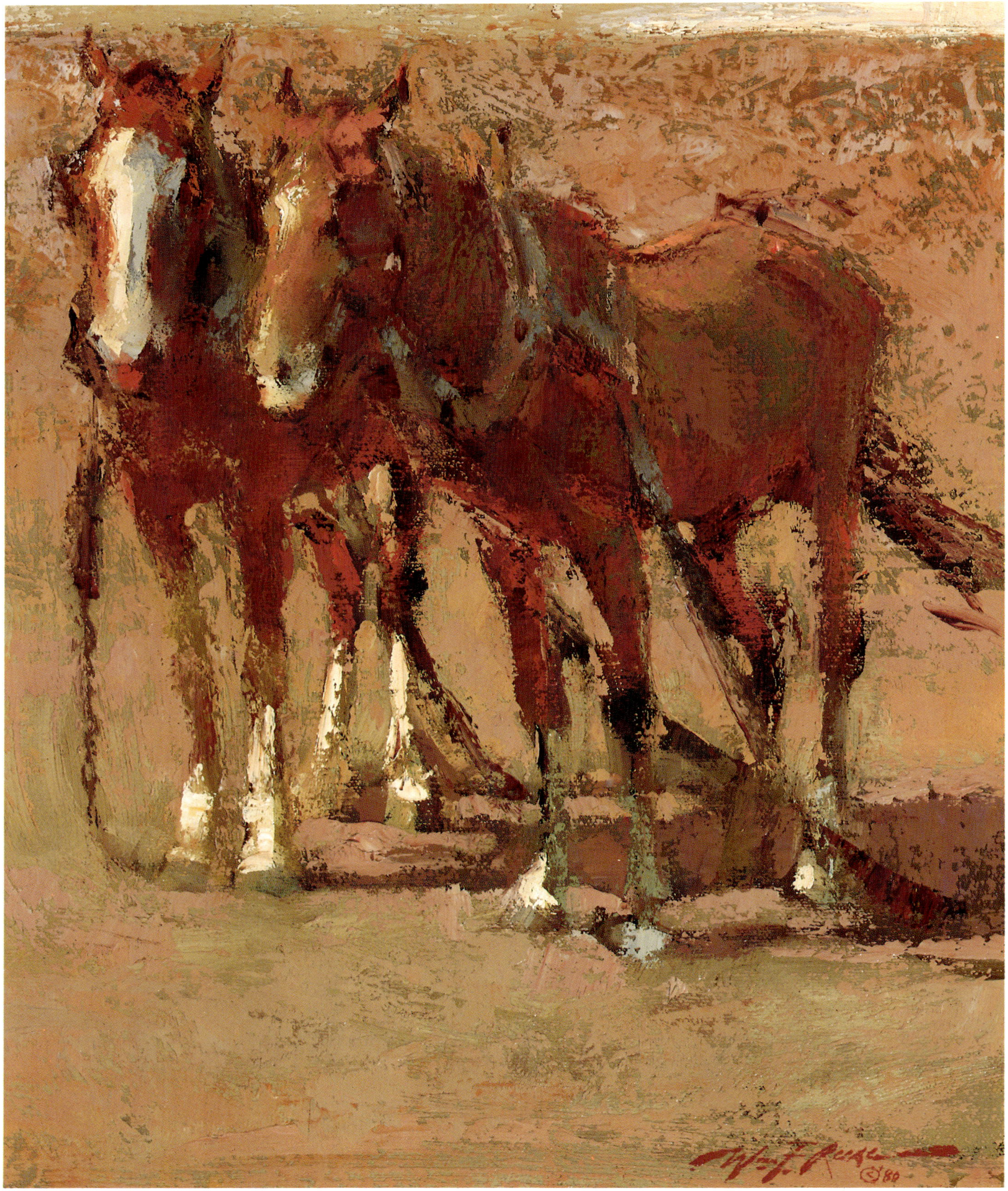

*Navajo Horse Team*
Oil, 15x12″
Collection of
Raymond E. Mesple

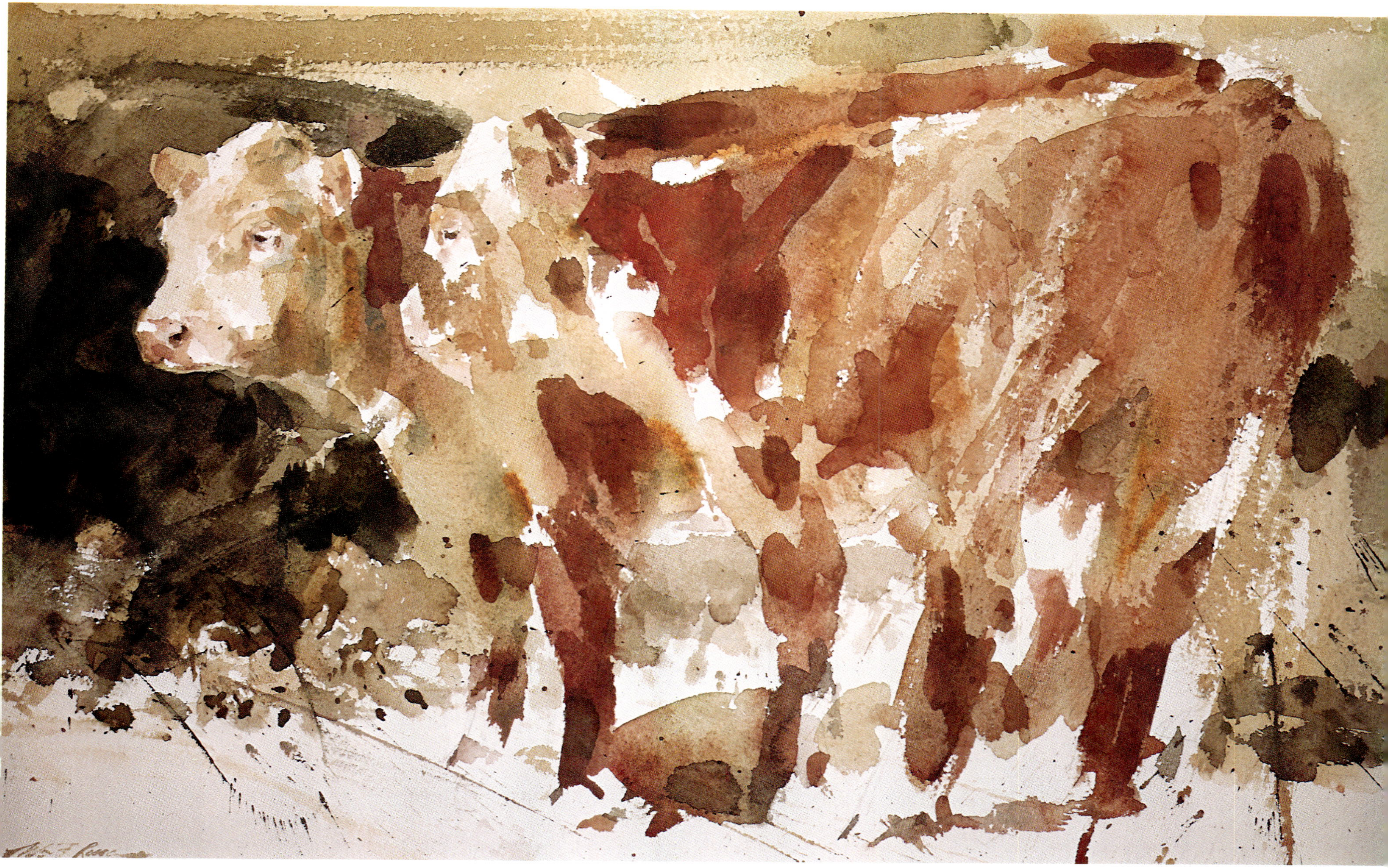

*The Yearlings*
Watercolor, 13½x21½″
Private Collection

"All of a sudden it was as if somebody turned on a bright light, and we stopped talking." Everything seemed hushed and still as if anticipating a momentous decision or happening; finally Bill broke the silence by saying, "You know, we can't accept. This is almost like setting out to walk from New York to Los Angeles and then somebody offers you a ride in Palm Springs. We've come so far by ourselves, I think we ought to walk the rest of the way, too."

Fran looked at Bill for a moment and then quietly said, "I was thinking the same thing."

The next day Reese went over to thank Gene and to tell him about their decision. "I think he always respected me for that. But if it hadn't been for Gene, I don't know what we would have done. From that point on, when we were down to our last bean and didn't know where the next one was coming from, Gene was always there. His secretary would call to say Gene needed a sign, or wall graphics for a new hospital, or another painting for a nursing home. I always suspected that he had an 'in' with my banker. I don't know for sure, but it seemed so coincidental. I owe Gene a lot."

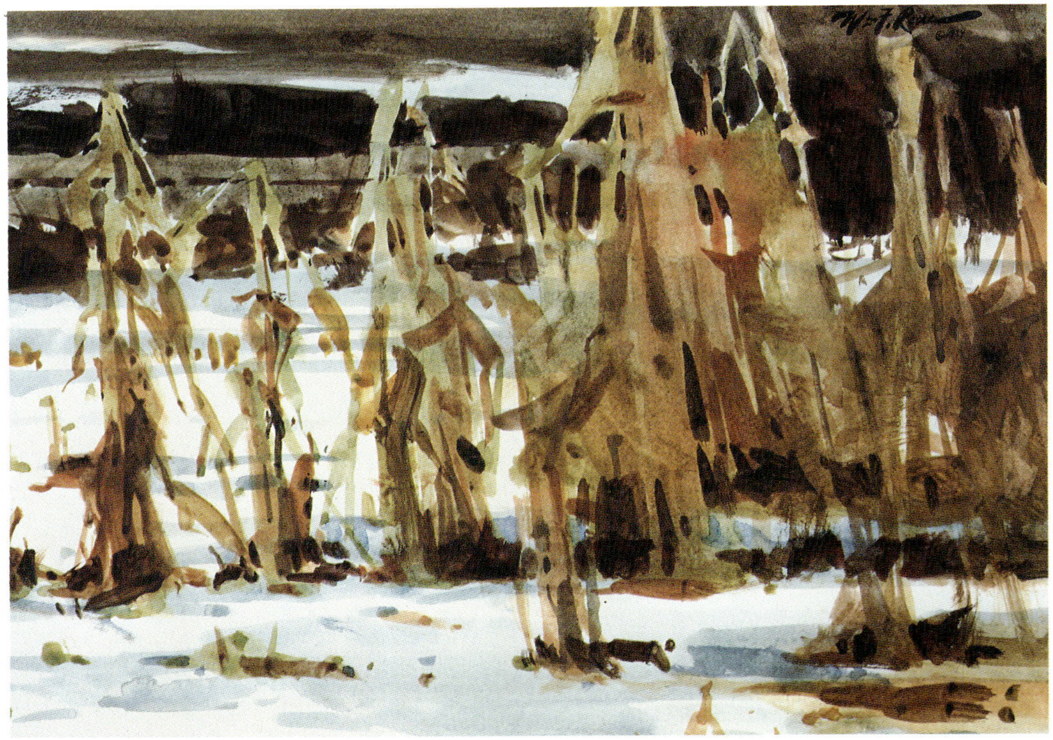

*Early Winter*
Watercolor, 11x15"
Private Collection

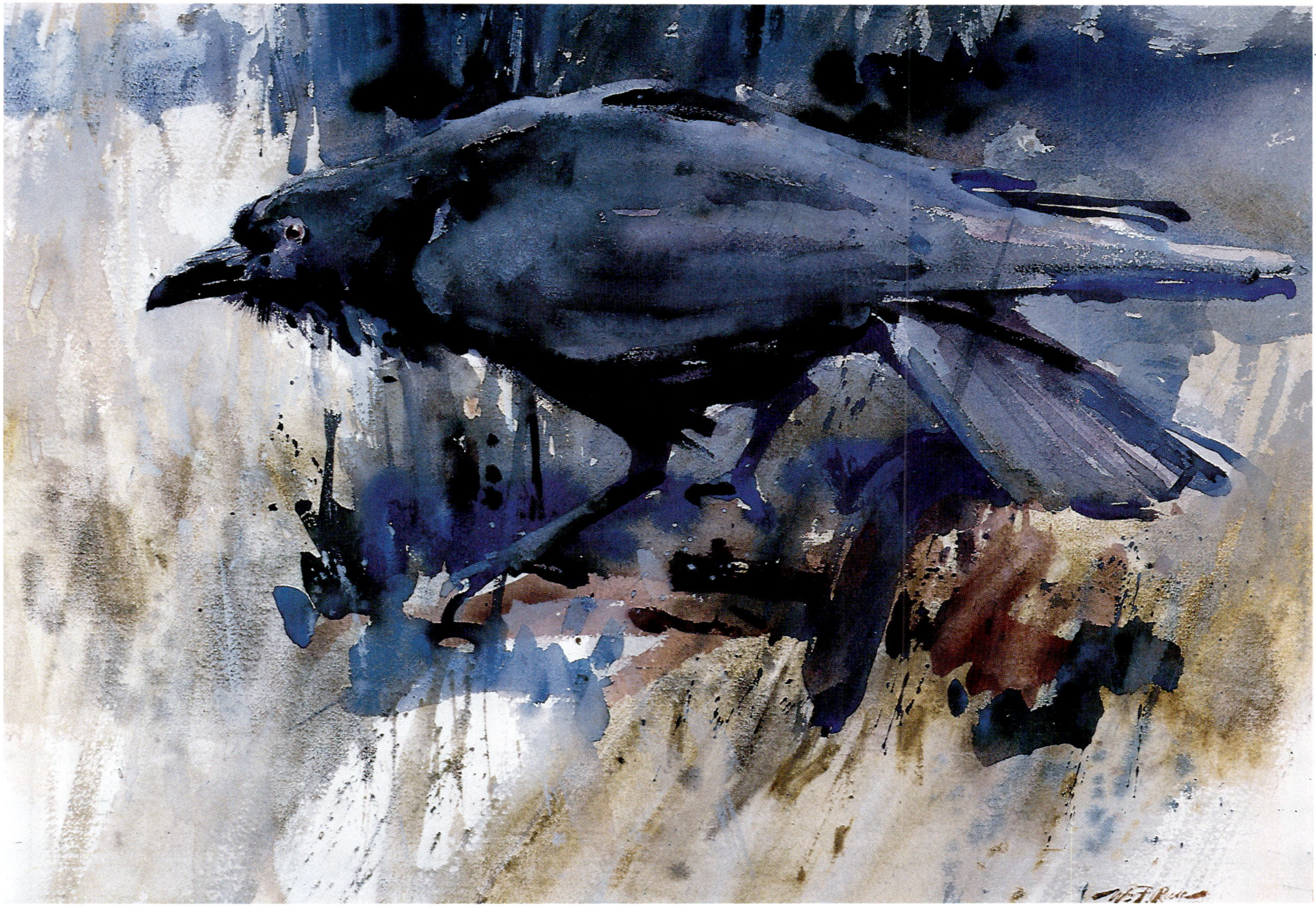

*Camp Robber*
Watercolor, 21x29″
Collection of Rex and Lu Walker

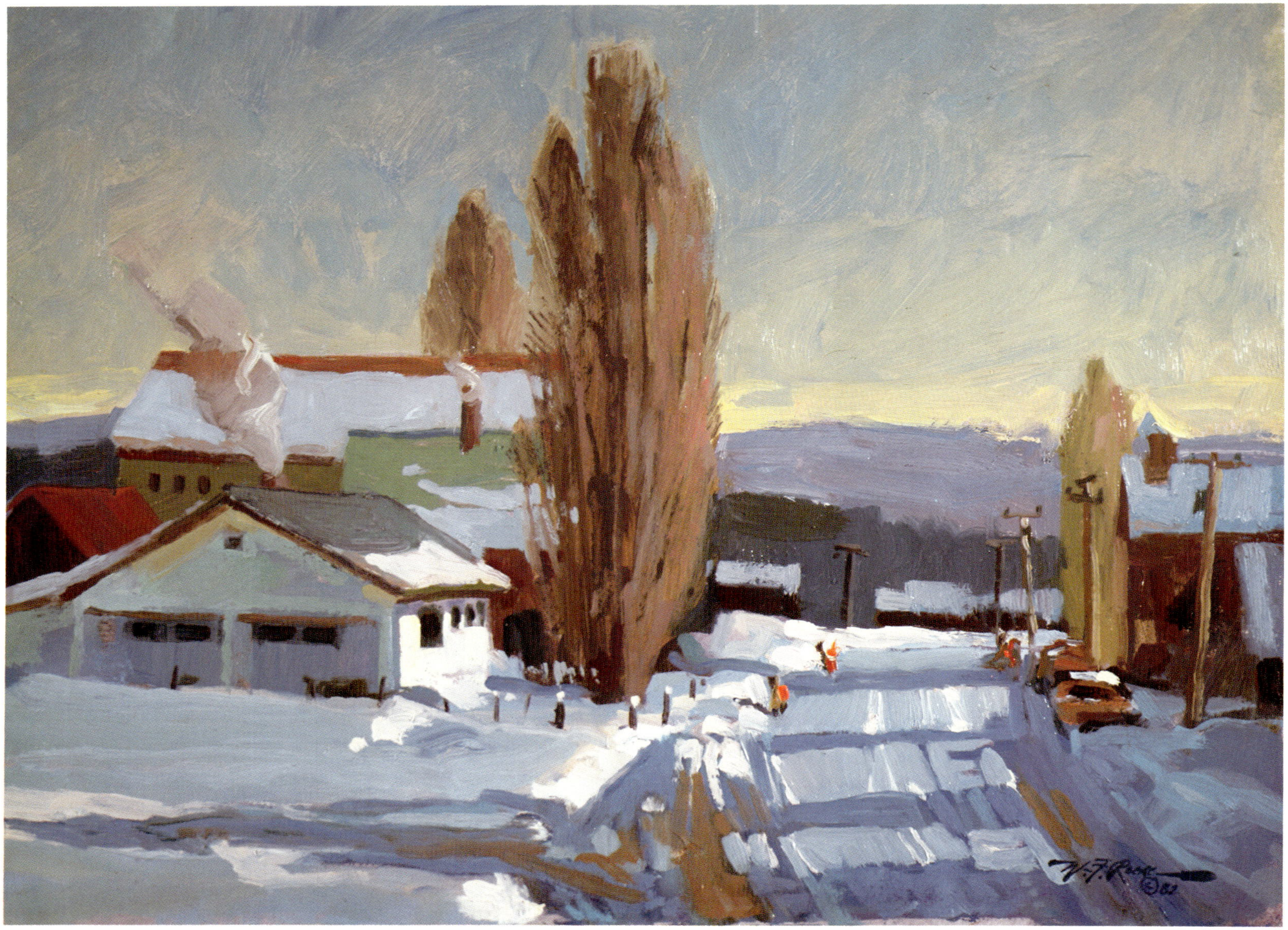

***Winter Afternoon***
Oil, 12x16″

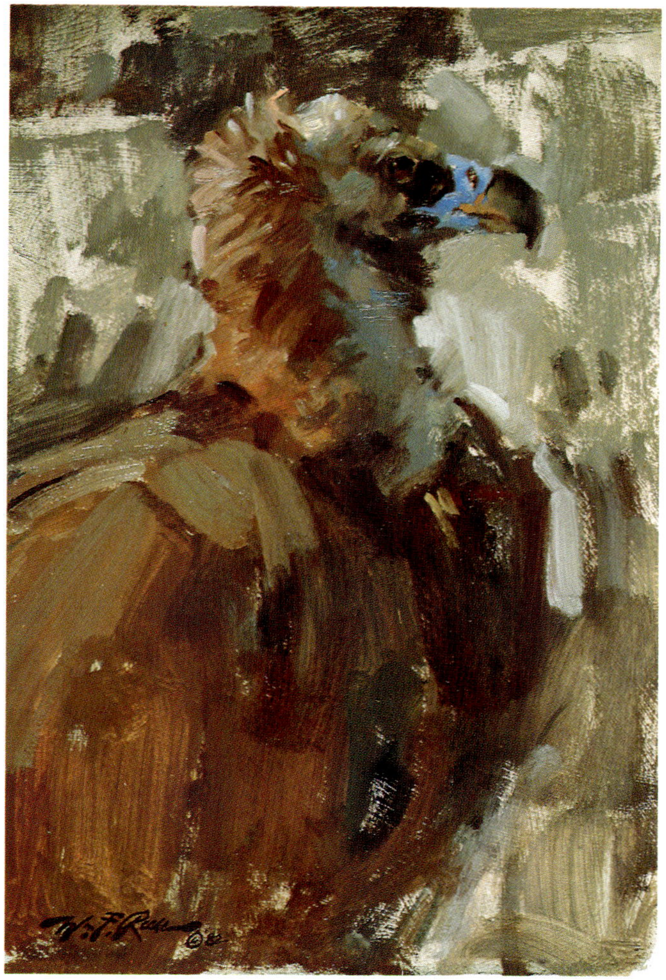

*Chinese Vulture*
Oil, 12x8″
Collection of Gene E. Lynn

# 4 *The Business of Art*

"In order to make a living from your work, you need to have it known that you are a painter. But, if your main reason for going into art is to make money, you shouldn't do it. You have no business being in art," Reese said adamantly. "Even if you make a lot of money at it — that's all you will have — you will be painting junk. An artist has to be dedicated. He must work hard like any other professional, and the interest must be continual — it can't be turned on and off like a faucet. Paint first and later figure out how to sell it.

Art differs little from any other business in which a product is to be sold. Finding the best and largest exposure is essential, involving advertising, publicity, personal contact, telephone calls, gallery exhibitions, art festivals, and art auctions — these are some of the most common methods of telling people about one's art. The work might be of the highest quality, the most imaginative and creative possible, but if no one is aware of it, only the artist can enjoy it in his solitude. He will have to find an income in some other field.

"The artist must aggressively explore all marketing possibilities. Young artists must participate in street fairs, mall shows, competitions, and so on," said Reese. "I've done them all. You do what you have to do short of prostituting your art — survival is the goal."

He and Fran suggested that auctions and collaborative art shows are excellent ways to meet large numbers of people and to expose one's work. Beyond exposure, the Reeses feel it is important to meet the people who buy one of their paintings — to learn why they buy it, what they like about it — "An artist needs to know that," Fran said. "It is nourishment for him. Some artists don't like to meet their collectors, but we really enjoy it. They all seem to be super people, highly interesting, and it gives us great pleasure to know where each piece is going. It's almost like sending your children to live with someone — you want to know if they will have a good home and will be treated well.

"If collectors are able to meet the artist, they will understand more about *why* he is painting, what his background is, what his future plans are. In this way they will have a greater appreciation for the work. They will know that it was done by someone who really loved and believed in his work. After all, as Bill says, 'Art is a form of communication, a chain that isn't complete for him until he knows who is listening.'

"It is important for people to know why an artist paints. They need to know that artists are intelligent people who work in a highly disciplined way which requires technical knowledge as well as intangible, creative thought and skillful use of tools. An artist is not just some weirdo leaping toward the easel for the entertainment of others."

The three-day art shows, in which the Reeses have been exhibitors, are usually collaborative efforts by a number of artists brought together through an arts organization or a special group for mutual benefit. The organization approaches artists, prepares a prospectus which includes information about the show (dates, size limitations of paintings, number of pieces to be shown, amount of commission), prepares publicity, and arranges for exhibition space. Invitational shows, requiring election to membership, are more prestigious, more publicized, and more widely attended.

The first important national art show in which Reese was invited to exhibit was the National Academy of Western Art (NAWA) Exhibition in 1977. Held annually at the National Cowboy Hall of Fame in Oklahoma City, NAWA gives artists recognition and prizes for creativity and technical achievement. Capacity audiences of over 600 academicians, dealers, patrons, and lovers of art come to applaud and bestow medals, cash, museum trips to Europe, and western wardrobes to the chosen honorees at the awards banquet. Preceding the ceremonious feast, guests are treated to seminar programs of events, which typically one year ranged from "the sophistication of Ward

*"I want to paint a picture with nothing but a soul, with nothing other than a spiritual meaning..."*
*— N.C. Wyeth*

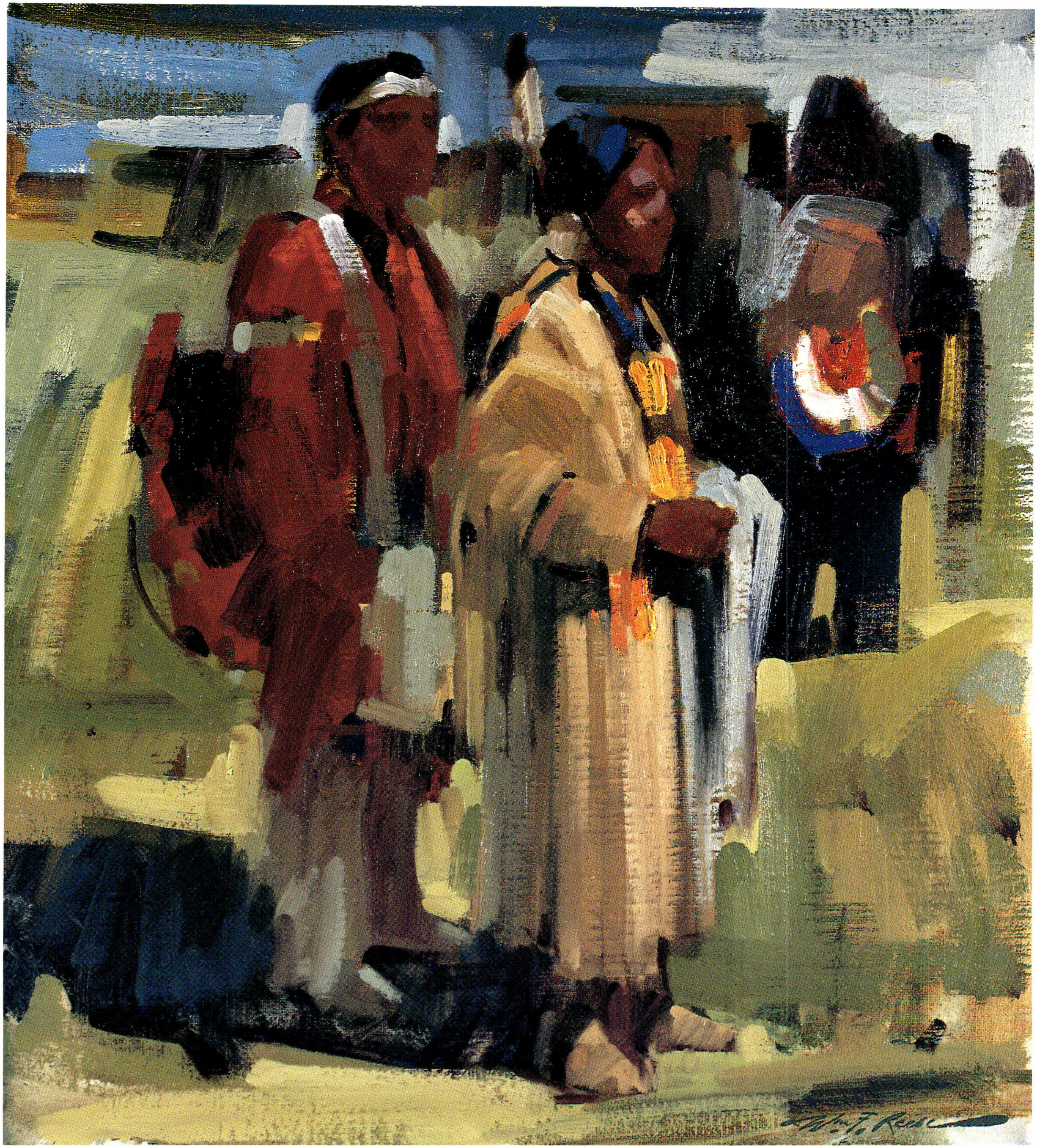

*Drum Song*
Oil, 18x16″
Collection of James and Allene Lee

Landrigan's New York jewelry market to a history of the West traced by artist-author Paul Rossi through the evolution of the saddle . . ."[5] to artists' field demonstrations. (Reese was a 1983 participant; his demonstration, a portrait of a cowboy, prompted artist Joan Marron to remark, "A lot of people can color them out of books and photographs but there aren't many who can stand on a bald prairie in front of hundreds of people and produce a work of art.")

Sometimes the audience response to the invitational shows is so tremendous that buyers must purchase the art by the drawing of names from boxes placed next to each artist's work, as in the "Artists of America" show held each autumn in Denver. This is another art exhibition of national caliber, showing the work of "the best representational artists working today from across the country."[6]

No matter where the exhibition or who the audience, the Reeses make a point of visiting with as many of the guests as they can.

"We have observed Bill during these events," say co-exhibitors Kathy and Les Perhacs. "He walks around and introduces himself to people and makes them feel welcome. He talks about his paintings, what inspires him, his ranch, his love of painting outdoors, his technique, the reason he doesn't work with photographic detail. He is very easy going. He has a knack for tuning-in on the other person's point of view, and he is able to direct his discussion to include that person — to involve the visitor in the conversation.

"If someone should remark, 'I really like your work, but I just can't afford it,' Bill turns it around from a negative to a positive by saying, 'Well, I'll do something specifically for you.' By that, he means that he will custom paint or draw something to suit that person's pocket book. He will not paint a piece that is similar to the one displayed, selling it at a lower price — that would be unfair, unethical practice — but he will paint a smaller or different piece or make a sketch of high quality, yet more suited to the individual's budget. It is not a high-pressure pitch, but rather an extension of his life: everything he does, everywhere he goes, he is thinking about his art, and if someone expresses a desire to own it, he tries to find a way to fulfill that wish."

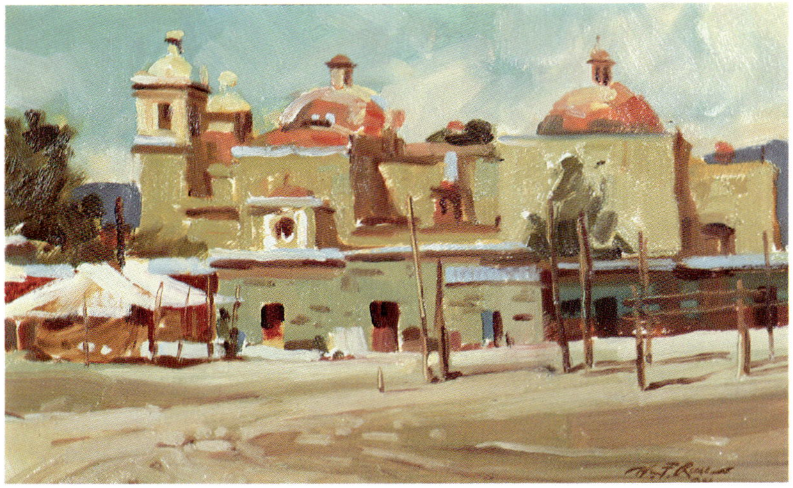

*Mexican Church*
Oil, 8x12″
Collection of Brill and Charlene Lee

*Boy From Acoma*
Pastel, 13x15½″
Collection of E. L. Johnson

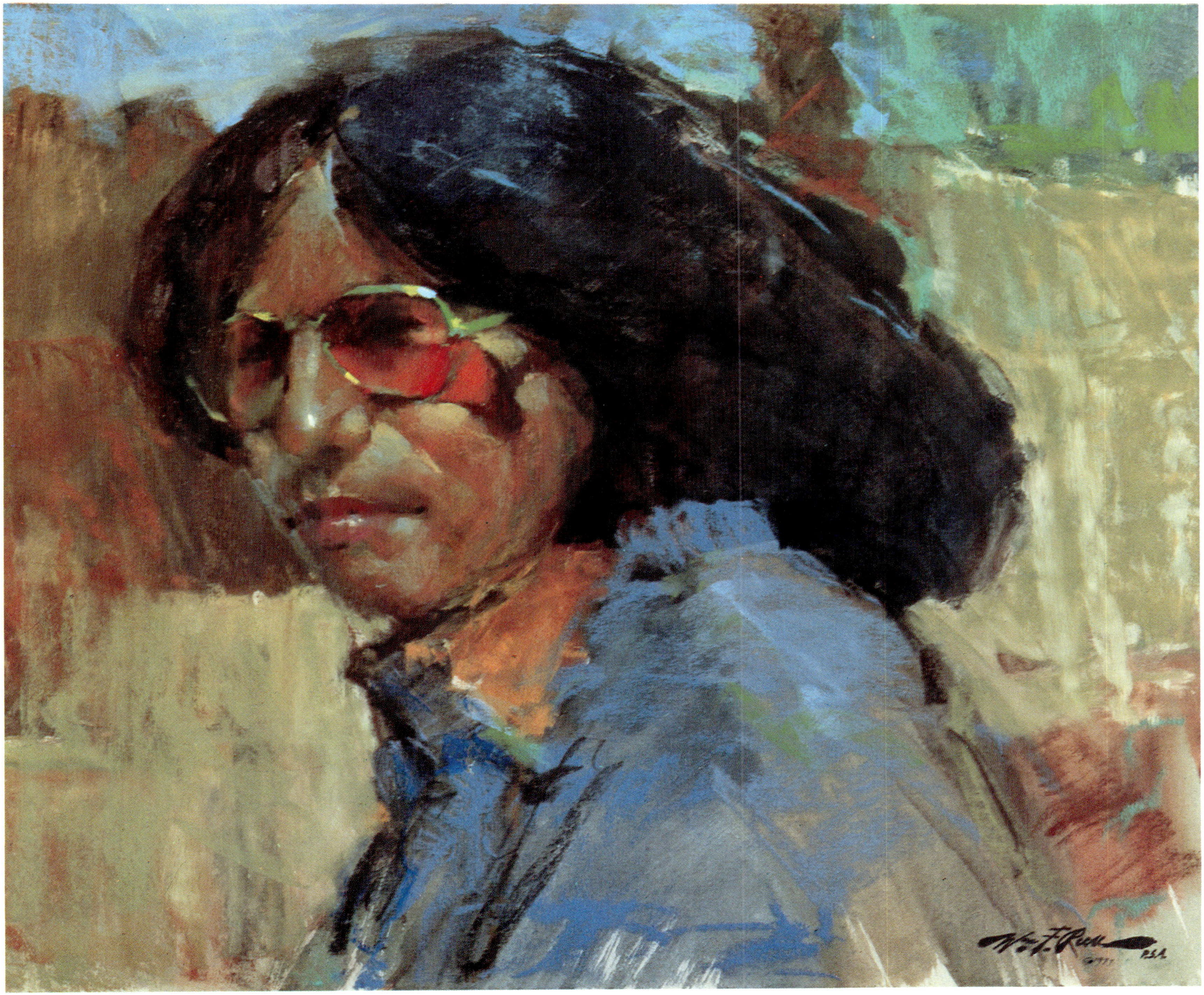

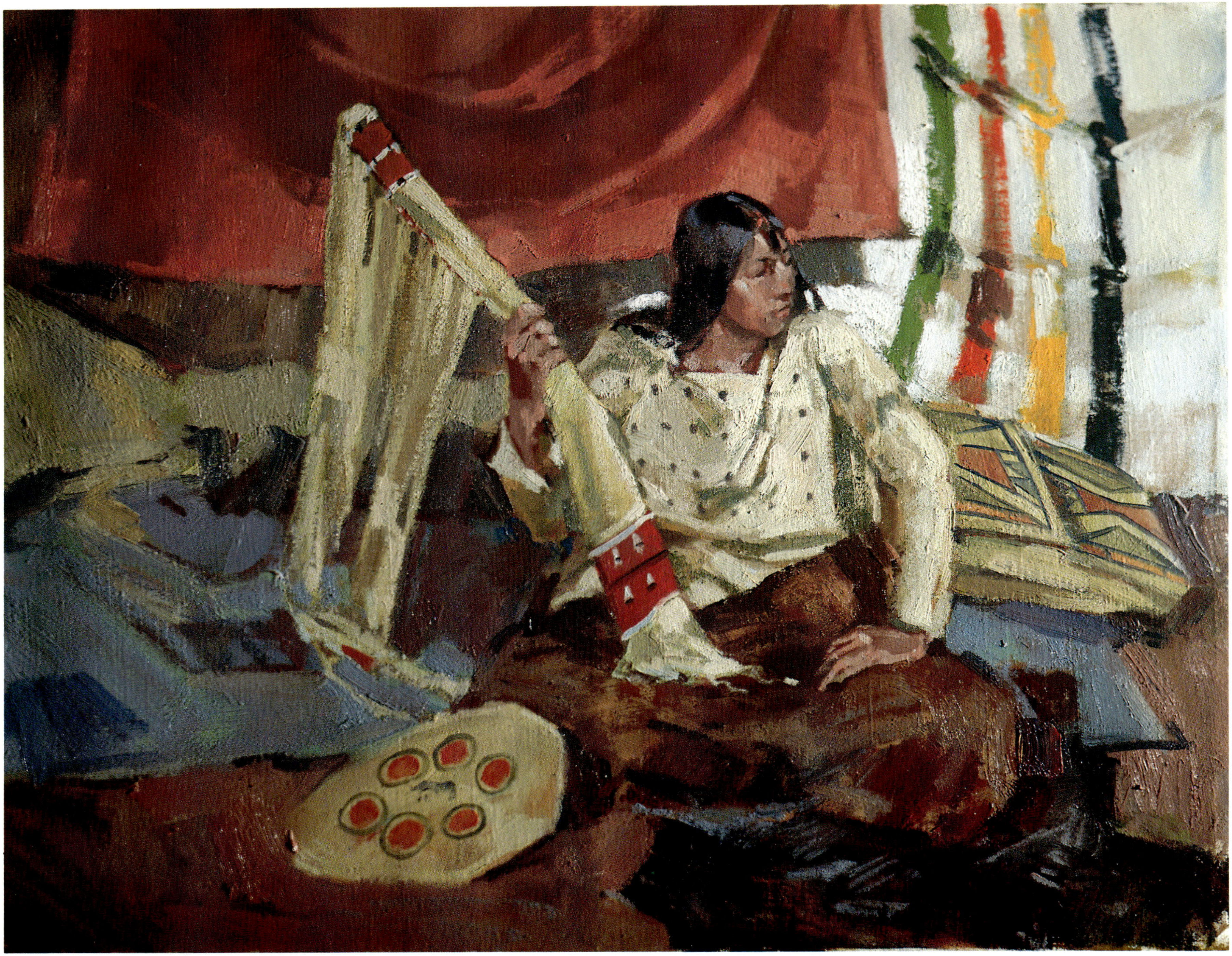

*Bear Shirt*
Oil, 16x20″
Collection of
Mr. & Mrs. Steve Honnen

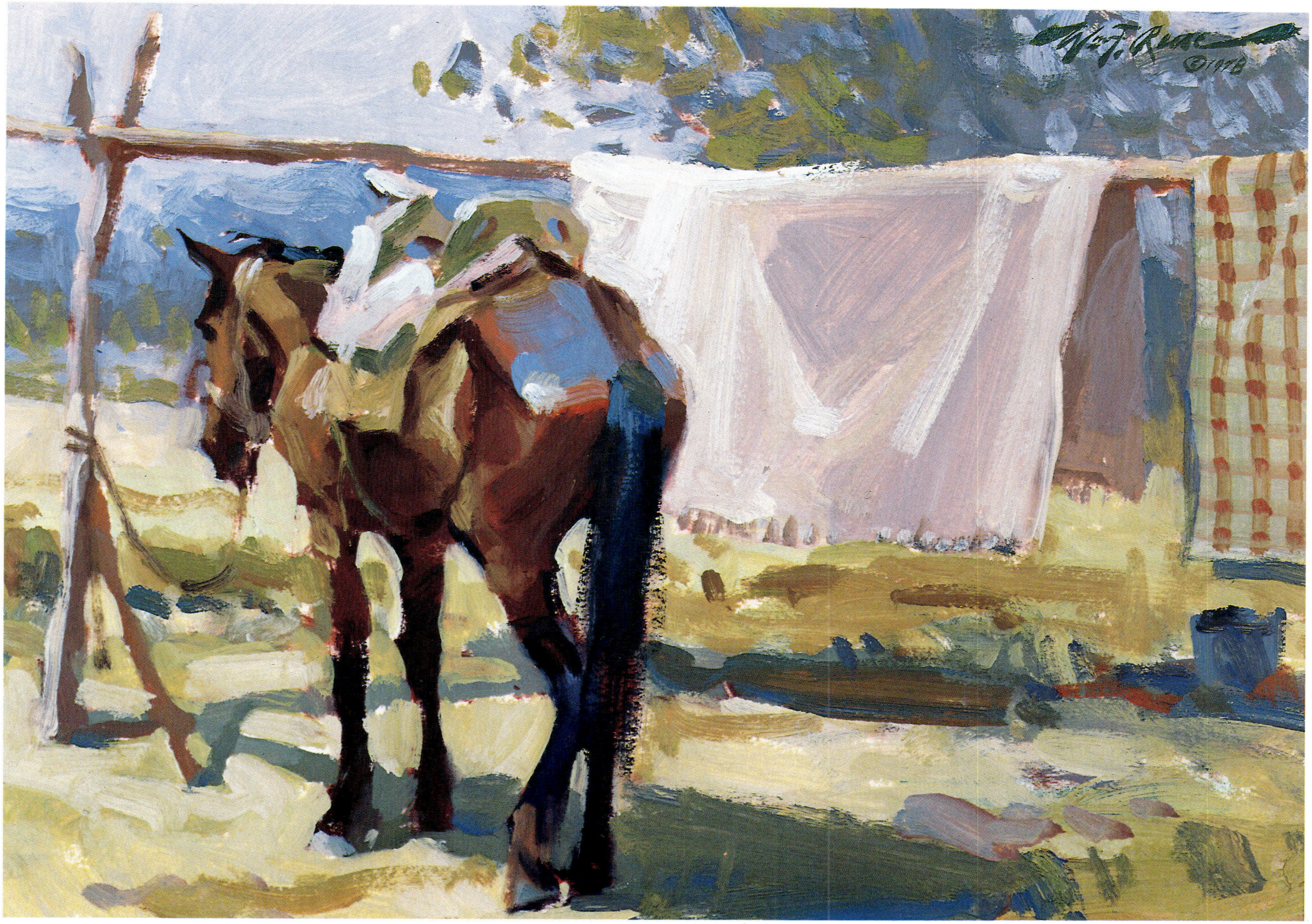

*Siesta*
Oil, 9x12″
Collection of
Mr. & Mrs. Richard Owings

The Perhacses continued, "He is a good role model for us. If one thing doesn't work for him, he tries something else and just keeps right on going. He has built a good solid reputation by constantly building, perhaps not always by leaps and bounds, but by persistent effort and attention to quality.

"He supports good artists, even those who aren't big names. He doesn't feel threatened by competition — he loves art and anyone who is a good and committed artist. He is willing to help in any way he can.

"What makes Bill a unique and prolific painter is that he doesn't try to do a great painting every time he paints; he paints because he loves it. He paints wherever he goes, on location, and then keeps adding to those. They are like building blocks, each painting builds on the other, helping him perfect his craft and vision; and the result is that he probably produces more great paintings than if he had photographed all the material and then painted from those photos.

"For example, when we were in Corpus Christi with him for a show, we were invited to a Longhorn ranch, the largest in the world. Bill immediately began painting Longhorns. And, he didn't paint just one steer but composites of ten or fifteen, study-sketches for paintings which he will do in the future."

Because he was there, working on location, he was able to capture a sense of texture, attitude, true color, and the behavior patterns of the Longhorns, as well as gain a feel for the sun-baked earth and sultry south Texas air. The essence of these emerges in one form or another from time to time.

In regard to being a role model and an assister of others (promoting other artists, helping them gain admittance to shows, and buying their work), Reese would quickly say that he is perpetuating the acts of kindness and assistance given to him.

"For example, to name just a few . . . Connie [Conrad] Schwiering was instrumental in getting my work submitted to the NAWA board and for my election to membership; to my good friend, Sergei Bongart, I am indebted for inspiration and my intense love for art — from him I learned of the soul of art and its true purpose and the relationship of all the arts, from painting to poetry to ballet — and to

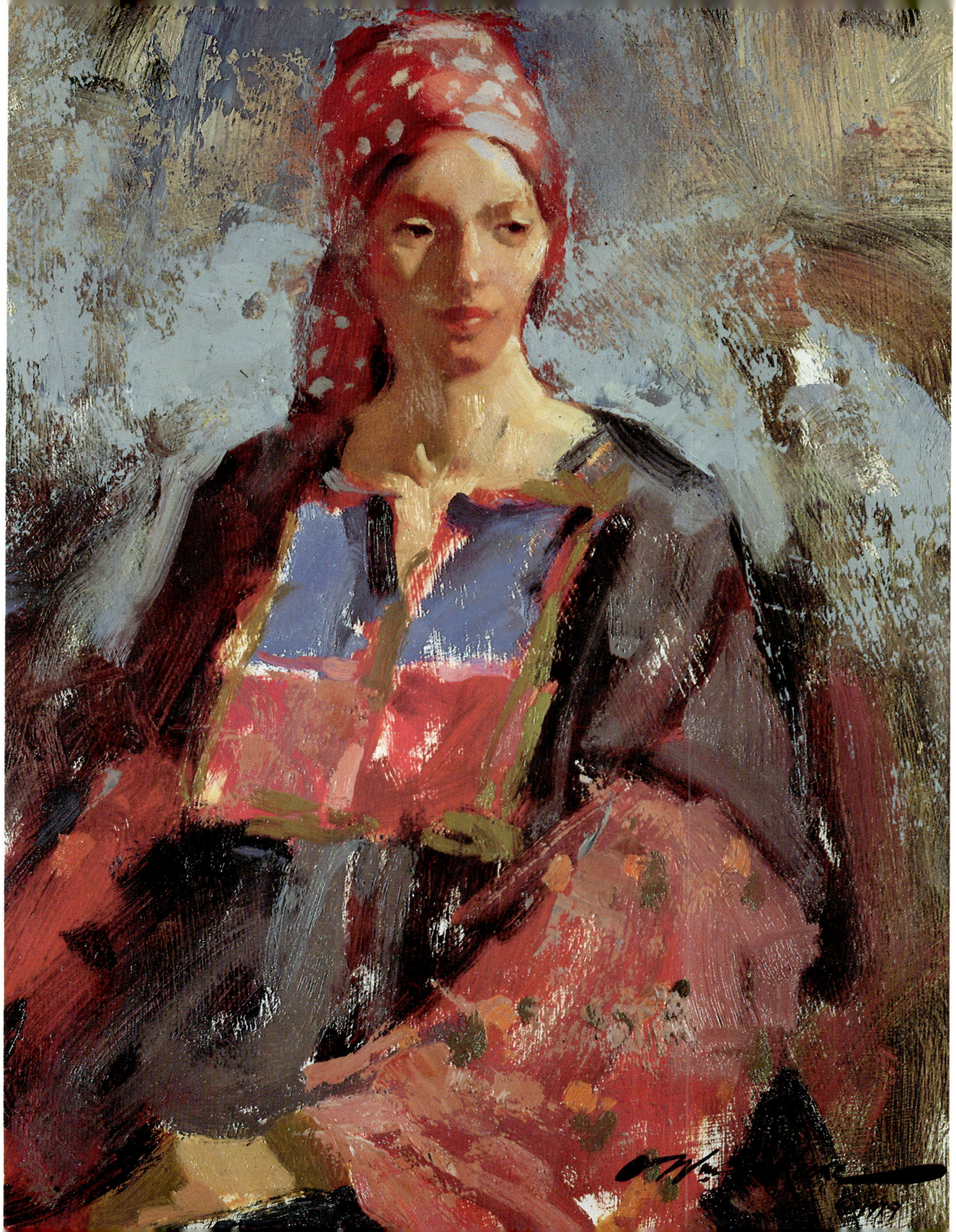

*Brenda*
Oil, 12x9″
Private Collection

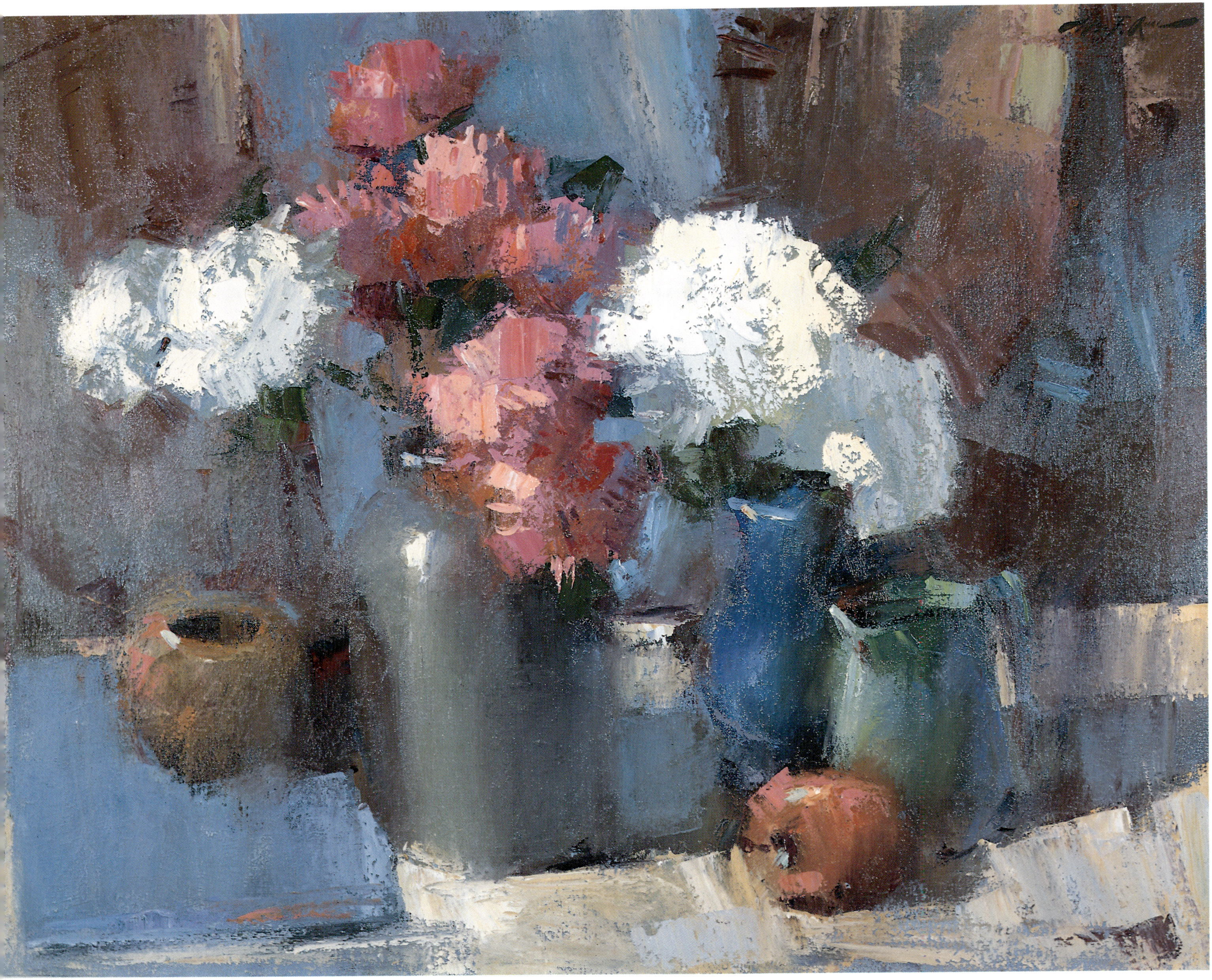

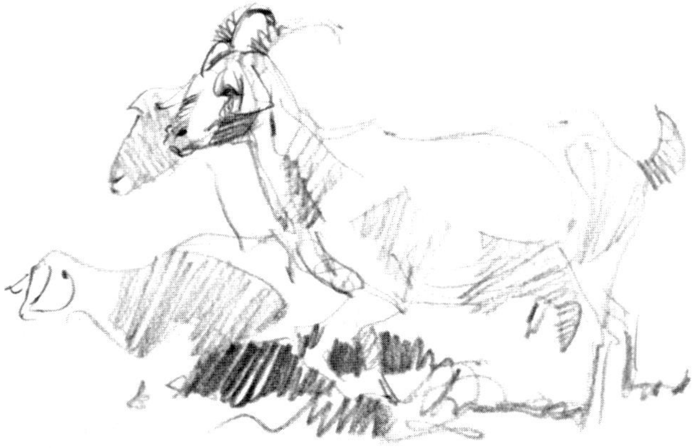

life itself and the importance of being true to yourself and your art. And, Ramon Kelley... he's done so much for me. He's given me contacts that I would never have gotten any other way. He is a good business man and has made me realize how important it is for me to think of myself as an artist in business — someone who conducts his affairs with order and consistence just as any good business person.

"It is not enough to live in the woods, create art, and leave things to blind chance. Art isn't just a game. If you must make a living at it, you have to try to make others realize that it isn't just a fun hobby. You must think of yourself as an artist in business! You have the right to be treated a certain way — to be respected for your efforts and talent — and in return, you have the responsibility to show that respect for the people with whom you do business.

"Learning to think of myself as a business man was not only a big lesson, but a hard one. I had difficulty for a long time in trying to figure out how to ask people to pay *money* for something I had so much fun doing. I found myself apologizing for enjoying what I did for a living.

*A Special Kind of Melody*
Oil, 24x30″
Collection of Mr. & Mrs.
Robert B. Hevly

"Another thing is that you have to learn to cope with everyday interruptions and problems and thoughts of failure. You can't let them stop you from working. Eliminate failure from your mind. Even if a project didn't work, it still had something positive about it, a new learning experience or result from which you will gain in the future. Henry Miller once said, 'Sometimes a setback is as good, or better, than a push. We seldom realize how much the negative serves to induce the positive, or the bad induces the good.'[7]

"Everyone has problems of one kind or another," Reese continued, "but many times they can be avoided or eliminated by thinking or planning ahead. When I worked for that ornery man in Oregon, he kept yelling at me because he could see that I was concentrating on the letter I was working on, and he'd say, 'If you're thinking about the letter you're doing right now, you're too late. You should have been thinking about it when you were doing the last one.' He drilled that idea into me so much that I am still thinking ahead of myself and sometimes I miss the enjoyment of the moment, but I think I avoid a lot of mistakes and problems because of it. So, you see, even with that man and that experience — out of all the negatives, the shattering of dignity and the goading to violence, all the yelling and drill — many good things emerged and have worked to my benefit. You just have to sort out the venom or bad parts, extract the good, and go on with your work and your life."

As to the mechanics of their business, Fran is the manager, the partner who keeps track of the numbers and creates an environment which enables Bill to paint. She makes careful arrangements so that business affairs, family life, social obligations, and the creative process commingle smoothly; and because she and Bill believe so firmly in full-time parenting, their commitment has resulted in a busy, rich life. She communicates with galleries, picture framers, suppliers, art organizations, and airlines. She calls collectors to keep them "up-dated" because she has discovered that they like and appreciate knowing about the events in regard to Bill's work; and she keeps a card file on each painting, listing information about its history, medium, size, where it has been shown, who purchased it, and its price.

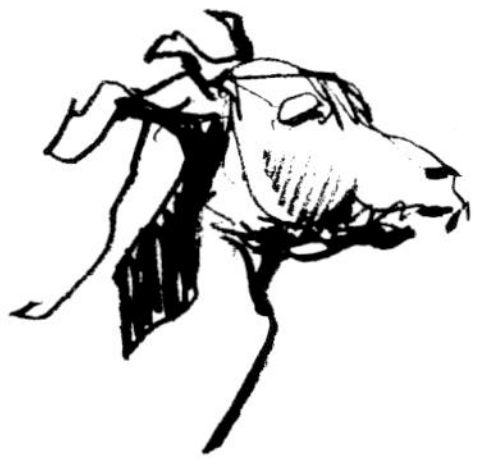

*Las Cabritas*
Oil, 24x30″
Collection of J. W. Gordon, Jr.

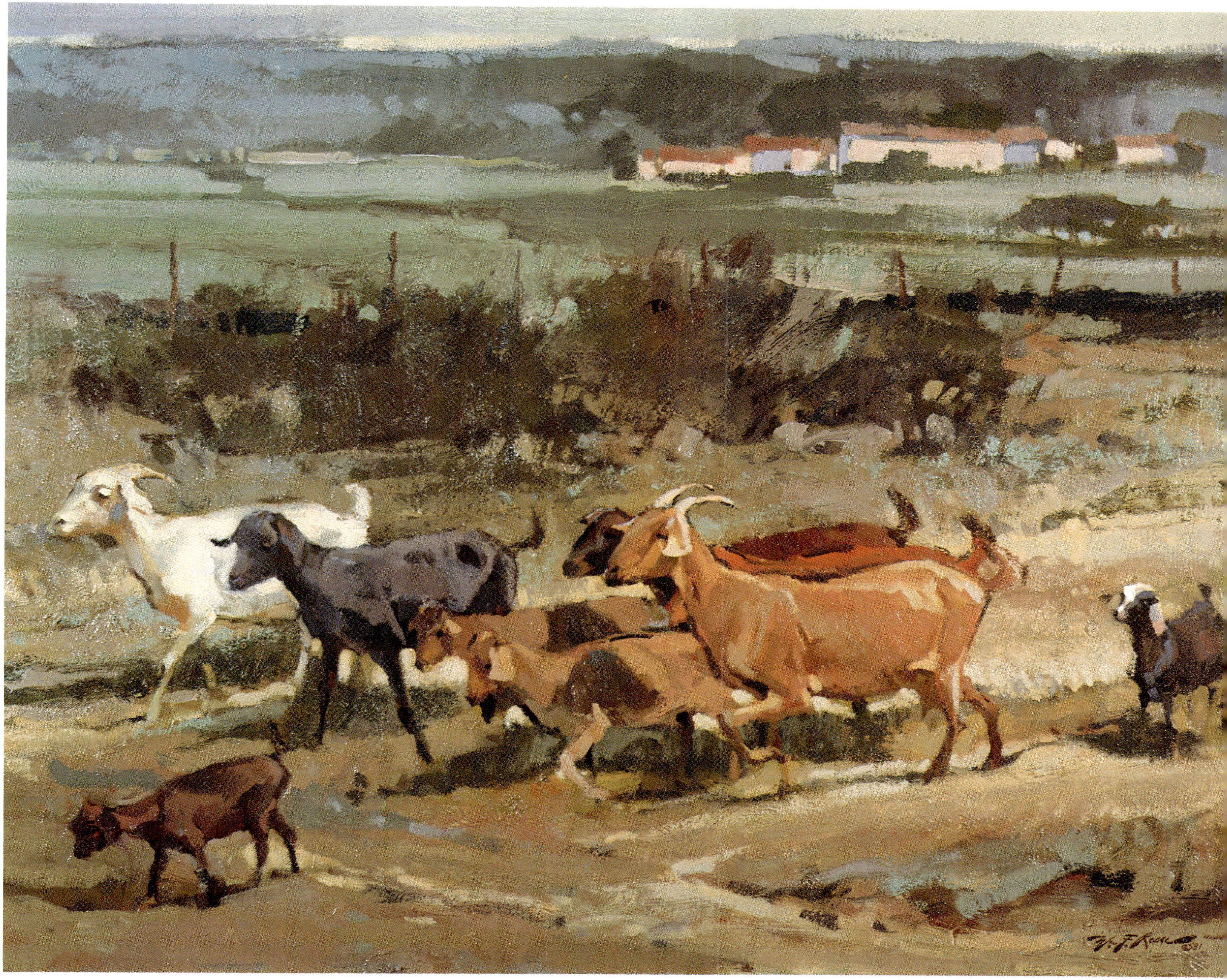

"We both make decisions about the prices," Fran said, "but Bill decides what goes where (to galleries and other shows). He insists on showing the wide range of work, not just selected pieces that are guaranteed to sell. He says that if the whole spectrum isn't shown, it's like asking someone to understand an entire book from reading a few randomly selected pages.

"Whenever we went to a show to exhibit our work, and this still applies, we always made sure that we had new paintings to present — and new frames. Many times the frames were more expensive than we could afford, but a good presentation is important and it has paid off. Now we use several different framers located in various parts of the country — Bill's paintings are so diverse that one type of frame just doesn't suit them all."

*"If the whole spectrum of paintings isn't shown, it's like asking someone to understand an entire book from reading a few randomly selected pages."*

Fran said that due to their upbringing, they never admitted to their lean years at the time. "It was much better to keep a positive attitude. When people asked how the art business was doing, we always said, 'Just fine.' We never came back from the shows with the report that nothing sold, the show was awful, nobody came — even if true. At the first shows, nothing did sell, but there wasn't anything to be gained in talking about it. Besides, there's a lot of psychology involved. You never know who your customers are going to be, and nobody wants to buy the work of a loser."

Along with her keen perception, Fran is refreshingly forthright, a quality which makes transactions, and interactions, much easier; one doesn't have to cope with hidden meanings or covertness, for she speaks her mind in a wonderfully apt manner. She has an uncanny intuition, a baffling talent for being able to sense or foresee aspects of an idea, event, or occurrence — not in an oppressive or foreboding way, but through a casual or amusing circumstance — and she finds specific objects within set time limits: an antique sofa for Bill's studio and a hard-to-find double-oven range for the farm kitchen just five days before dinner for twelve on Thanksgiving, just two of the many examples.

Bill mused about an incident in which Fran's intuition as usual proved correct. It occurred in the early days when they were alarmingly short of funds. He was working in the studio when Fran came

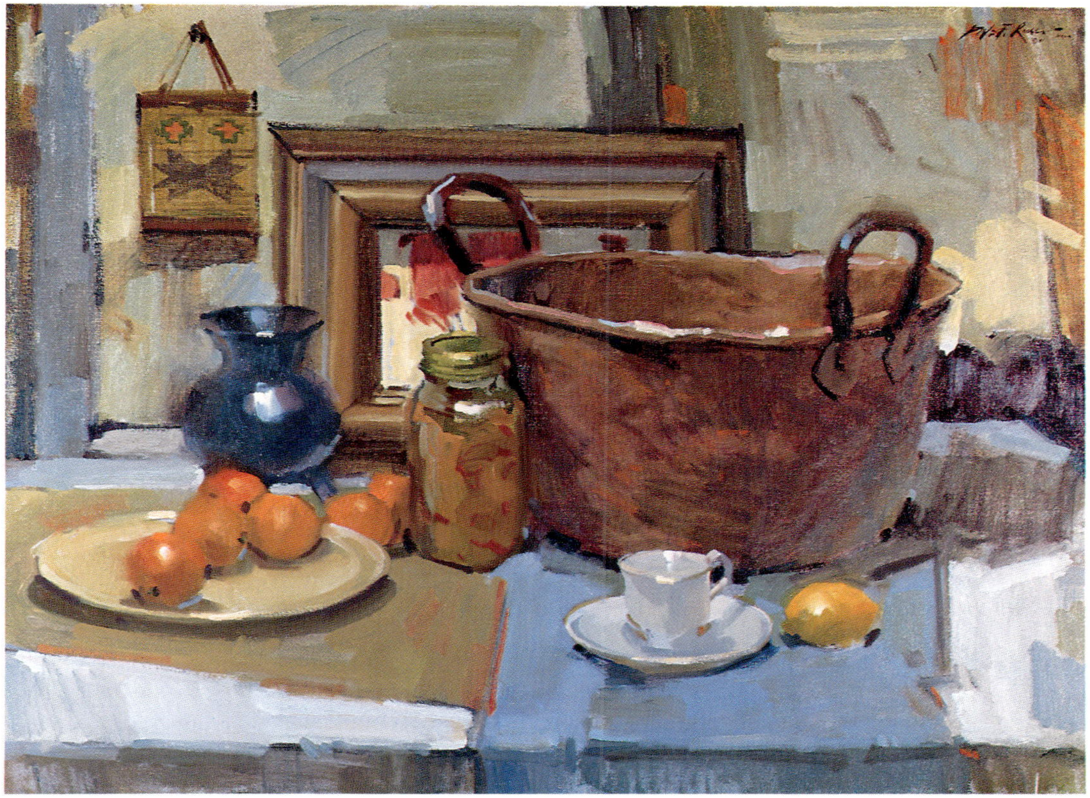

*Studio Arrangement*
Oil, 30x40″

running down the stairs shouting, "Whole mushrooms! Whole mushrooms!" And she produced an open can as evidence.

"Big deal," Bill thought and then asked, "What's so special about whole mushrooms?"

"The label on the can says 'Pieces and Stems,' the kind I always buy because we can't afford the whole ones. But these are *whole*! Our luck is going to change." With that, she went back up the stairs, a new spring in her step and a smile on her face. Then she broke open a half-dozen eggs for the dish she was preparing — they all had *double* yolks! That cinched it. There was no question in her mind that the dry spell was over.

The next day, two major paintings sold.

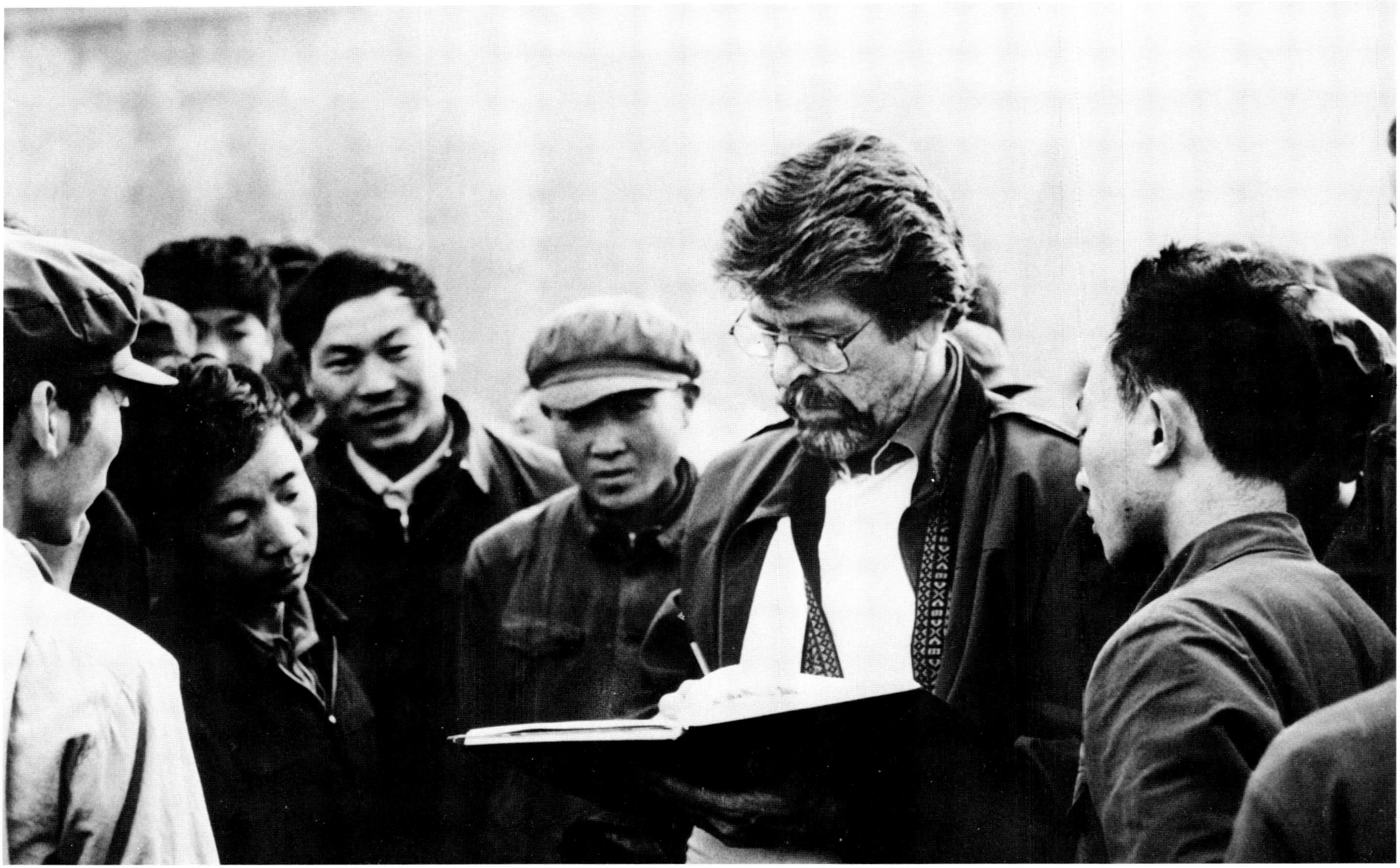

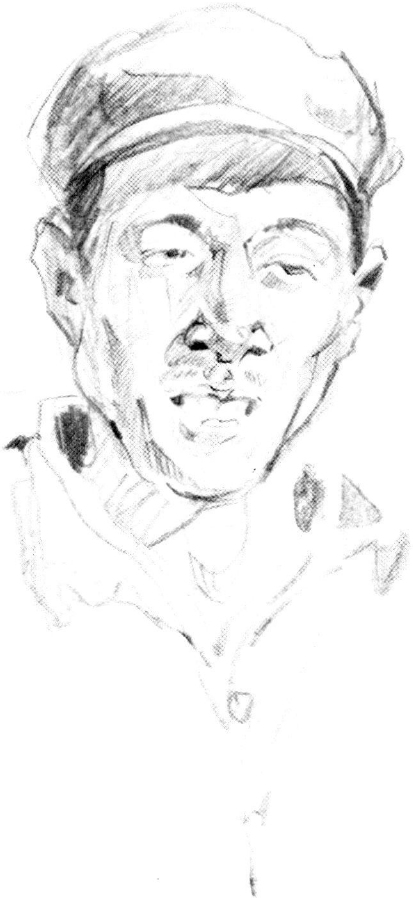

# 5 *Journey to China*

"If I wanted something, all I had to do was to take out my sketchbook and draw what I needed — I communicated by drawing — the sketchbook always seemed to fascinate them.

"One day I went to the market to sketch the buildings and the people, people with yokes carrying heavy loads of vegetables or other products just as they had for centuries and people pulling rubber-tired carts or pedaling 'pick-up bikes'; anyway, the minute I took out my sketchbook people started to run toward me.

"Soon a crowd of about two hundred had gathered. One man asked if he could practice his English by serving as interpreter. Of course, I had no objection to that. He was sort of like a sports announcer in that he kept the crowd informed about my progress with the drawings, a blow-by-blow description, you might say! The crowd at first kept politely closing in, but the frontliners, realizing I needed 'breathing space,' pushed the others back and kept an aisle open to see my subject. They were such an appreciative audience, I had a ball!"

Enthusiasm glowed in Reese's face as he talked of his experiences in China. One of a selected group of artists invited to participate in the "First American Western Art Exhibit" of contemporary artists to be shown in China, Reese accompanied two of his paintings to Peking. The show, conceived by Driscol and Knox of Denver, was sponsored through the governments of the United States and the Republic of China, taking two years to arrange.

Glowing enthusiasm, however, wasn't the case at the beginning of Reese's trip. Although he had been excited about sending his work, and he wanted very much to see the Chinese people, he wasn't able to muster up a lively interest in making the journey himself. Stories of China's political upheavals and the regimentation of her people, combined with the months and months of anticipation waiting for the arrangements to be completed, had dimmed the glow of the initial invitation and further contributed to his reluctance.

He found it convenient to make excuses about the costs, inconveniences, and considerable time the trip would take away from his work — all atypical of him — yet, despite such misgivings, the reservations were made, and when the time came he boarded the plane for San Francisco. Delays in departure made arrival time into the Bay Area later than scheduled, and he sighed with relief as they landed because he was certain he had missed his connecting flight to Manila. No such luck. Authorities informed him that the Philippine Airline's jet was still at the waiting gate, and they rushed him through.

After several stops in different cities, and several days later, Reese and the thirteen other American artists arrived in Peking, taking time to rest and adjust before opening night. The gala was held in the Peking Exhibition Hall, a building constructed by the Russians in the 1950's. A huge red star, high above the facade, commemorated its builders, while an imposing colonnade with Corinthian capitals paid homage to the Ancient Greeks.

At the opening, the large foyer glittered with hundreds of lights cascading from multi-layered chandeliers. Excitement filled the air as Heads of State, Ambassadors, distinguished guests, and the artists began to arrive. When they had all convened, they were directed to the exhibit for a thirty-minute preview, making this the first time for the artists, too, to see their work collectively displayed. After the brief survey, the guests were directed back to the reception area for an introduction and short biography of each artist with the help of an interpreter. Formalities completed, the guests were again invited for a second viewing, this time prepared with some knowledge about the artists and their work. It was a momentous occasion ending with an American-style buffet.

"They served something that resembled hot-dogs! We didn't know what they were made of and they certainly weren't anywhere near the real thing, but the Chinese loved them. We drank their beer, only nibbled at the 'American' food, and just stood back and had a wonderful time watching them enjoying themselves."

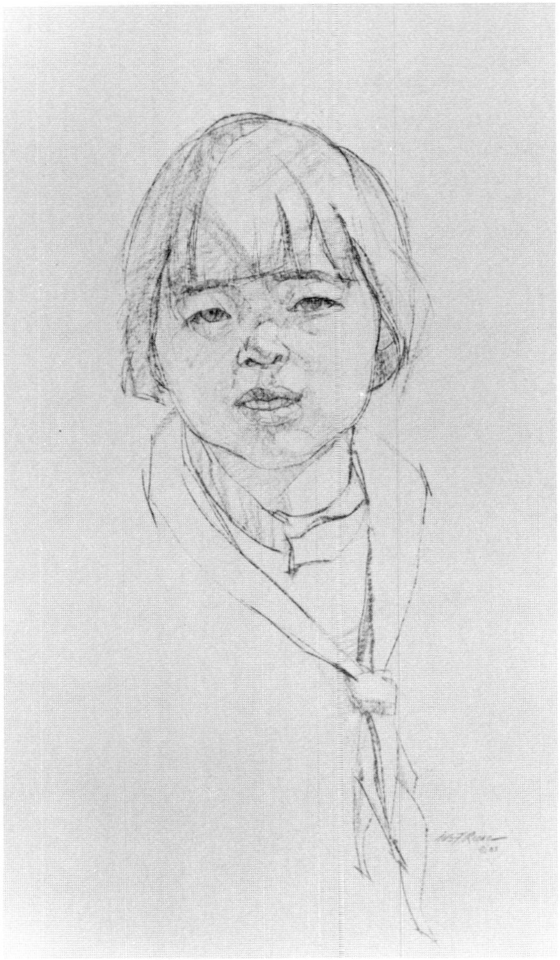

*Winter White, Ptarmigans*
Watercolor, 17½x17½″
Private Collection

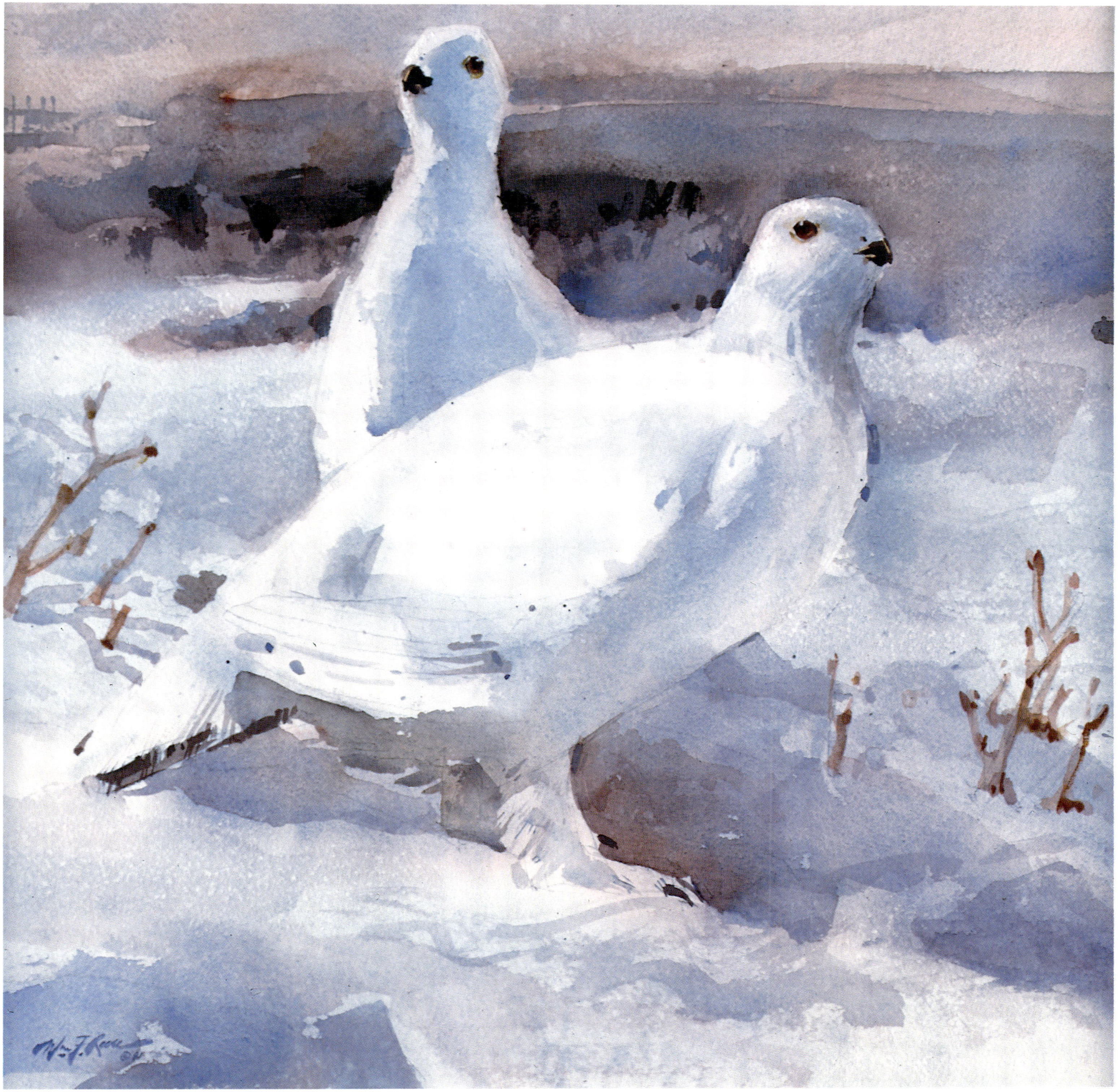

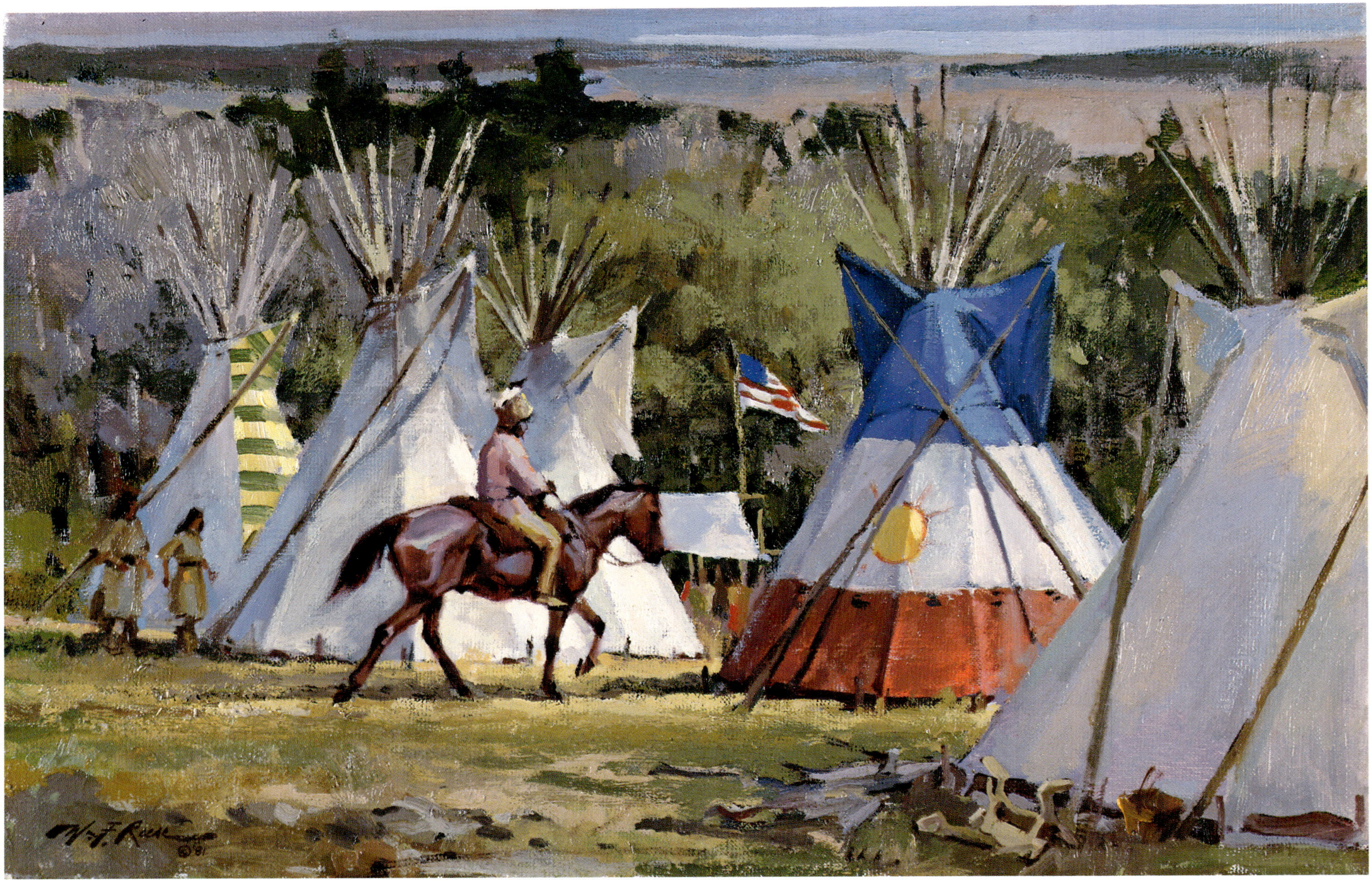

*Madison River Camp*
Oil, 16x24″

The artists were represented by two pieces of work each, ranging from paintings, sculptures, weavings, pottery, baskets, and Kachina dolls, all beautifully displayed. Reese's *Winter White, Ptarmigans,* a watercolor, and *Madison River Camp,* an oil, were well received, as were all the other pieces shown. Highly enthusiastic and curious, Chinese audiences arrived in droves for the run of the exhibition. It was so popular that, at the onset, visitation had to be limited to 10,000 people per day. Their artists made notes and drawings; their sculptors, especially, were excited to see all the bronze pieces because, as Reese learned, they rarely have the opportunity to have their work cast — it is perhaps a once-in-a-lifetime occurrence even for the best of them.

The exhibit opened on a Wednesday evening, and the following Saturday morning the artists were invited to visit the Central Academy of Fine Arts. In the meantime, they explored the sights and sounds in and around Peking. In the street markets they wove through displays of vegetables and wares: bok choy, rutabagas, long roots, potatoes, cabbages, and big mushrooms; embroidered items and handicrafts, tightly woven baskets — vendors and buyers — burros and *Chinese* horses transporting goods from one place to another. Steamed bread, naan, noodles, bowls of rice and vegetables, and cooking pork permeated the air. A hundred smells intermingled with the fragrances of herbs displayed in open burlap bags. Each object added to the multitude of colors and textures to form a three-dimensional, aromatic collage.

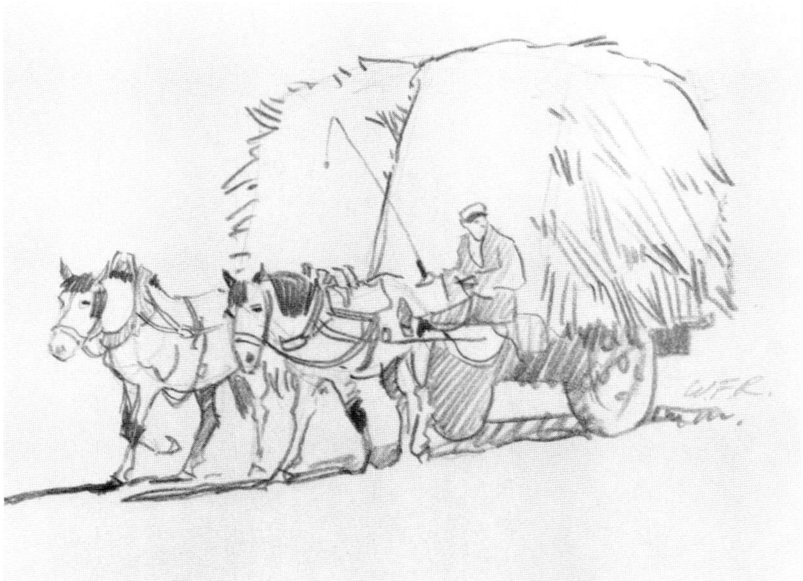


"We went into a hat store, away from the center of the market. I wanted a typical, soft-crowned worker's cap and asked for a $7\frac{3}{8}$ (through the interpreter) but I was told that my head size was 60! You can imagine the jokes and wisecracks my companions fired at me over that! I took my size-60 hat and left. Outside, dozens and dozens of people had gathered and lined up, waiting for a glimpse of us as we left the building.

"They are the most friendly, outgoing people of any country I have visited. They were eager to please and could anticipate our needs and wishes with an incredible sense of intuition. I never felt like an outsider. Yes, the language was an obstacle — for example, there is no western equivalent to the sounds — and when I went wandering off alone I always carried a note which our guide wrote for me in Chinese, saying: 'Show me the way to the Shanghai Hotel,' or wherever we happened to be staying at the time, but I never had to use it. People walked with me or checked along the way to make sure I didn't get lost." Peking and Shanghai are both large, with populations of over 5 and 7 million respectively. It would not have been too difficult for a foreigner to become disoriented in either city, at least temporarily; however, the neighborhood surveillance system would have put him on the right track posthaste.

"That day when I finished drawing in the market, surrounded by all the on-lookers, I wandered toward what looked like a marina or port a few blocks away. I examined the boats and barges and watched the activity on the shore for awhile. Suddenly I became aware that I still had an audience — apparently all the people from the market had followed me and had gathered others along the way. They had been so quiet that I just hadn't realized what was happening, but when they saw me looking at them they began to chant in unison: 'DRAW! DRAW! DRAW!' Talk about an ego boost and being touched emotionally . . . their responsiveness was one of the best rewards of the entire trip."[8]

Modern buses, with crocheted arm and headrest coverings (antimacassars), took the American visitors to outlying areas for sight-seeing and a visit to a commune. Although the community was primarily agrarian, factories dotted the green, terraced landscape. One such factory was the Kenington Shirt Company, where the workers were friendly and eager to meet the tourists and proudly showed their prowess in shirt-making.

Reese marveled over the privileges and freedoms he and the others of the group were given. "We sketched and painted everywhere we went on these special excursions. We took the back roads, so to speak, and were able to see and experience things that were not on the usual tourist path; and yet, we saw the spectacular sights, too — the Temple of the Forbidden City and the Great Wall, to name just two."

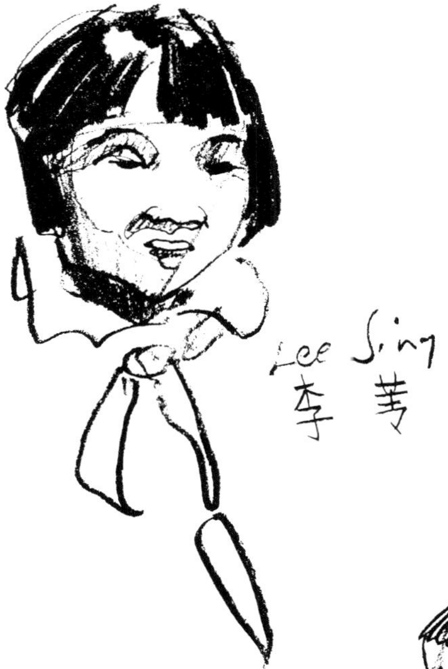


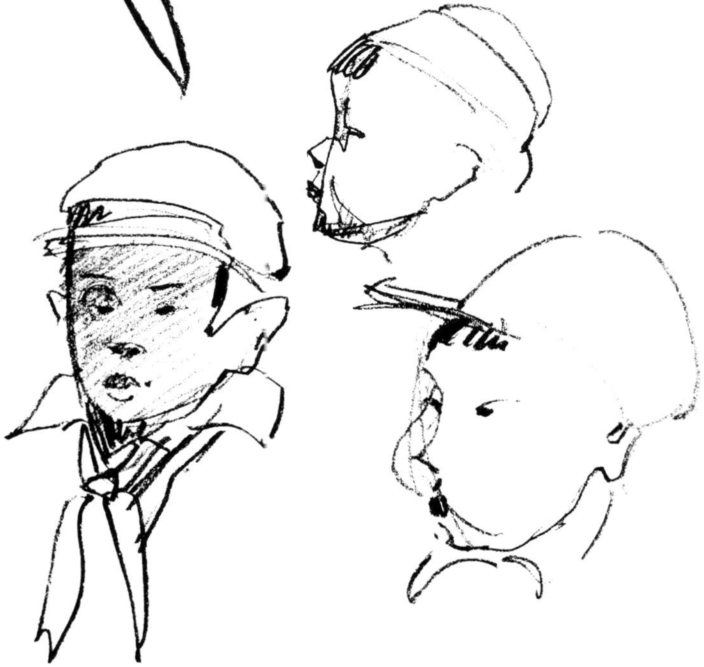

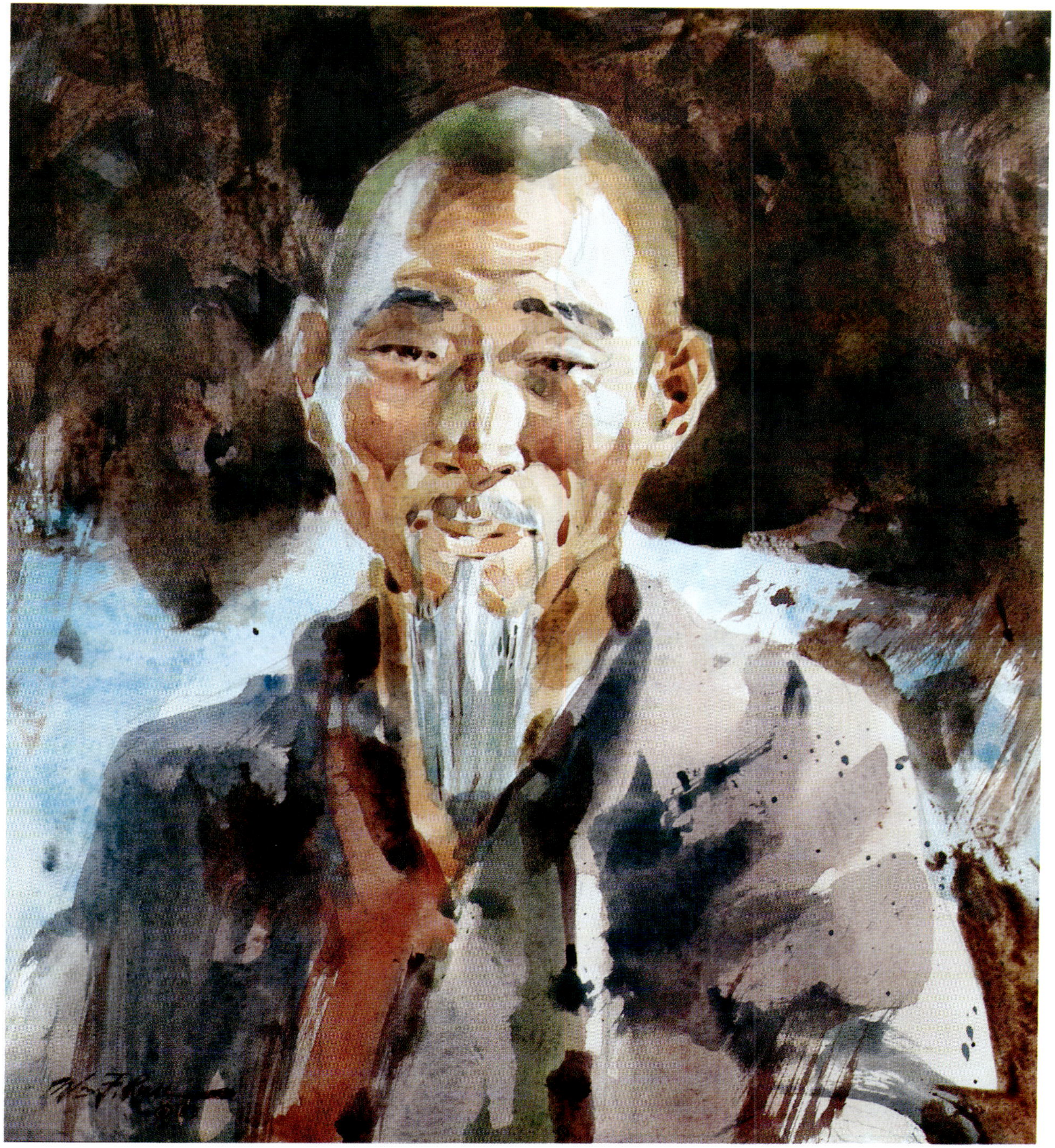

*Chinese Elder*
Watercolor, 11x10½″
Private Collection

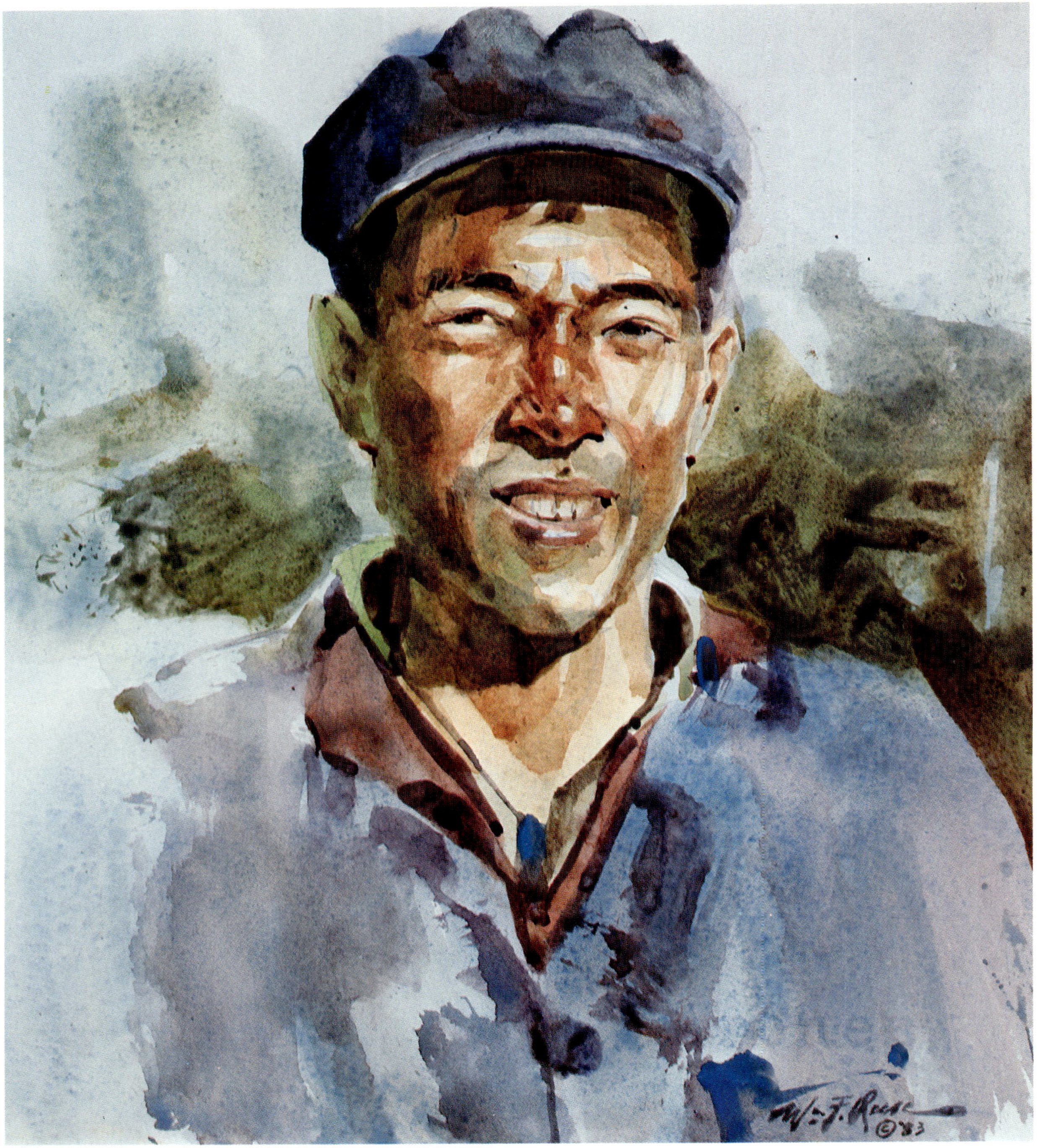

*Chinese Worker*
Watercolor, 11x10½″
Collection of John and
Glenda Dunn

The group visited the Children's Palace in Shanghai, a building used specifically for after-school activities in the arts and sciences, a place where children are able to create and develop their special talents. Perhaps because families are now generally limited to only one child, children are considered more like special gifts and are bestowed with respect, attention, and devotion. They are colorfully dressed, in contrast to the somber blue, grey, or green Sun Yat-sen suits of the adults.

"The children wore bright-red flowing scarves or ties at the Palace. They were wonderful and responsive — and beautiful. I drew portraits of as many as I could in my sketchbook; and when I was finished, they passed the book around and giggled and pointed to each other as they recognized themselves in the sketches. I had them autograph their portraits in their own beautiful calligraphy, and they loved it!

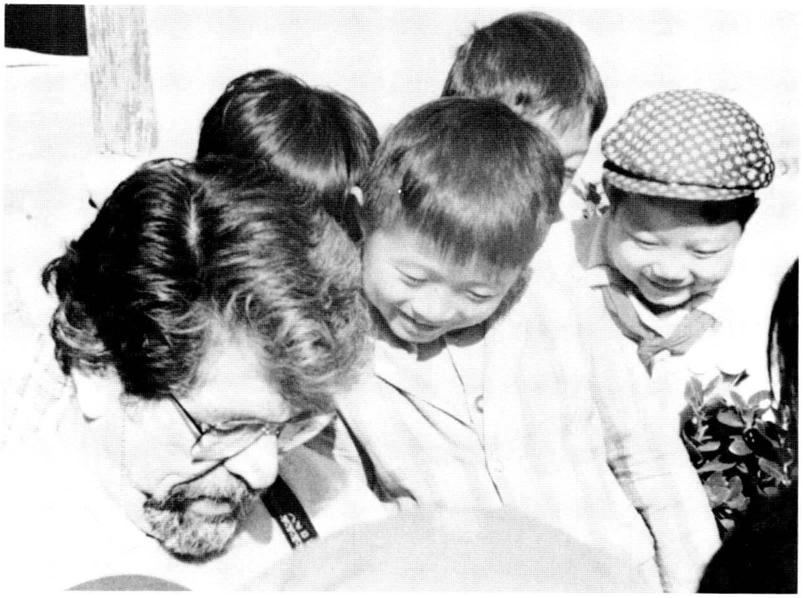

"While we were at the Great Wall, I painted several watercolors; but it was so cold that the paint froze and crystallized on the paper! When it thawed," Reese laughed, "the colors ran and displaced values in totally unintended parts of the composition."

On Saturday they went to the Academy with expectations of working with the faculty and students. As an introduction to the school, they were taken into the gallery to see the current exhibit, drawings and paintings, all products of the Academy.

"My immediate impression was that I had been dropped into Kiev! Most of the work looked like that of the Russian 'Wanderers' and the later influences of Repin, Serov, and Fechin — and some even reminded me of the Spanish Sorolla. The work was extremely well crafted, highly professional. I reacted subjectively to it, too, and wondered if the work was for sale — it would be wonderful to have a piece or two to enjoy on a daily basis. I asked one of the artists if they would sell a few of the paintings or drawings."

" 'What? *Buy* art?' he asked. 'Why would you buy art?'

"He just couldn't understand why anyone would buy a painting or drawing or why they should sell such work. Before we left, almost every one of our group expressed the same wish to buy a few pieces. At first the answer was always 'No.' One of our sculptors good-

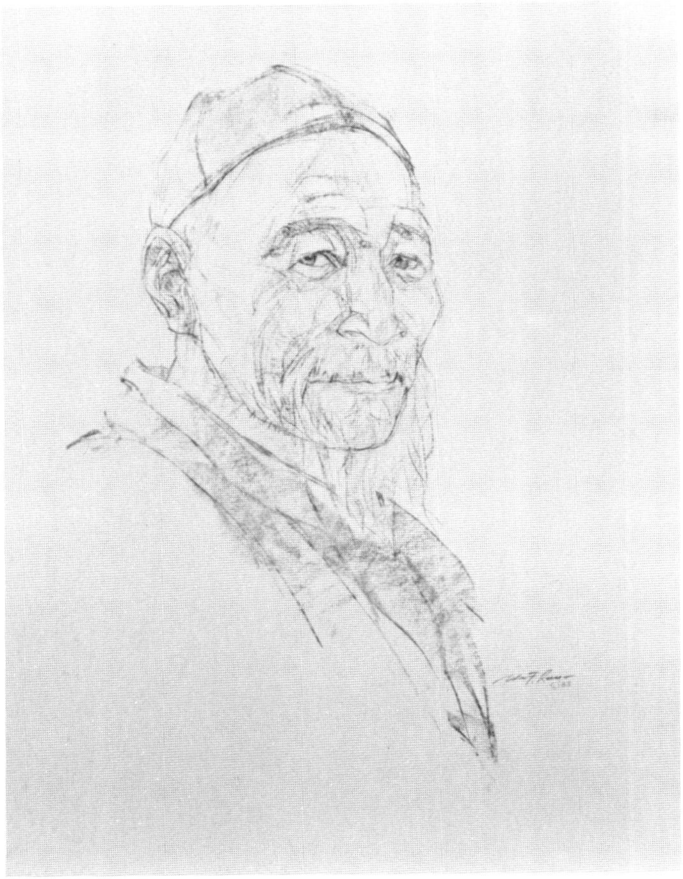

naturedly suggested that if they sold some of their work they could afford to build a foundry and cast their own work. Perhaps his suggestion had some impact on them because later their answer turned to 'Maybe,' and eventually they did consent to selling a few pieces. I was lucky enough to purchase two from this collection.

"Next, we went to another part of the school for tea; and the head of the school, along with some of the faculty, explained through an interpreter how the school functioned."

Applicants, perhaps 2,000 in all, are invited to apply, coming from the Children's Palace, the high schools, and the colleges and universities. They are carefully screened, and approximately 500 of those are then invited to submit their portfolios; but from that number only 50 are accepted into the Academy each year. The faculty numbers close to 200, almost equaling the total enrollment including post-graduate students, those who work beyond the standard three-year program.

"It is about a one-to-one basis, and the instructors must truly be superior because it was reflected in the students' work. When we visited the studios, it was difficult to tell the students from the faculty; they all worked side by side, painting together, producing work of equal caliber. Some worked from nude models; others, from plaster casts.

"I kept puzzling about the dominant Russian influences in their work. When the question-and-answer period arrived, I asked if all of their instructors were Chinese. 'Yes,' they replied. Obviously I hadn't asked the right question or phrased it properly; but I was hesitant, not wanting to come right out and say that the work had a strong Russian influence. Instead, I skirted around the issue and remarked that the work had Eastern European characteristics, to which they replied that they did have instructors from Russia about twenty years ago. My hunch was correct. Beyond the look of Russian work, the paintings also seemed to suggest that they had sent some of their instructors to Russia to study because the people in the paintings were definitely Russian — not Chinese.

"In one of the studios, I stopped to look at an artist's work, and right above his head was an exhibition poster with a self-portrait of Kathe Kollwitz. I said, 'Kathe Kollwitz.'

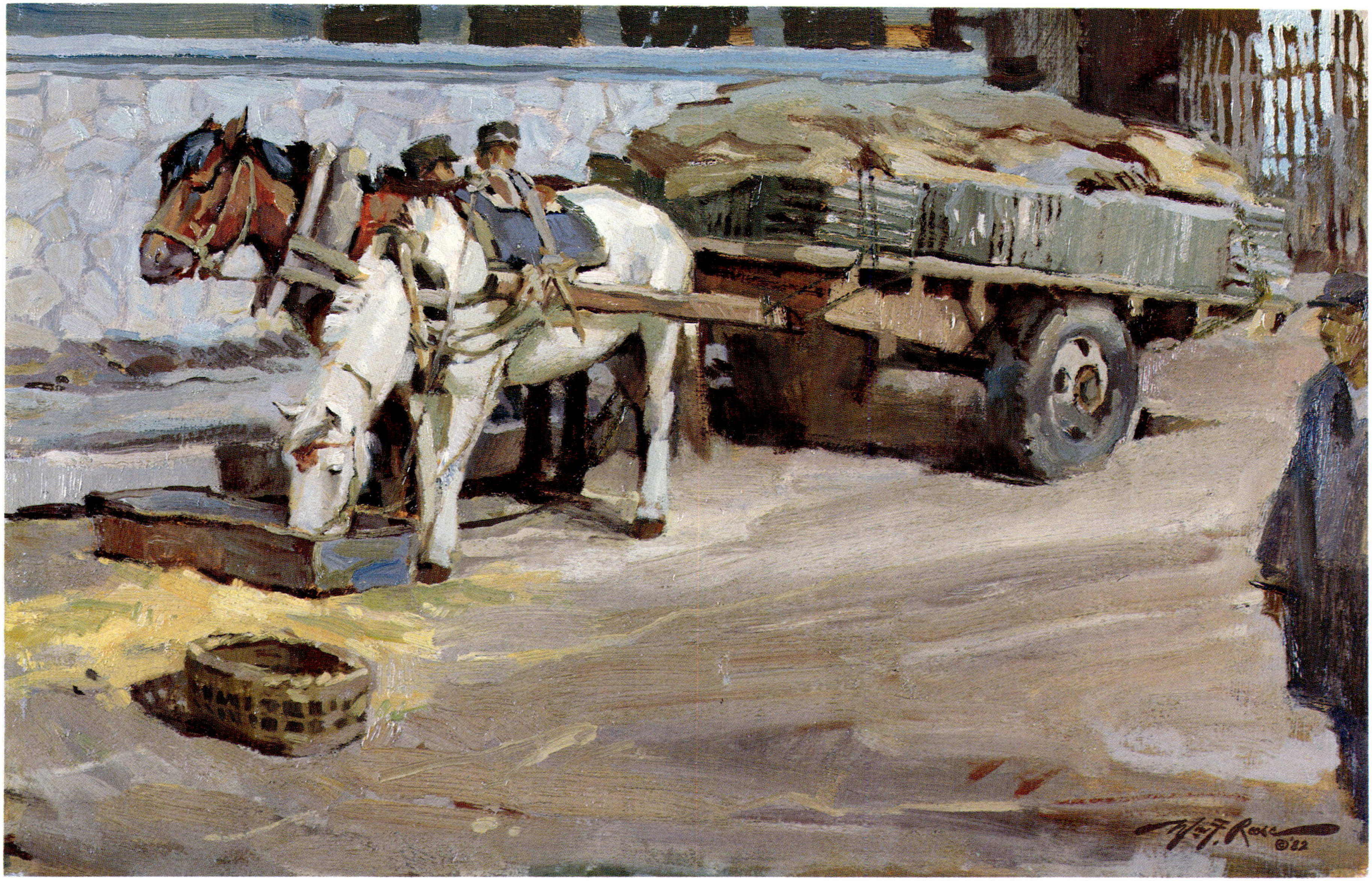

*Streets of Peking*
Oil, 16x24″
Collection of Mike and Kathy Phillipy

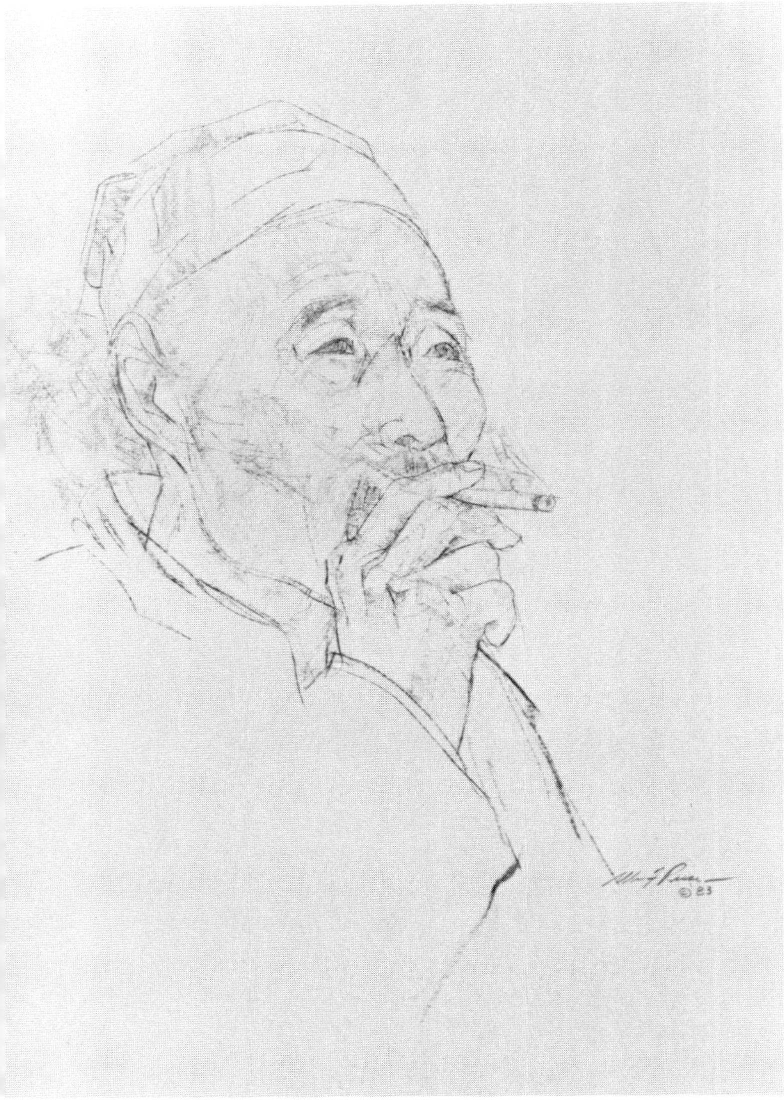

" 'Ya, ya, Kathe Kollwitz!' the artist repeated excitedly.

"We struck a familiar chord. He was surprised that I recognized Kollwitz and spoke the name — and that we could both say the same name in the same way and understand what it meant. I think it dawned on both of us that one could mention any of the masters in art and we would have a mutual understanding. I mentioned a few other masters and he smilingly repeated them

"Then he noticed my sketchbook and asked the interpreter to ask me if he could see it. Included were a few watercolors along with the sketches and brochures of my other work. I gave him a brochure when he had finished, and then he said something and ran off. The interpreter told me that he had gone to get his portfolio. His work was absolutely beautiful. I especially liked a charcoal drawing of a young boy done on mulberry paper, and would have liked very much to have it. The work strongly reminded me of Nicolai Fechin's drawings. It was through this mutual admiration for the same artists and love of art that we both felt a strong camaraderie or bond with each other. We were able to say, without actually verbalizing, how we felt about art — color, drawing, composition and so on, and about life and the world in general — merely by speaking the names of certain of the masters of art.

Time at the Academy passed much too quickly to suit the Americans. They had been intent on working with the other artists and on more of a mutual exchange of ideas; however, just the evening before, they learned that they had been invited to the Great Hall of the People for tea with the Deputy Premier. "We had enjoyed a State dinner there earlier in the week, but this was more like a 'command performance.' When our guide made the announcement to us, he was so excited he could hardly talk. He said the Deputy Premier himself wanted to bid each of us goodbye. *'Everyone must be there.'*

"I didn't fully realize what an honor it was — I had an intellectual awareness of sorts, but I didn't understand why the guide was so excited — I, too, wanted to feel some of the excitement, to savor the event emotionally. In retrospect, maybe the lack of excitement had to do with the lack of foreknowledge and preparation, the lack of 'ritual,' like the simple act of selecting clothes for the occasion; in other words, there was no orientation, no advance plan or information, no historical base on which to start building excitement or emotional responses. We were told not to 'dress up' so nearly all of us wore blue jeans; that alone meant that it was nothing special, at least psychologically. Then, we were taken there by bus, tourist fashion. Again, nothing special. And, then we were deposited in a building and rooms that were stark, almost forbidding — they seemed so out of character for Heads of State.

"I wanted very much to get the full meaning, to appreciate, to *feel* the significance of the opportunity — I wanted to understand emotionally where I was and why. In trying to grasp all this I kept questioning the guide and finally asked him if he had ever been in the Great Hall."

"*Never!* It is a feat just to get to the door to look in. Not even many foreign dignitaries have been granted the privilege."

"It finally began to sink in, I now had a parallel — it was like an invitation to the White House but on a far more selective scale — and even if the preliminaries had been lacking, it was a celebration not soon forgotten. We were treated royally with great respect; and we, each, were thanked and toasted by the Deputy Premier and his cabinet. It was then that I felt I needed that size 60 hat!"

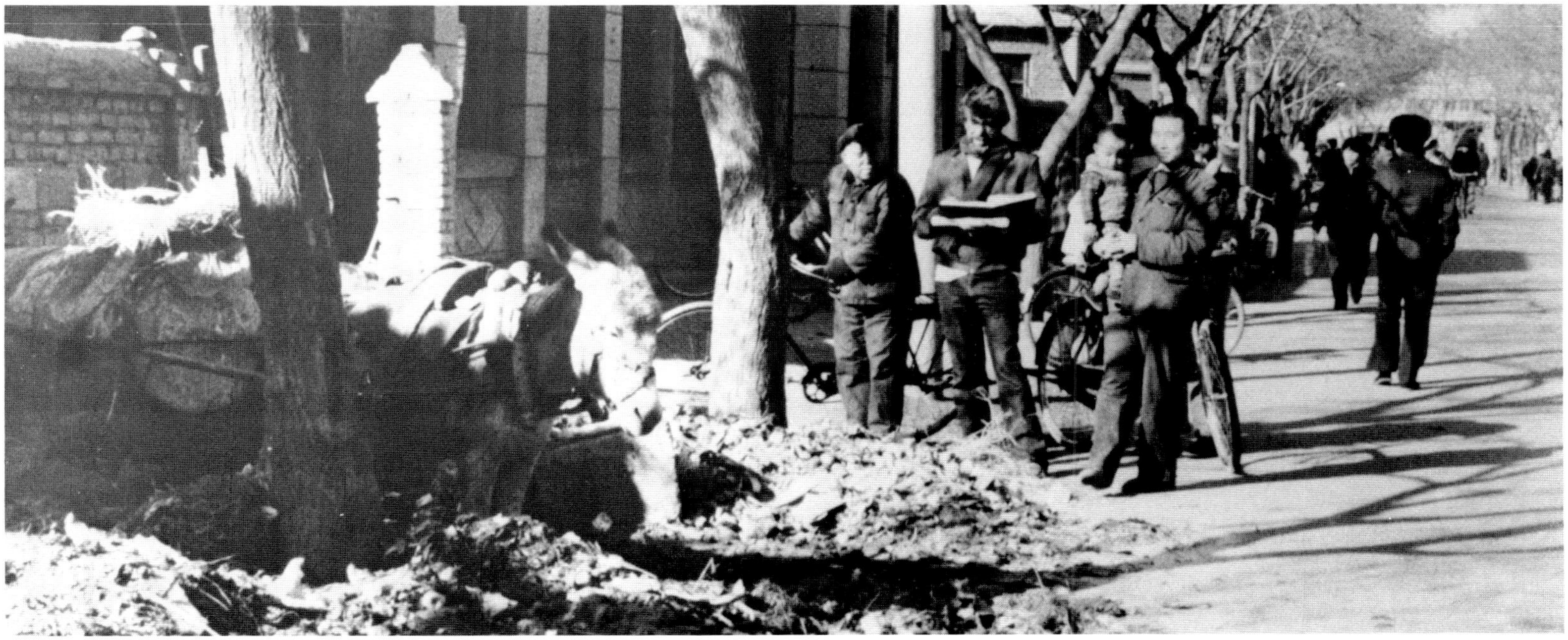

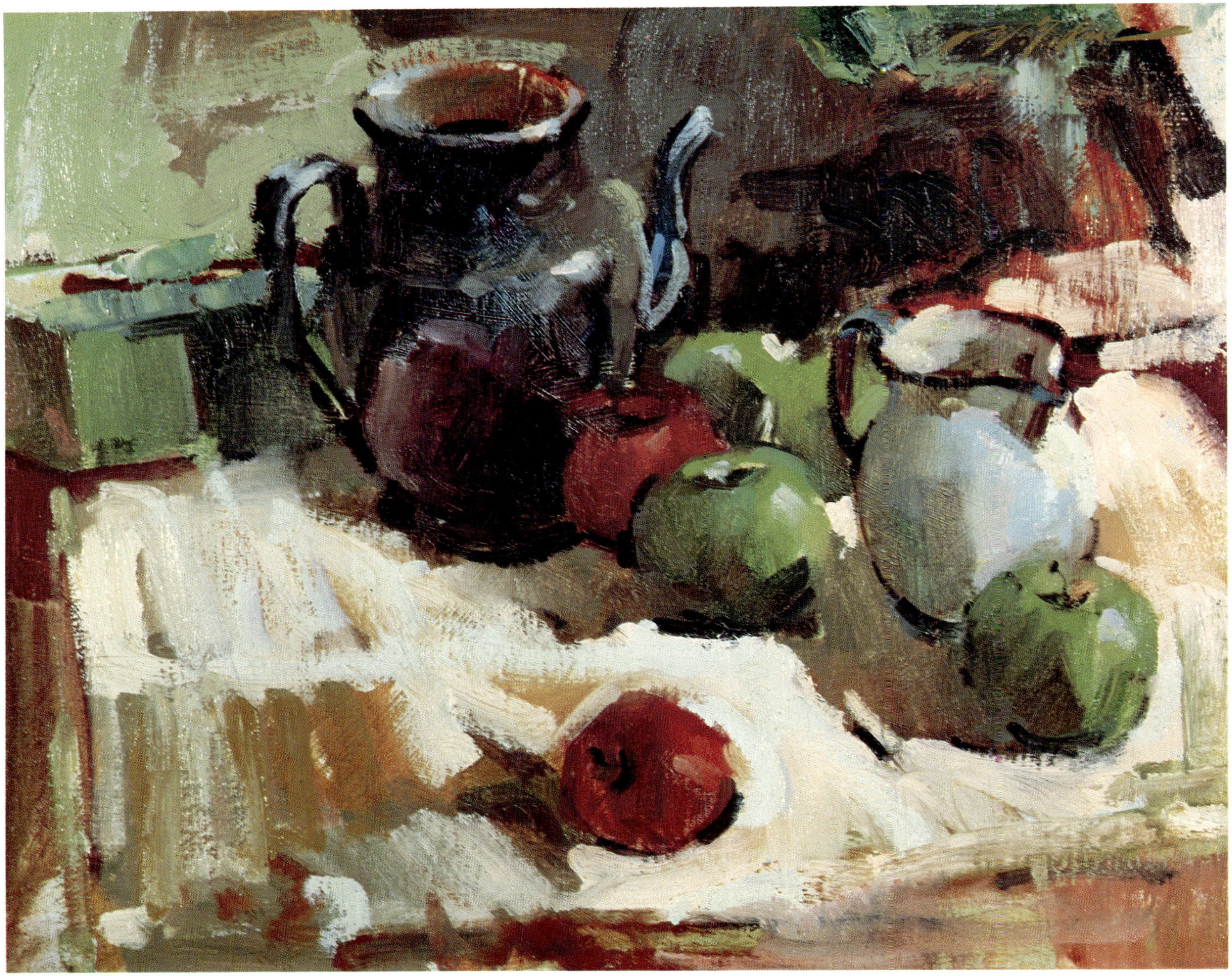

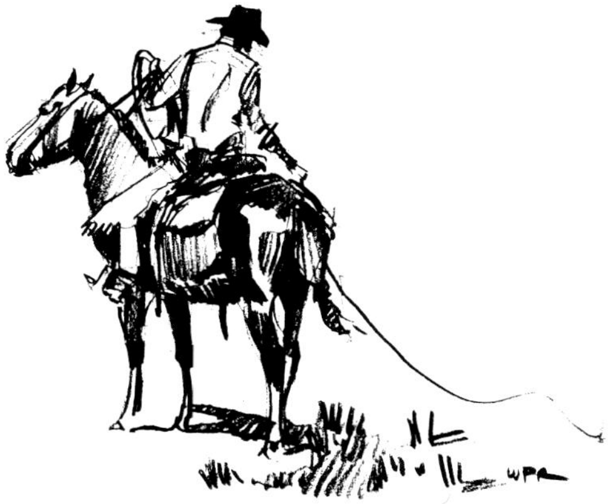

*Black Enamel*
Oil, 16x20″
Collection of Stanley H. Fink

# 6 *Apples For Butterflies*

"One of the rewards, the great highs of this business of art, is the association with other artists. That is the gratifying part — that's what makes it all worth it to me," Reese said.

"I have found a camaraderie with artists almost everywhere I have gone, in this country and elsewhere. Sometimes we have only twenty minutes together when we meet, but over a period of five or six years we've become close. We have developed a feeling for each other, a trust, as if we have known one another for a lifetime. We can talk on the phone and console or boost each other depending on the need at the time. Or we can bounce ideas off each other, be one another's sounding board. It's wonderful."

San Francisco painter Stan Galli said that his first acquaintance with Reese was through his work reproduced in art magazines. "I liked the directness and the richness of his color, and I liked his subject matter and the strong evidence of humanness and deep feeling. I later met Bill at an art show in Spokane, in which we were both participating. It was quite evident on the first meeting that I had surmised correctly, that I would like him personally. All the forthrightness and integrity came through clearly. It was plain also that he was dedicated to art and that it would be a forever thing. His influence on me comes through the stimulation created by his enthusiasm and searching efforts. There is a camaraderie that comes with traveling the same road."[9]

Sculptor Tony Angell recollects the time when he asked Reese to serve as a judge for an arts commission board to help select works of art for public places.

"The submissions for selection were reviewed, and one artist was asked to make a more detailed proposal. Once viewed, it fell short of the standards Bill felt were needed to qualify as 'public art.' The easy

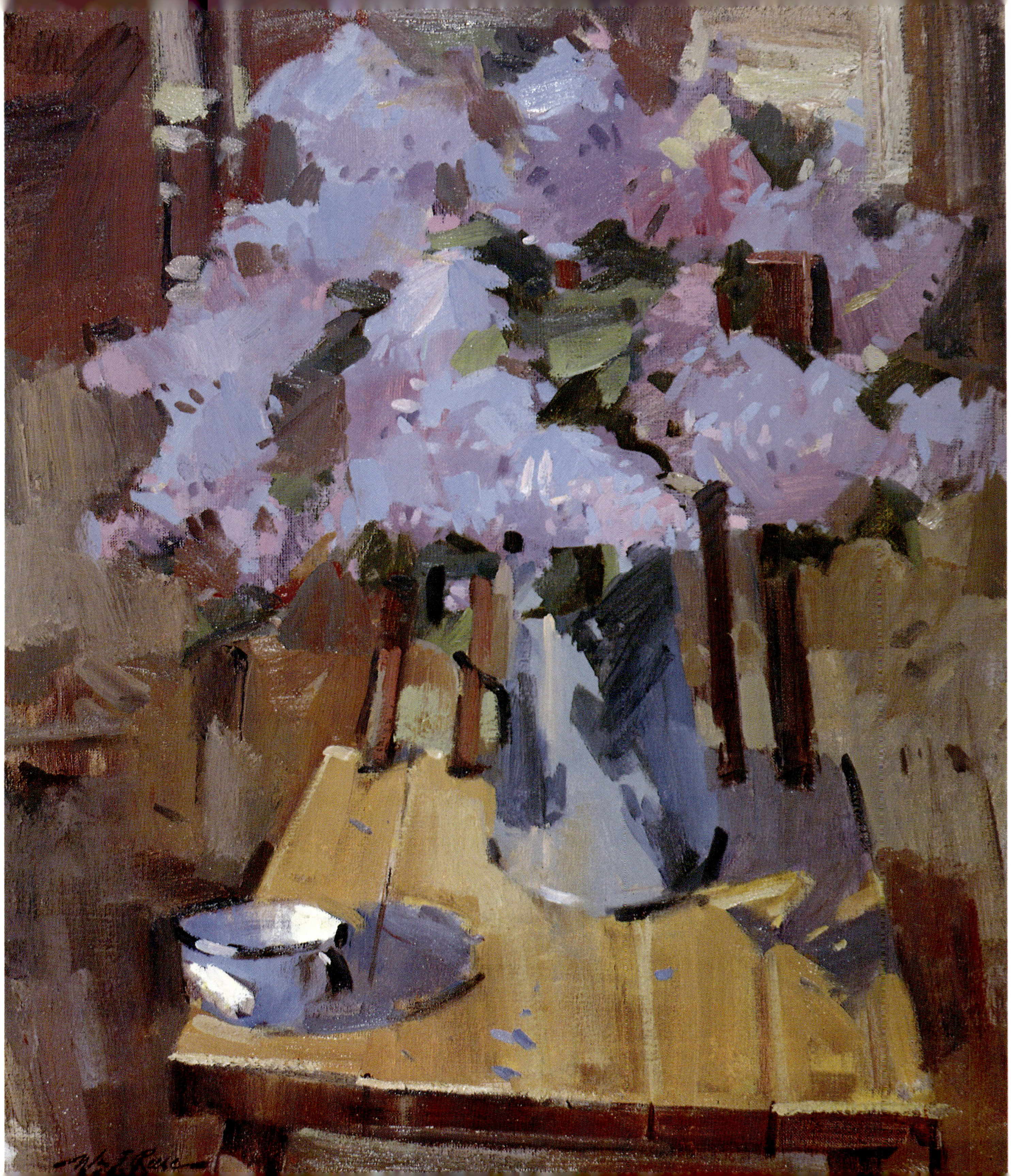

*Spring Lilacs*
Oil, 30x24″
Collection of Pattie
Welder Edwards

way out after the first meeting or two would have been to swallow hard and accept the work in spite of all the questions that remained unanswered. Bill challenged the other jurors to hold their ground and with others asked the hard questions that ultimately led to the rejection of the work, and a true exercise of the art jury process. I would argue strongly that because of Bill's conscientious commitment to artistic excellence, the community was served; the artist herself received an opportunity to strengthen her expression through realistic criticism, and the jury process (hard as it was to complete) was genuinely exercised."[10]

Reese talked of some of the many advantages of being in the arts, not only the friendships but the entree to almost anywhere an artist chooses to go. He contends that if one can show proof of ability and wishes to paint or sketch in specific places, any door can be opened by merely expressing the wish. "And, many times you will be provided with assistance — someone to carry all your stuff!" He reflected on some of the special invitations presented to him, including the exhibition and travel in China, a mid-winter snow coach adventure in Yosemite, and a rare week at a working cattle ranch in Oregon.

He also spoke of the relationships among the artists' wives and how he is amazed that they, too, have grown close to one another. Fran attributed it to mutual interests. "We all seem to have similar lifestyles and feel very comfortable with one another. We have the same likes and dislikes and enjoy going to the same places for the same reasons. Almost everything we do is art-related. It is just a way of life for us.

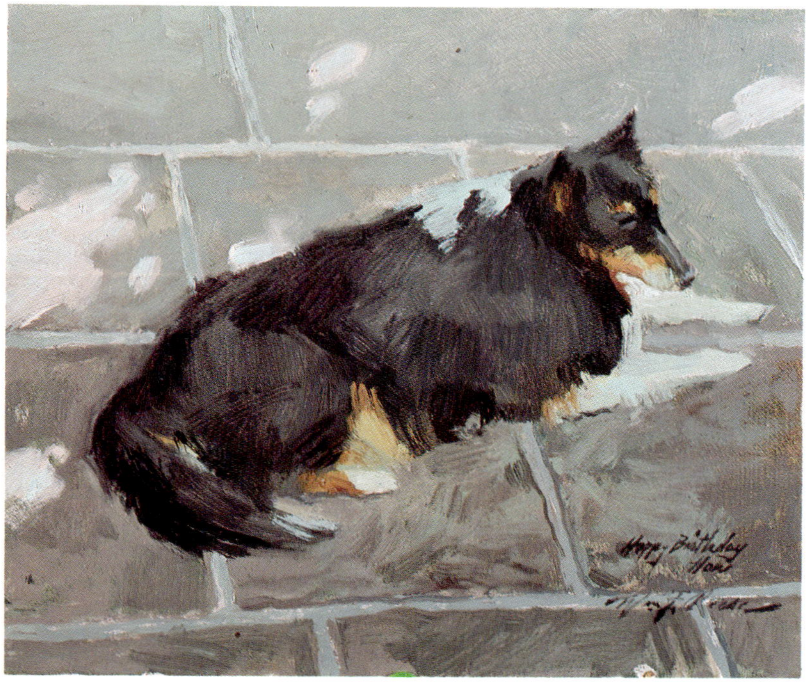

*Dandy*
Oil, 7x8″
Private Collection

"And, the children have found a unique kind of companionship with other artists' kids. They've discovered that they have the same problems and concerns; and consequently it's easier for them because they can share these situations with their peers, who also are used to being asked to 'sit down and wait' — at the shows, for example. But it's been a lot of fun for them, too." Shelly and Dean agree that the fun parts of the shows were the large motels, the swimming pools, and the other kids.

Dean said that when he was younger and attending the receptions and exhibits, he often was puzzled about people gathering around his father, waiting for an autograph. "I just couldn't understand why on earth anybody would want *his* signature! If he had been with the Sonics or some other sports team, I could have understood it, but he was just an ordinary guy — a great dad and all that, but he was just my dad, that's all. Now, of course, I can see what it's all about." In response to his teachers' inquiries about his father's occupation, Dean astonished them by saying his father didn't work. When pressed further, he would reply, "He doesn't work. He paints all day."

"What does he paint? Houses?"

"No, fruit and horses."

Dean's room was adjacent to the studio as he was growing up, and he recalls lying in bed listening to the activities of the classes, which were held there in the evenings, and to the numerous discussions about art. His father proudly said that both Dean and Shelly have drawing ability, a good sense of proportion, a knowledge of color and composition, and selective tastes. They have not had lessons beyond the few art classes in junior high and high school — making a strong case for knowledge through "osmosis." Neither one had expressed interest in choosing art as a career until a few casual remarks during the last year. In retrospect, Fran and Bill, just as parents everywhere, both wonder if they should have tried to influence their son and daughter more directly — after all, the development as an architect of Frank Lloyd Wright by his mother began at age five!

*Still Life with Oil Can*
Watercolor, 21x29″

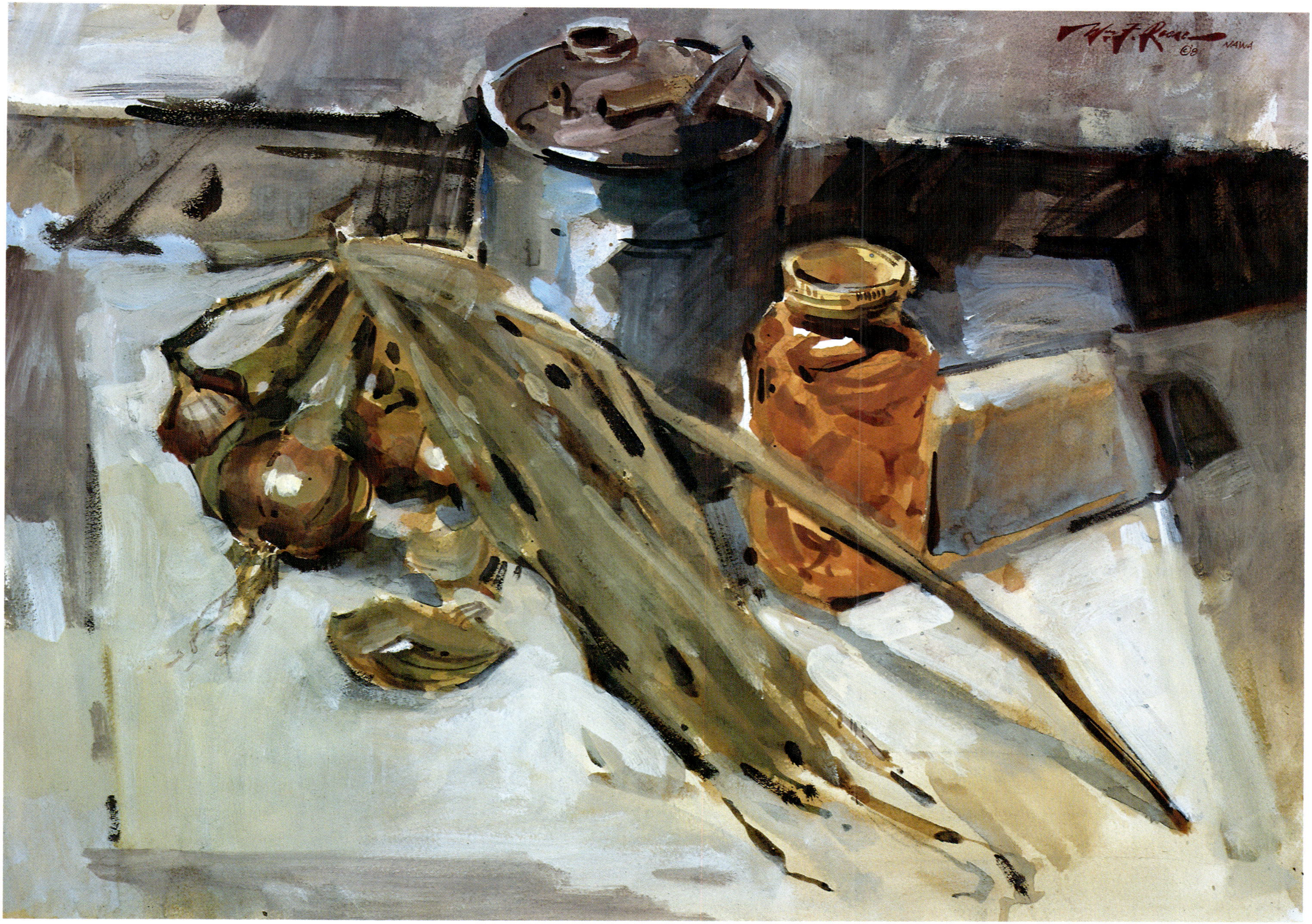
NAWA

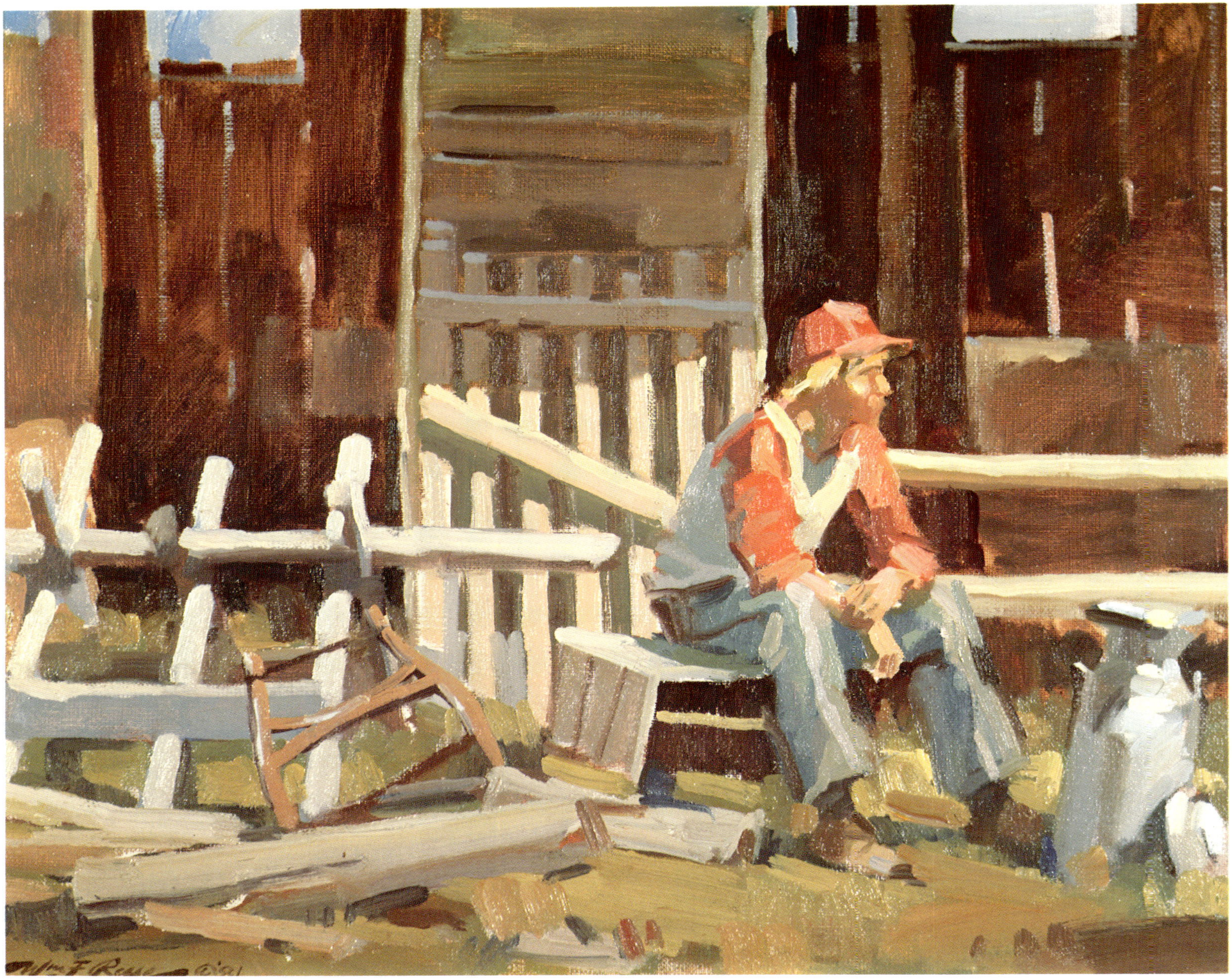

*Wood Chopper's Break*
Oil, 16x20″
Private Collection

*Freedom Lost*
Oil, 20x30″

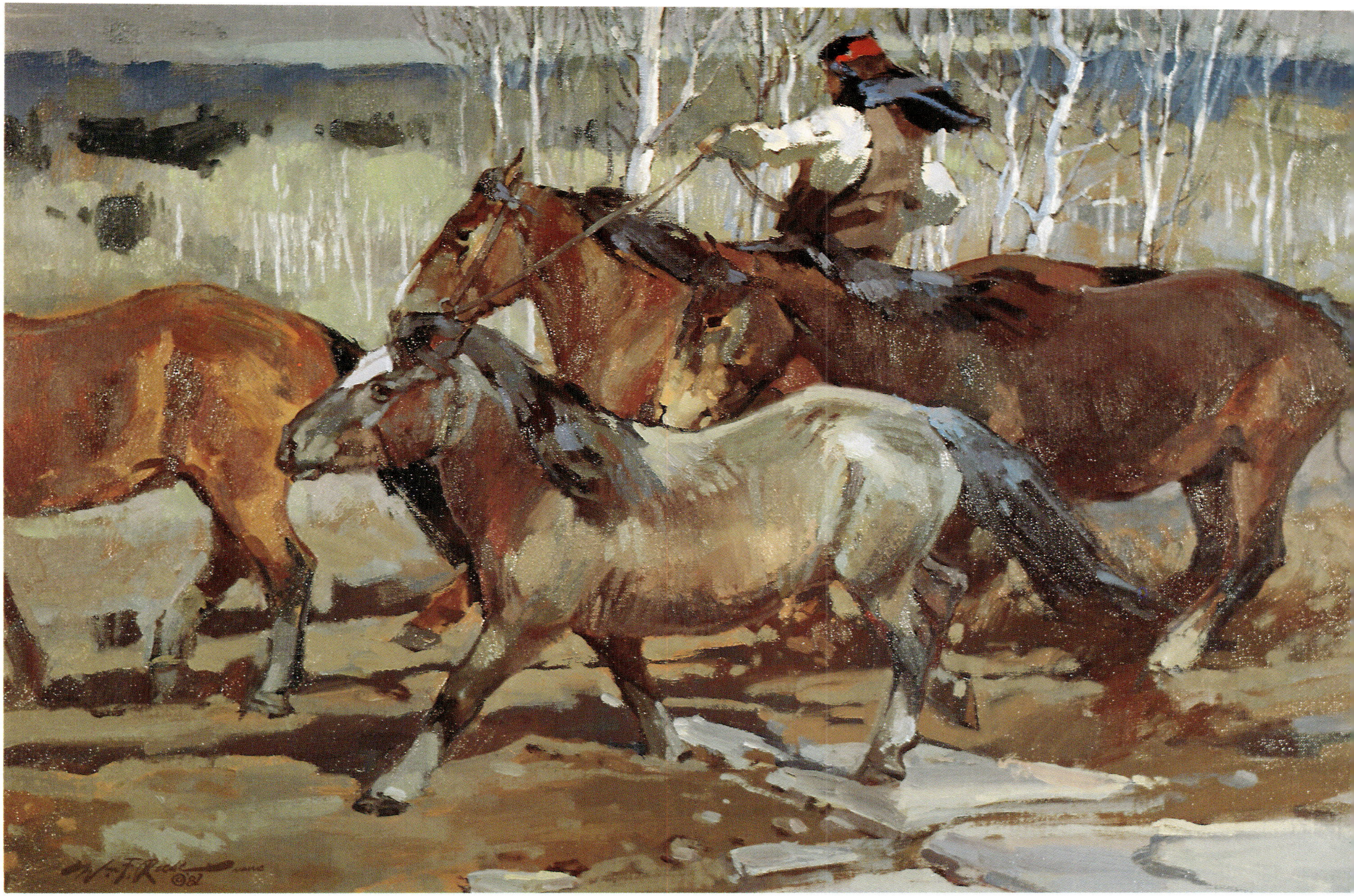

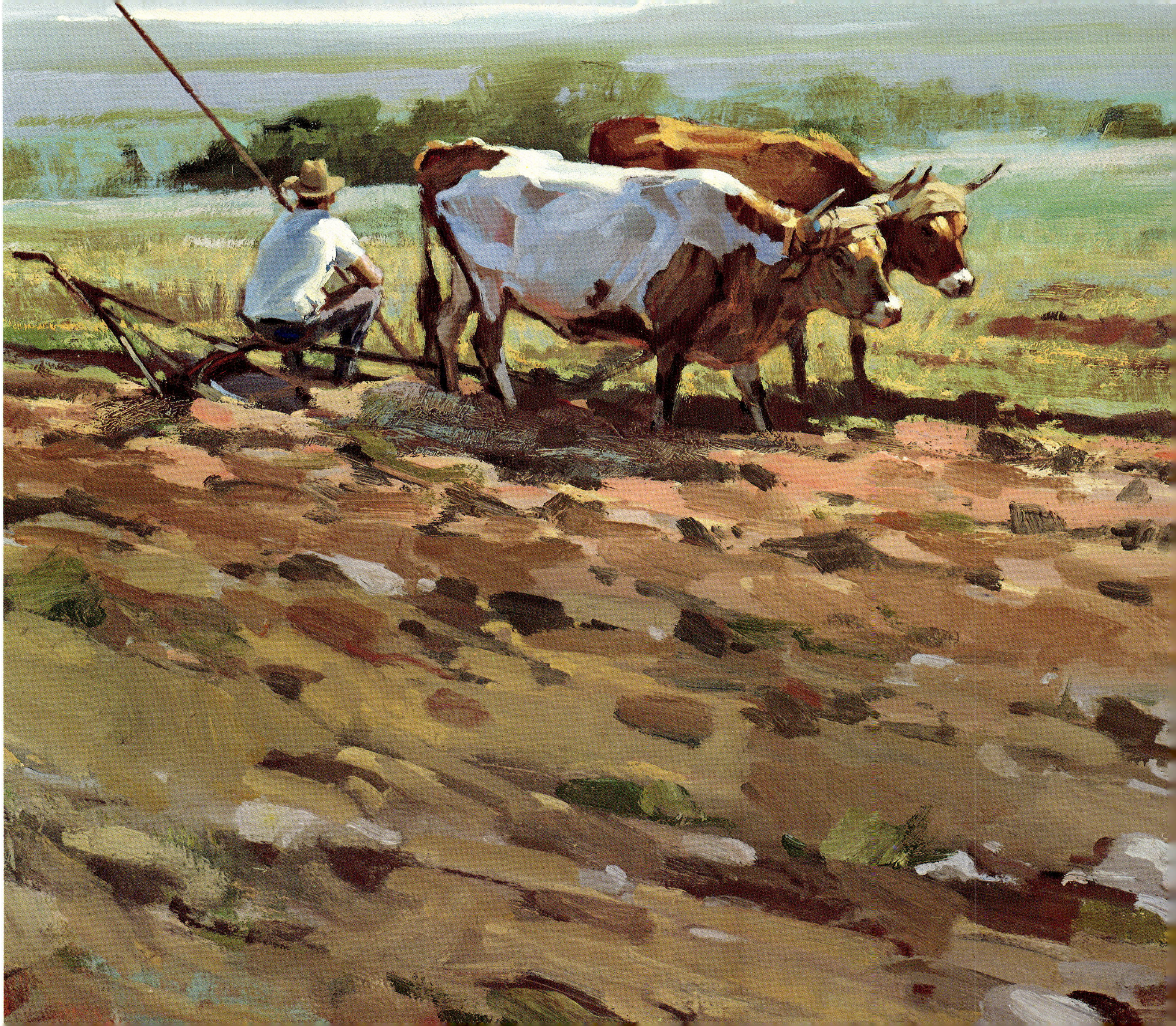

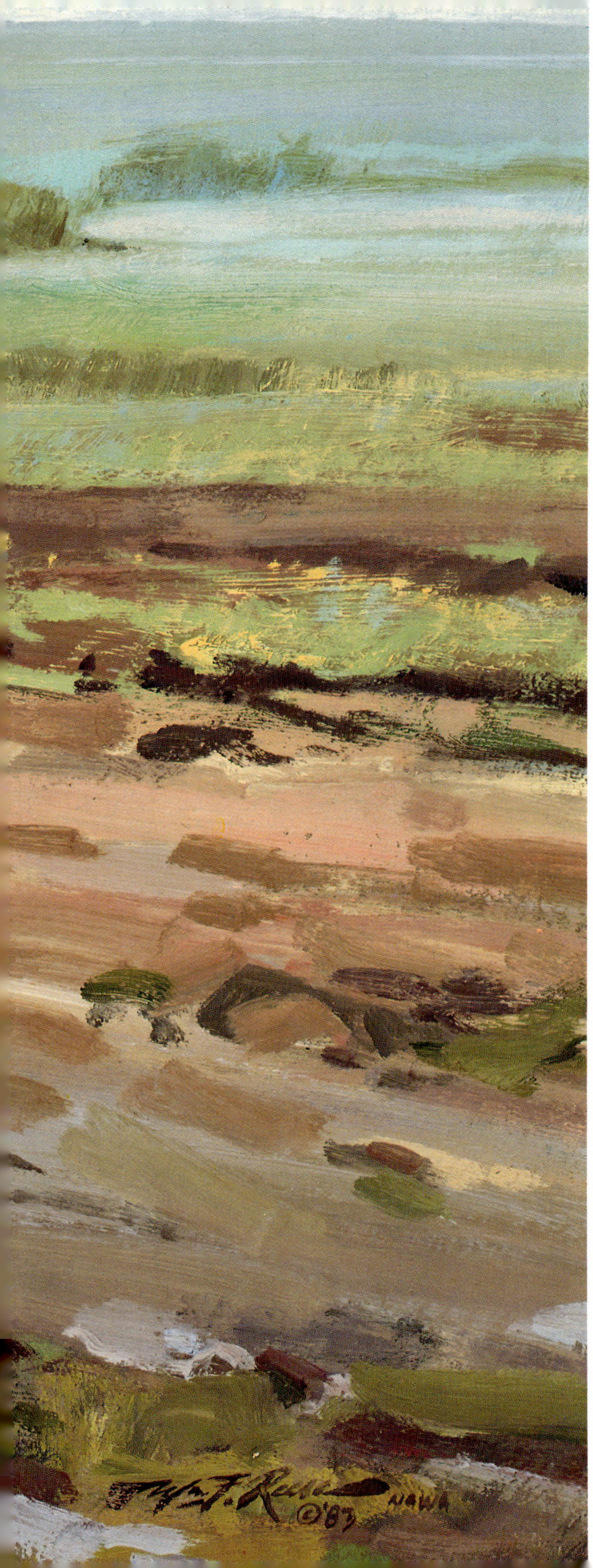

*Amora de Tierra*
Oil, 16x24″

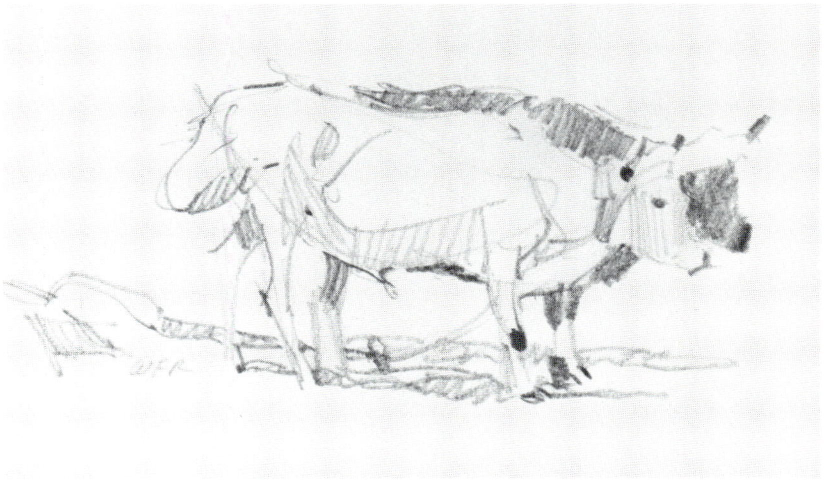

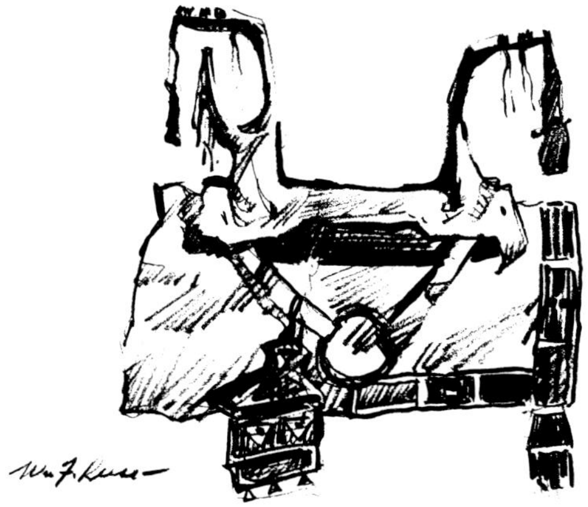

Reese took the two for a visit to the home of a butterfly collector, whose extensive collection included extinct species as well as the more abundant varieties. Dean was especially impressed with them as well as the exotically beautiful displays composed in small glass cases. He spoke of them almost reverently for weeks afterward.

One day when he came home from school he found such a display on the front hall table. He expressed his surprise and pleasure as he excitedly examined the butterflies from all angles. Finally, it occurred to him to wonder about the price of such a marvelous exhibit, and his father told him that he had traded a small painting of a green apple for the butterflies.

The boy was shocked, "Da-a-ad, ya mean you traded that little picture of a green apple for those beautiful butterflies! How *could* you? Dad, you really ripped that lady off. How could you do that?" He just couldn't believe his dad would do a thing like that. No amount of explanation sufficed to reinstate the "good guy" image of his father. It was not until weeks later that the "butterfly lady" was able to convince him that she considered it a truly fair trade: her display had been priced at approximately the same price as the painting, which in her eyes was a fine work. "She was as happy with her apple as Dad was with his butterflies."

Through that experience Dean finally began to realize that his dad's paintings had value. He had taken them for granted because they had been an everyday part of his life. He had assumed that everyone lived with original art, and never gave much thought to why and how the paintings were accomplished.

Reese's father, too, never really had understood the merit of painting nor how Bill went about his daily "job" until one time when he was confined to his son's home with a broken foot. Always an active man, he could never justify sitting still — but he had no choice. Day after day, he watched Bill create his paintings; and now, after all the years of only peripheral knowledge about his son's work, he finally understood what it involved. The forced immobility was a gift in disguise, resulting in a greater understanding — appreciation — and a closer bonding of father and son.

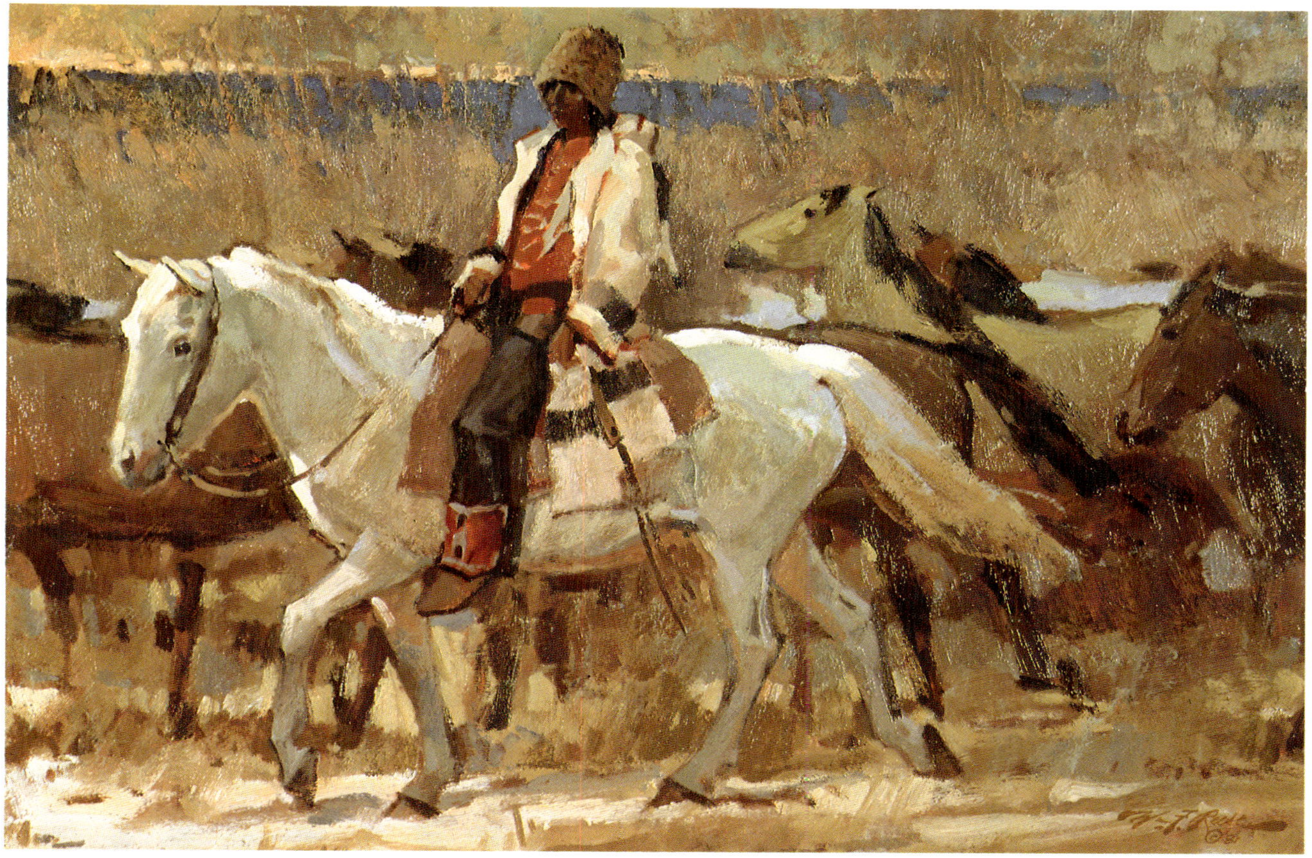

Even the slightest twinge of doubt about the decision to give up sign painting (long gone from Bill's mind), was erased. Of that momentous decision, a forceful vow quietly made in a hospital bed, Reese said, "Winning or failing in painting mattered little. Having been given an extension of life, the only tragedy — the only failure — would have been if I hadn't tried at all."

*Moving the Winter Camp*
Oil, 16x24"
Collection of Dr. & Mrs.
Terrence Coyle

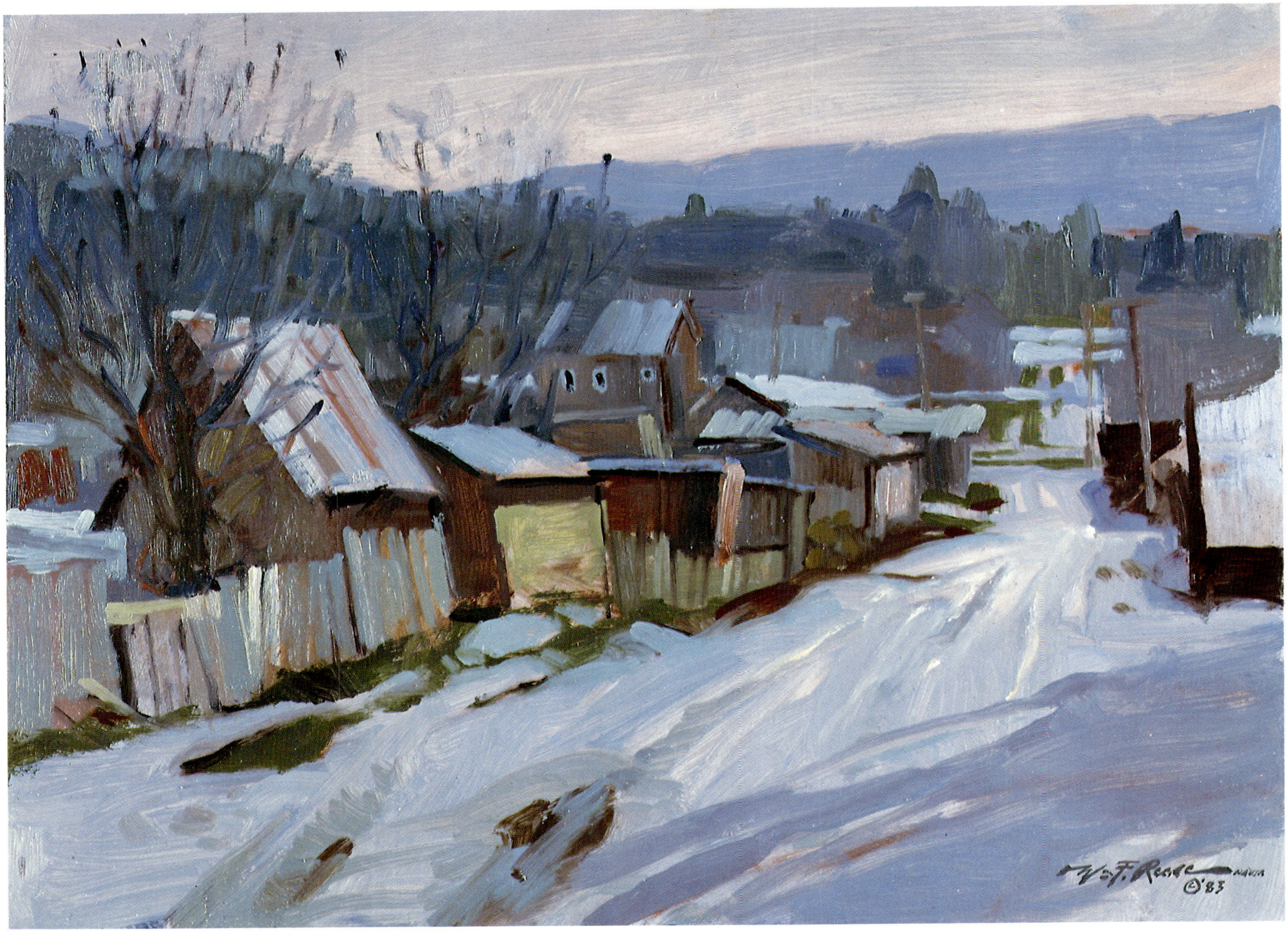

*Ronald Alley*
Oil, 12x16''

# Art as a Profession

*"One must know how to work hard for a long time, but in such a manner that nobody would notice the amount of labor and sweat on that painting."*
*— Valentin Serov*

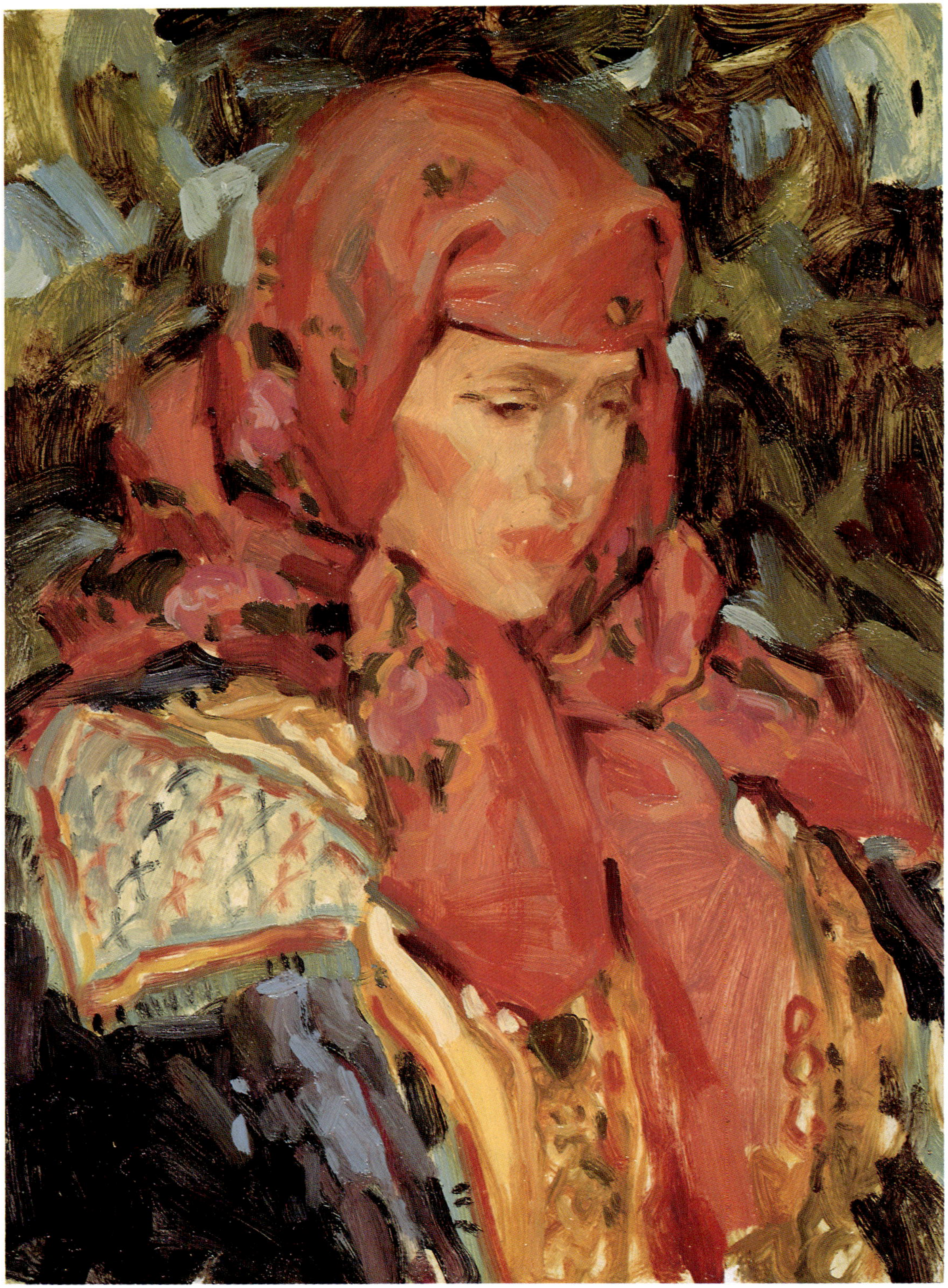

*Janie*
Oil, 14x10″
Collection of Dodson's
Gallery, Oklahoma City

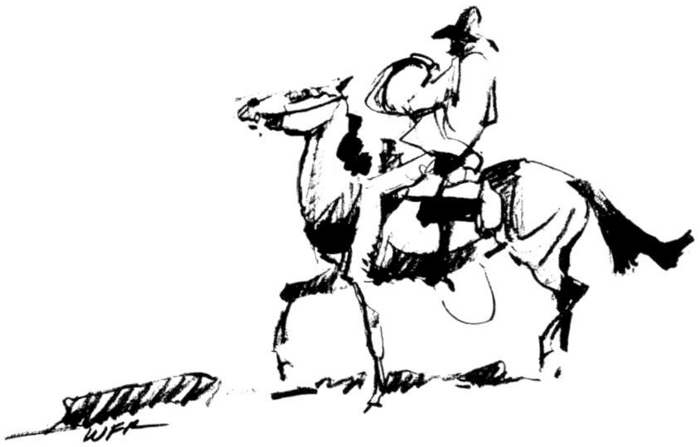

# 7 *Materials, Methods, and Techniques*

"You have to paint at least three days a week just to keep from getting worse!" Reese said. "And, you're going to have to paint five or six days a week if you want to get better." While certain individuals require specific times set aside for painting because a regimen works best for them, Reese is an instinctive, spontaneous painter who works at random times during the day.

"I have a compulsion to paint, so I don't have to worry about logging enough hours in front of the easel. I always have so many ideas going around in my head that I can't wait to get them all down; therefore I paint nearly every day during some part of the day — usually about four hours at a time, which is enough. It exhausts me because it's such an emotional drain. I do like to paint in natural light and this provides a good incentive to get an early start."

*Before his brush ever touches the canvas, he sets the stage the night before, mentally working out the generalities of the painting after he has gone to bed and has lapsed into the 'theta' state, an intuitive, creative, relaxed period which precedes sleep. 'All intellectualizing must be done, all logic must be applied, before you start to paint, be it ten hours or ten minutes in advance — just as decisions must be made on the subconscious level, without thinking, throughout the whole painting process. The artist must call upon the sum of all his senses. When a musician is called upon for a concert, that is not the time to learn to play the piano.*[11]

As the painting session begins, Reese studies the subject at hand, whether a carefully arranged still-life or model in the studio, or a landscape or animals on location, letting his emotions react to it — allowing it to speak to him through his senses — allowing it to emerge through its own color, texture, fragrance, quality of light, mood, and temperature. Then, composing directly on the canvas as he paints, he works out the details, making decisions instinctively, without forethought.

Attributing his ability to compose directly on the canvas to more than a decade of laying out billboards, Reese discussed the importance of negative space in composition. "In sign work, that is vital — the whole object in making a sign was to form the letters properly in space — if those were graceful and well-formed, then the letters were correct. I use the same principle in painting and drawing. I paint negative shapes, one against the other, and things fall together much more evenly. I'm aware of it every time I paint. For example, if I paint a forest of trees, I'm aware of the spaces between the trees. I make sure the spacing isn't the same so that the painting won't be monotonous or dull.

"It's amazing how learning one thing helps you somewhere else. Ten or twelve years ago I started studying the guitar (I had played the violin when I was a kid) and I became aware of the values assigned to each note. If one thinks of those values as positives and the rest as negatives, it makes you realize why trees have to be spaced at different intervals to make a painting of them more interesting — or the spaces among most things have to be different to be interesting.

"Frequently I make musical notations under the spaces students have left in their paintings. A whole note represents the largest space, a half-note represents a space half the size, and so on. Sometimes the painting shows nothing but whole notes or too many half-notes to be interesting. They seem to understand this analogy more readily than just a verbal explanation.

"On the other hand, you can become too technical with art. The math and complexity of Dynamic Symmetry, for example, are boring and can ruin your work; however, understanding the basic theories and mechanics can be helpful. Art must be created through the emotions."

No one medium or method is sufficient to express the wealth of feeling — the hand cannot execute what the soul dictates — the mind envisions wonderful images only to find the hand stumbling along unable to fulfill the expectations. This elusive gap between the eye and the canvas, between appreciation and execution, is often a source of high frustration. That is why one should have only a general idea of the result, allowing it to evolve through the creative process.

*The King*
Oil, 12x18"
Private Collection

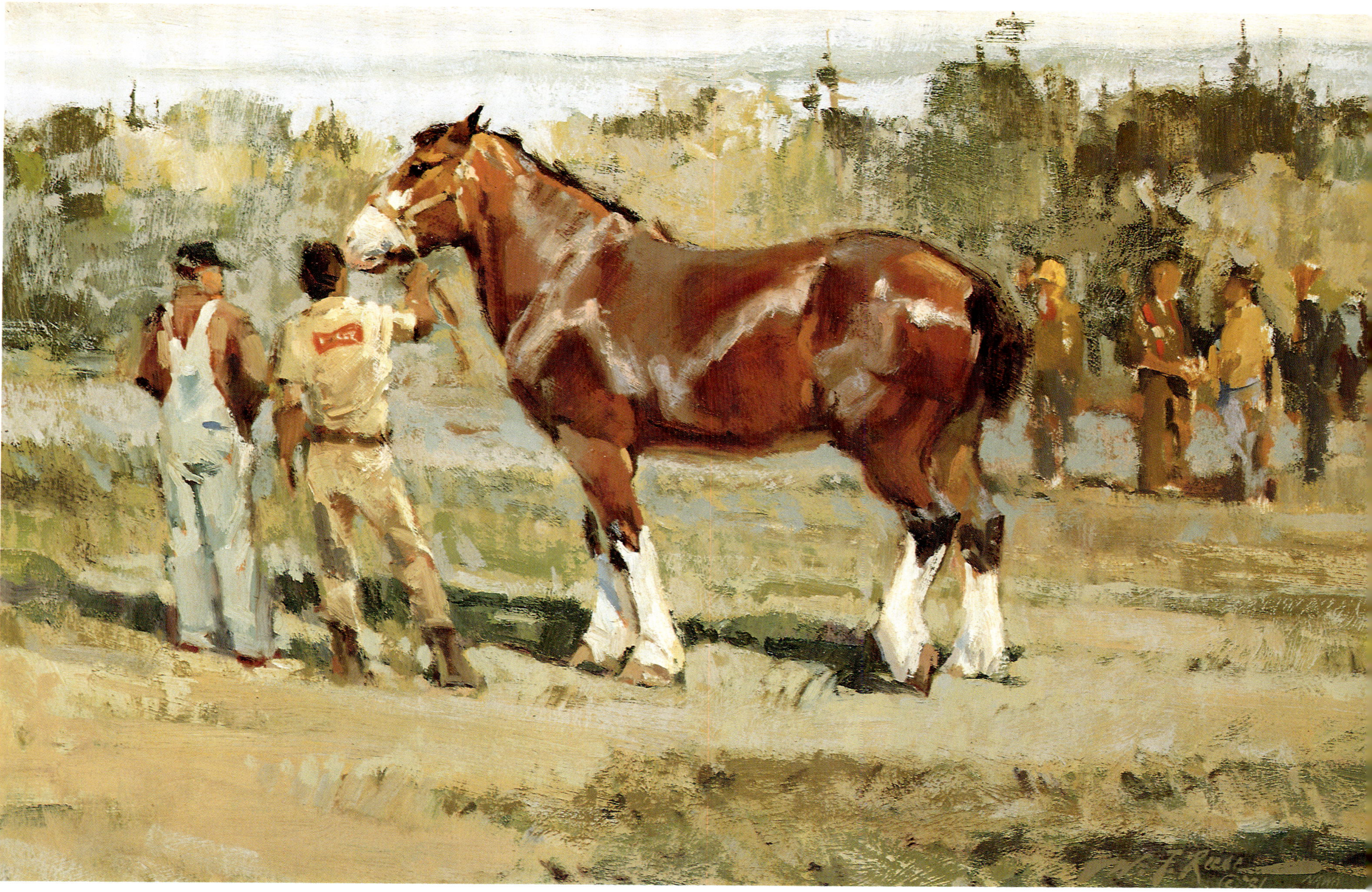

"If you just paint what the subject is *doing* — move your strokes in the direction of the action — pretty soon you'll capture the essence of it. Forget rules. Paint intuitively. Don't worry about exact proportions, at first; approximate them and the various positions or parts by blocking them in in general terms only.

"I start the painting with large washes and build the drawing through the use of large shapes and movements and not so much outline. I concentrate on the 'inline.'" Once the forms have been blocked-in on the entire canvas, each with its own local tone or value, then Reese begins to refine them by pushing forms closer to where he wants them in the final composition. Each form is then built up through a more accurate definition of planes, the 'inline' (the parts that come toward you and the parts that recede), to give solidity and a three-dimensional quality to the object. The thin pigment washes become progressively heavier, as the painting advances, through the means of a loaded brush, so that the paint, rather than the bristles, touches the canvas and creates the stroke — edges are softened or hardened (defined) to direct the viewer's eye in and out of the forms.

Inspiration for the canvases comes in a multitude of ways, from something as spontaneous as the wind blowing a model's hair or making her costume billow as she stands in a field of wild mustard, or from such sources as a string of yellow onions, a jar of homemade preserves, blue iris nodding on the edge of a marsh, or the sleek summer coat of a horse — all can become subjects or parts of subjects for a major work. Some paintings are begun and finished on the spot; others serve as idea-sketches for larger compositions.

"Often I do little studies while I'm warming up to a subject whether in the studio or on location. They are my fact-finders, memory refreshers, and well-springs for many other paintings. Because I am studying as I do them, they are sometimes tighter than the larger paintings which result from them. Some people actually like them better."

*"A work of art must be the orchestration of all its parts, a symphony."*

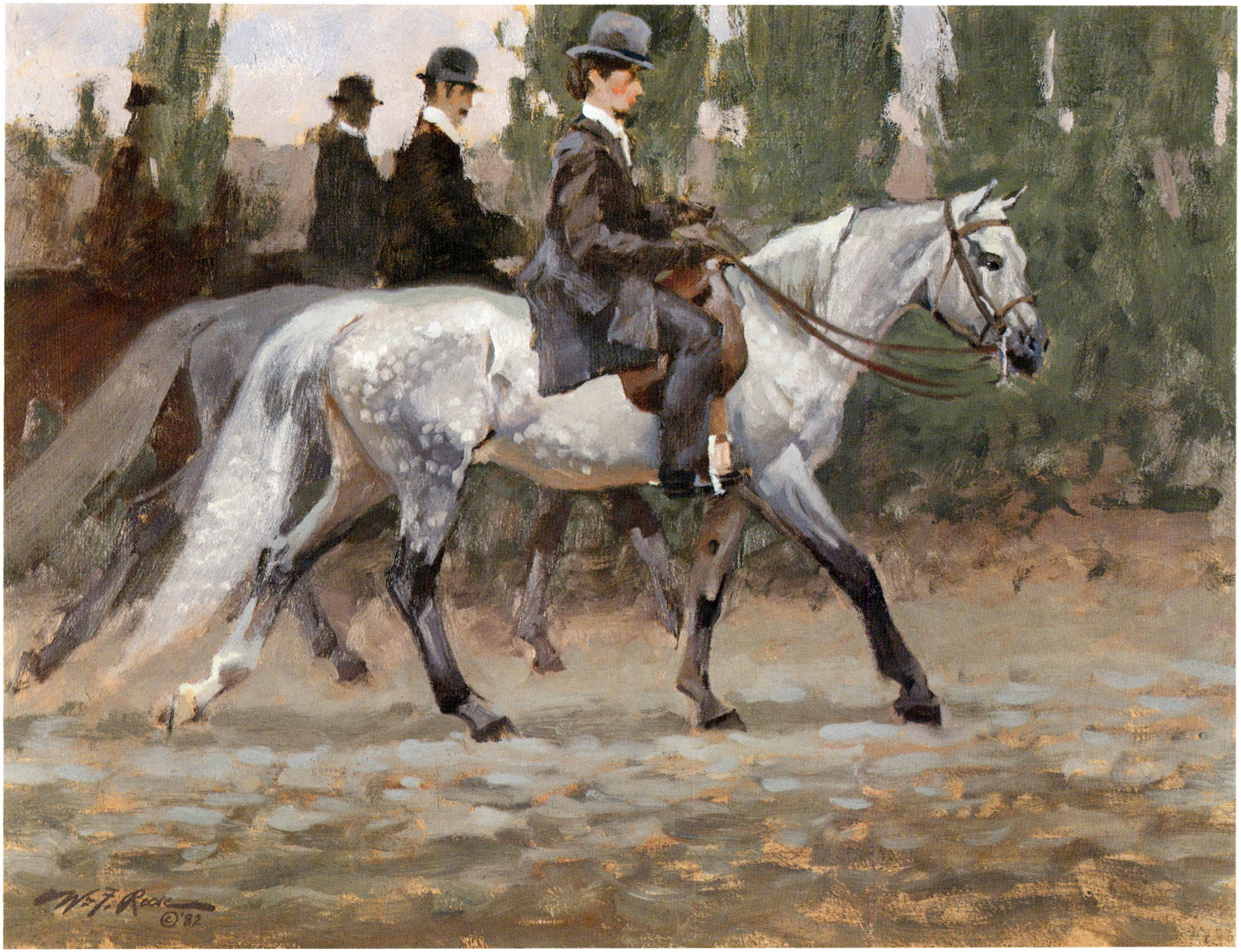

*High Brow*
Oil, 16x20″

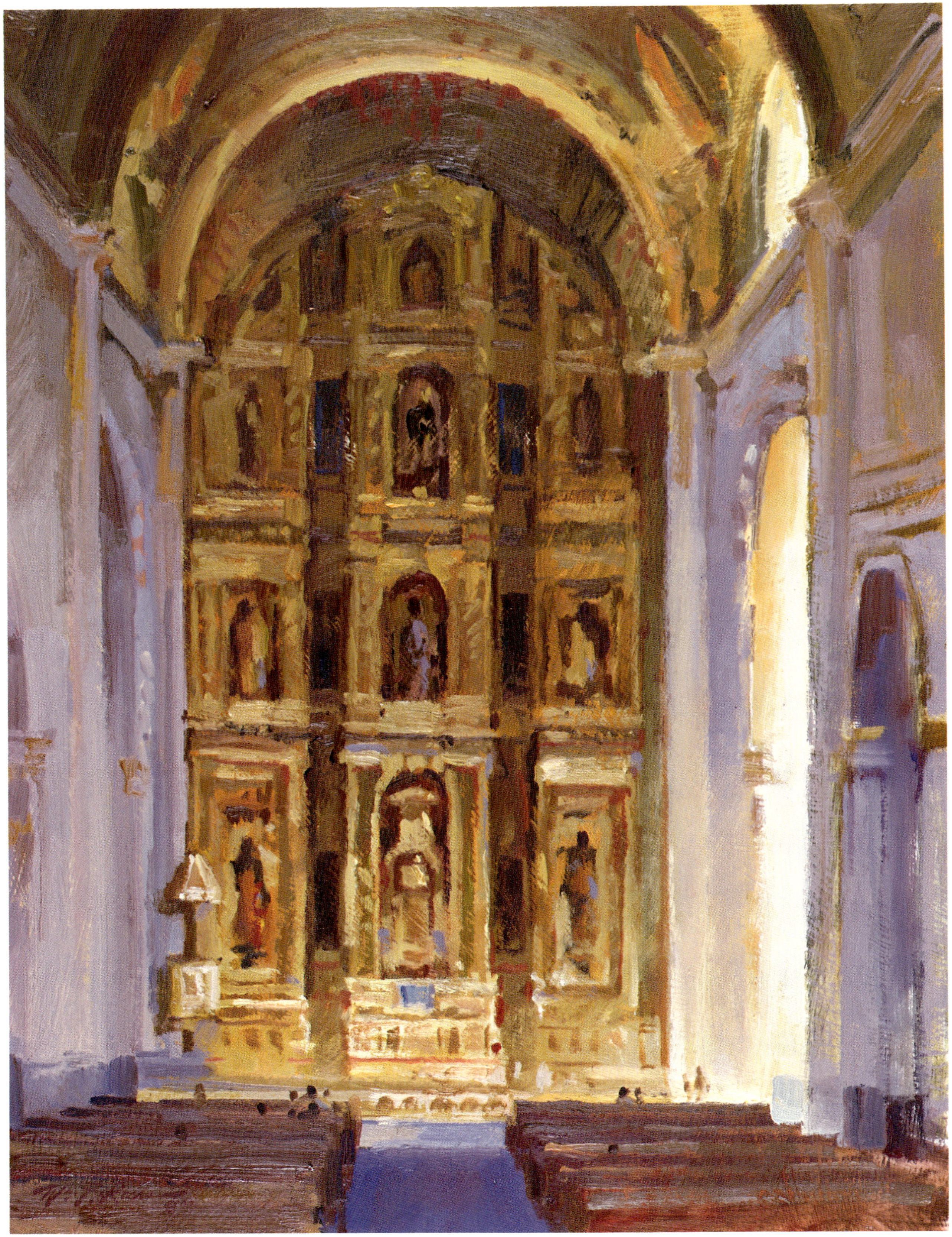

*Divine Light*
Oil, 16x12″

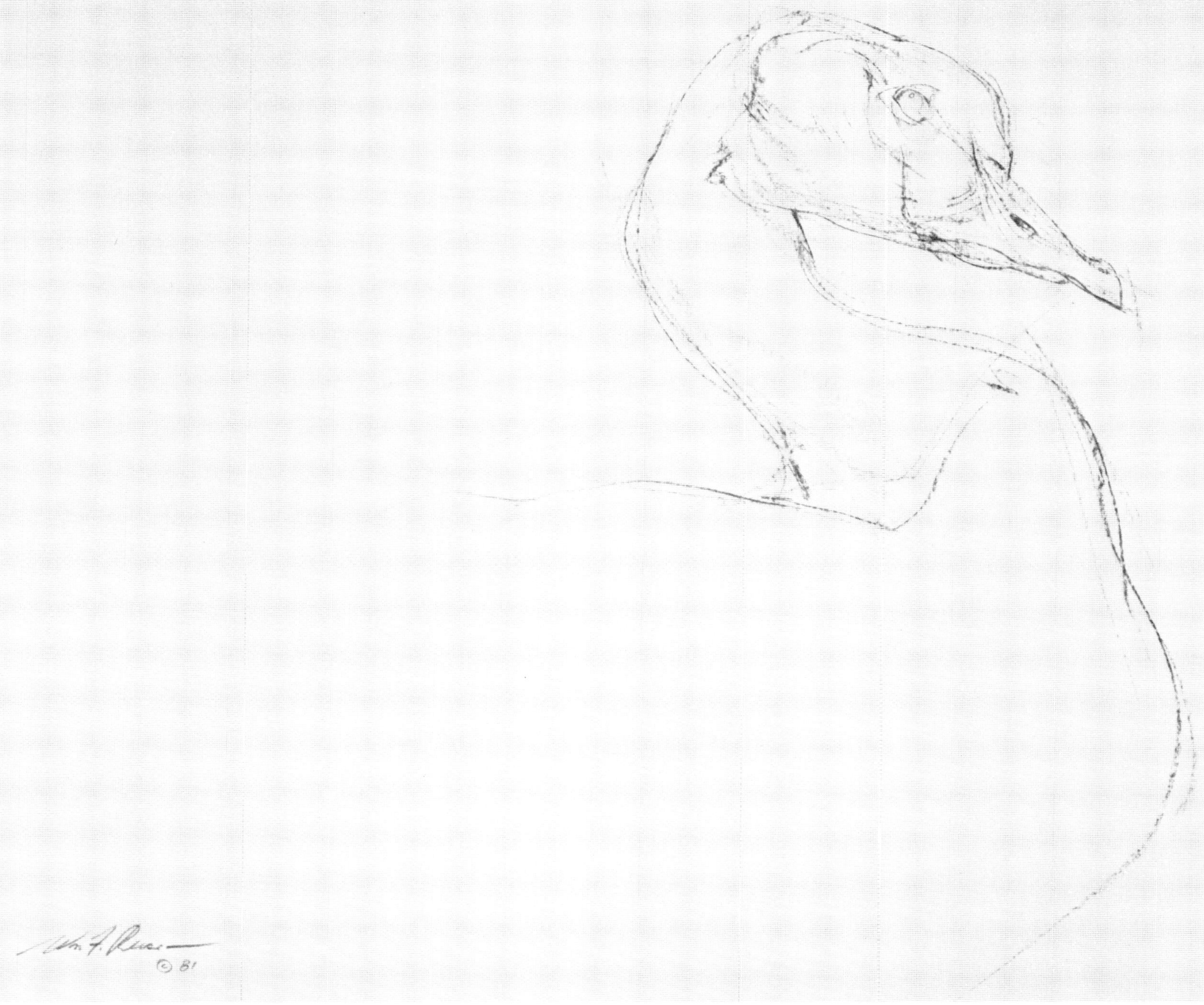

The studies are in demand and sell as quickly as he is ready to let them go; however, they are purposefully painted to serve an artistic end. The idea-sketches for *Winter White, Ptarmigans,* for example, were the impetus for several paintings: one, an oil, was commissioned for the cover of a sporting-goods store catalogue; another, a watercolor, was part of an international exhibit that accompanied Reese to Peking in 1981, and later was the subject for a large print — and it may well be that not all the Ptarmigans have yet seen the light of day but are still "stored" in Reese's head.

Another example is seen in *Sounds of Silence,* commissioned for a hospital lobby. Innumerable studies preceded the final work and subsequently germinated into additional, totally different paintings. In preparation Bill went into a marshland, equipped with sketching materials and bags full of bread crumbs, and followed the resident geese for several days. He observed their habits and actions and simultaneously produced a wealth of visual information. The large painting, a gaggle of Greater Canadians, is an august presentation paying homage to nature's magnificence.

*"Paint the essence, the mood, the chill in the air — rather than making a census count of the trees in the forest."*

One is drawn into the muted blues and greys of a boggy marsh, to smell the salt air of Puget Sound and to eavesdrop as the geese chatter and preen. Yet, the geese are not painted with realistic, photographic detail. They are impressions — ideas that reveal the spirit and essence of the geese — accomplished by Reese's sure, loose strokes that flow with the forms and their parts.

When Reese was commissioned to do this painting by his long-time friend and patron, Gene Lynn, he was not instructed to paint geese. In fact, there weren't any instructions or restrictions beyond "It should be something of Bellevue, Washington. It must be the biggest and best painting you've ever done — and you have two years in which to do it."

At first glance it sounded like the kind of a commission everyone dreams about. Almost no limitations. Almost complete freedom. But the more he thought about it, the more puzzling it became. What would his subject matter be? How could he typify or depict Bellevue in a painting? Should it be about a historic event or building, or perhaps a scene, a landscape or the surrounds?

He simply could not become inspired about the history of the 35-year-old city with its new, square buildings — "plastic boxes" surrounded by pavement — streets and parking lots crammed with automobiles.

Then he remembered an office park which had been built on a reclaimed slough south of town. Considerable marshland and lagoons juxtapose and meander through the park, making it a haven for birds and other wild life. In the spring, the geese and ducks parade their goslings and ducklings and train them in the ways of the urban world, teaching them to keep a sharp eye for crumbs and breadcrusts from their human compatriots, the hundreds of office workers and salespeople who inhabit the park's buildings each day. The humans have learned to make concessions as the wayward birds idly waddle around the lawns and streets. It is a captivating setting — the one which, with its entourage of resident birds became the subject for the commissioned work.

"My idea at first was to do the painting on several panels which would project from the wall at various angles, much like an Oriental screen. I stretched canvas on several identical frames and started in. But after several tries, and then more trials, it just didn't seem to mesh. The geese never looked right. Their necks always came out in the cracks or folds — nothing wanted to fit — even the paint refused to go on as it should. I had to give it up.

"I let the whole idea rest for some time and went about my other work, until one day I decided to try the painting on a single, flat plane, a 40″x 70″ canvas. It worked immediately. Everything just fell into place. Sometimes it happens that way — you know right from the beginning whether or not it's going to jell. If it doesn't, you might as well not waste your time. Try a different approach, different materials, or put the painting aside for a few days."

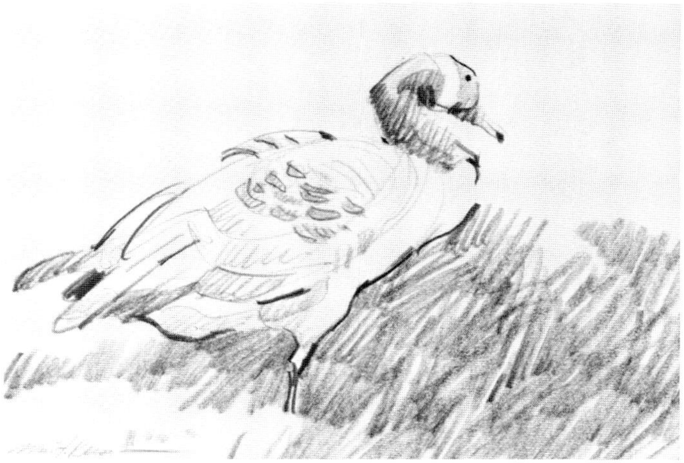

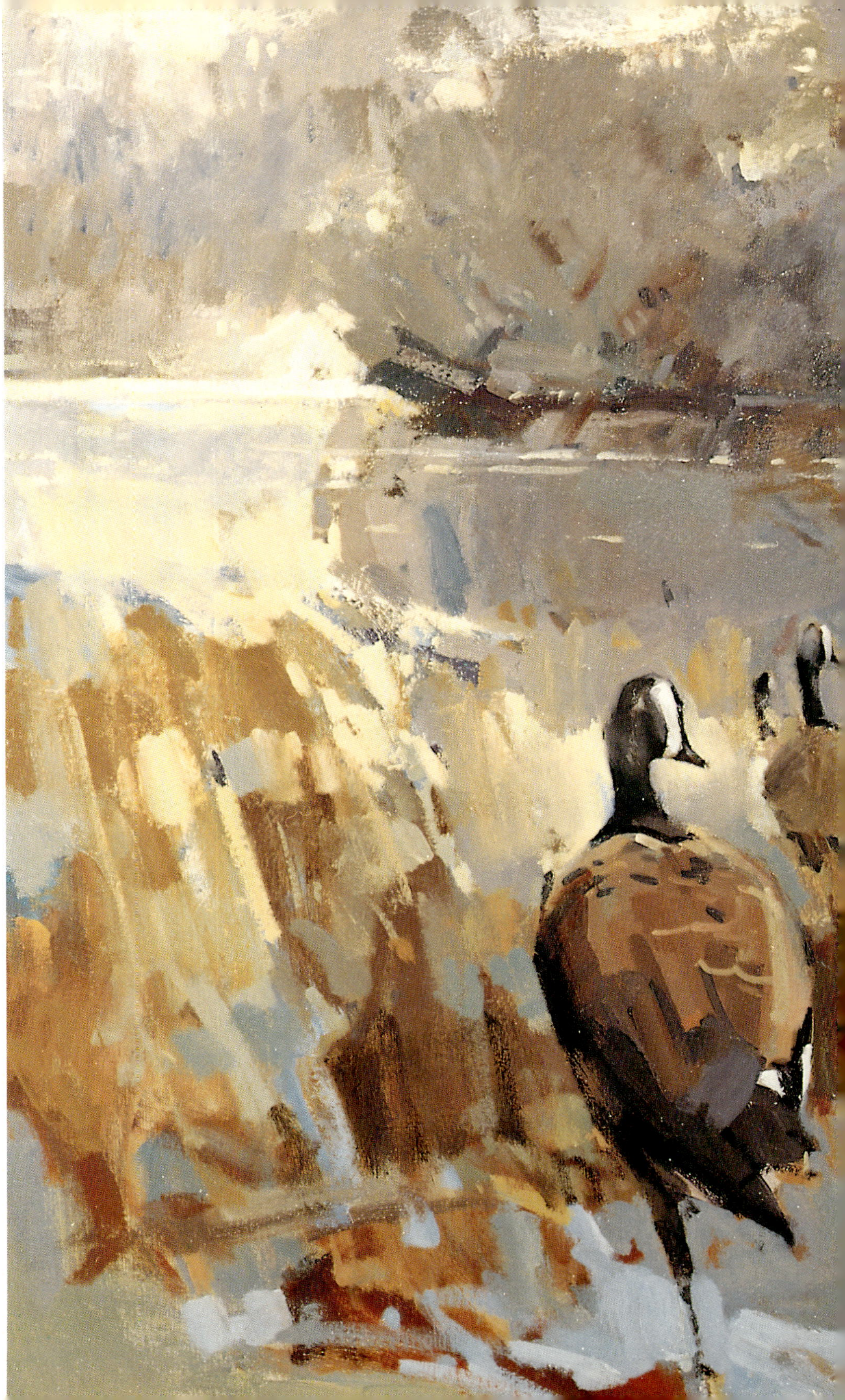

*Sounds of Silence*
Oil, 40x70″
Collection of Gene E. Lynn

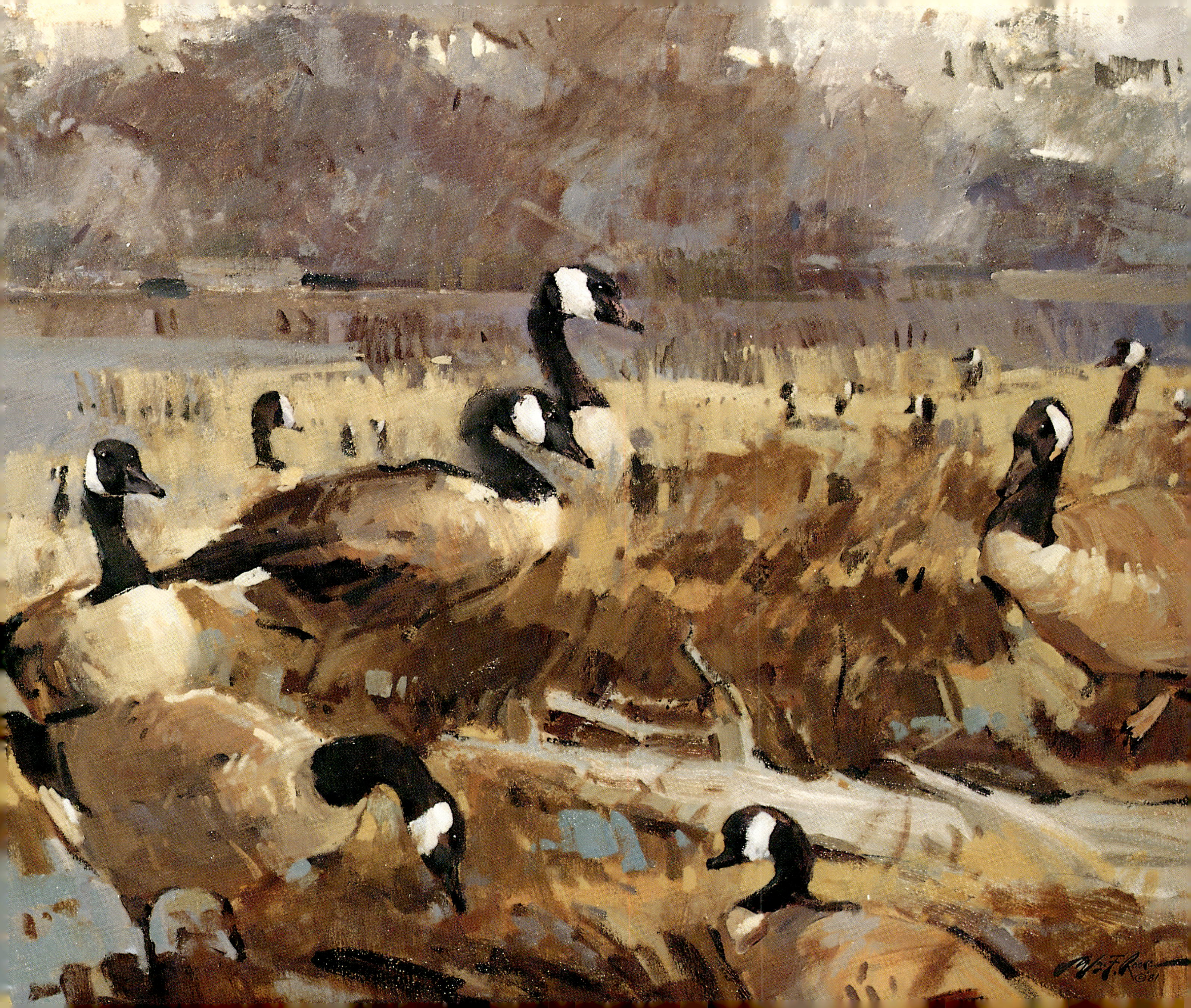

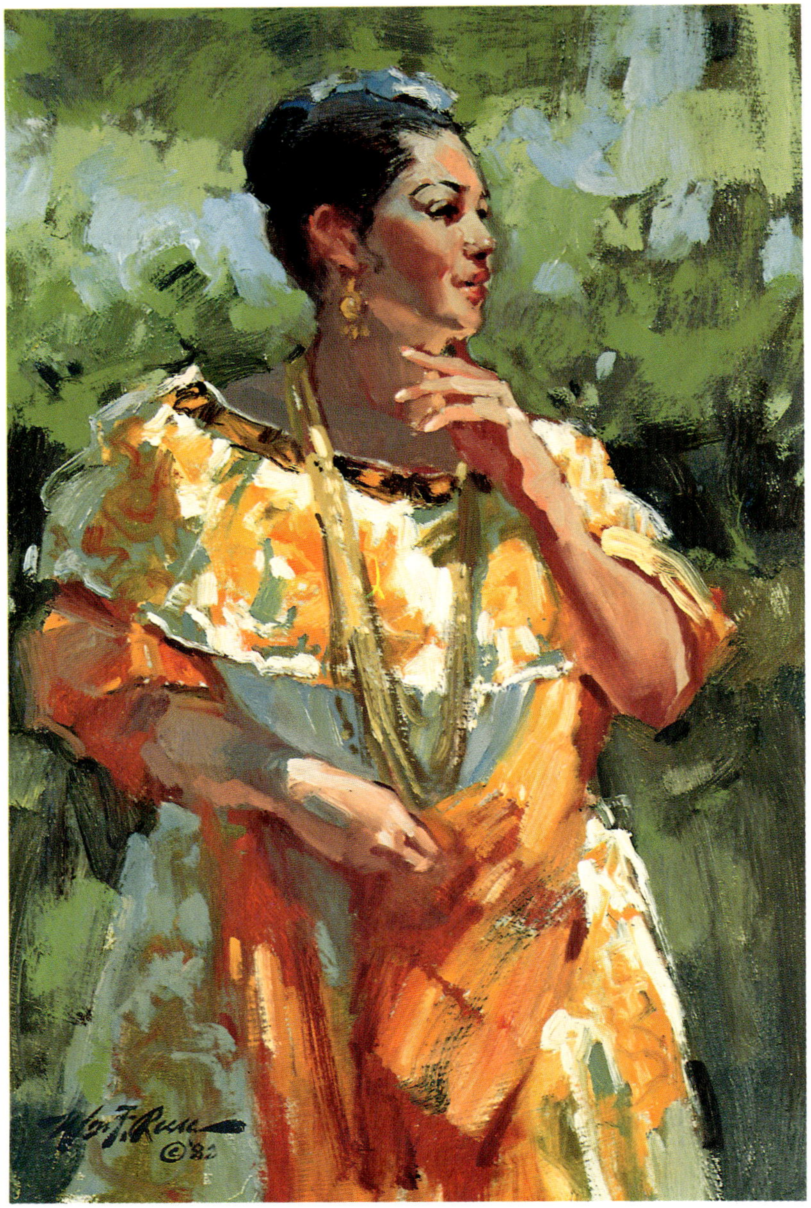

*Rebozo de Naranja*
Oil, 12x8″
Private Collection

A prolific painter, through personal necessity, interest, and desire, Reese paints a wide variety of subjects; and because of this output, restriction to one or two subjects would be too confining. In addition to variety, he searches for new ways of approaching subject matter to keep the spontaneity, excitement, and momentum at peak level, changing or alternating palettes, brushes, mediums, and supports and sizes. Frequently, he introduces a new color to the palette to find out what its effect will be on the others or to create a problem situation; and because the outcome is an unknown, it produces an additional challenge and vitality.

"I'm not interested in a set, never-changing system or procedure — it is more exciting not quite knowing what the next step is."

Aside from the concerns of tools and materials, the development of the painting must be exciting at all stages. The visual excitement of a new subject — the high energy level of the beginning thought process — must be transferred to the canvas and must be maintained throughout. In part, this is accomplished by maintaining the relationship of one area to another; *e.g.,* all areas of the canvas must be worked on almost simultaneously so that it evolves, unfolds, and "moves" as a unit rather than in isolated parts.

*"Try to let your painting tell you how to paint it."*

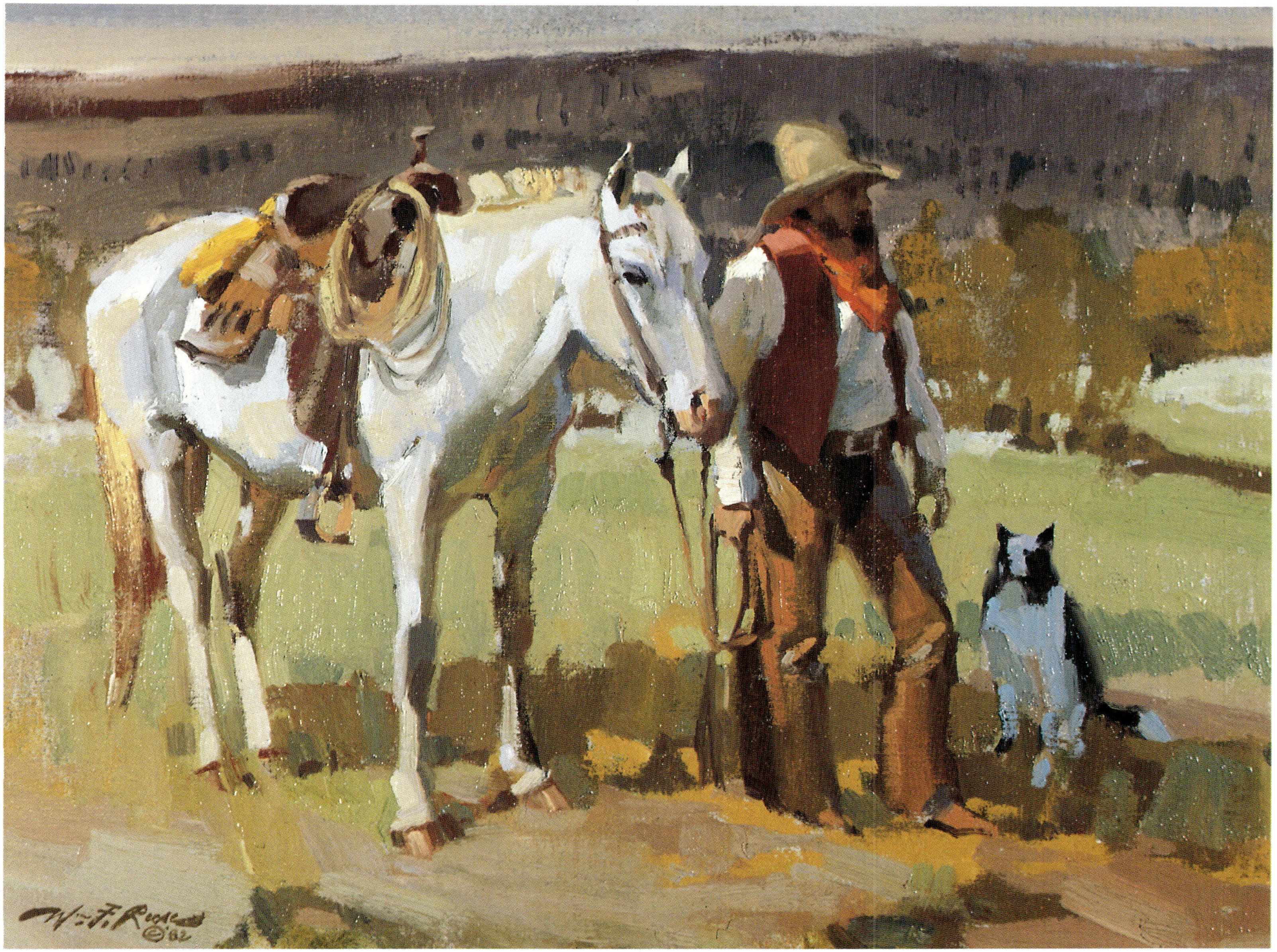

*The Drifter*
Oil, 12x16″
Collection of Mr. & Mrs. John Clum

Extensive travel is one method Reese uses for finding new subject matter, logging a number of air and road miles annually to paint with friends or to conduct workshops in other parts of the country. This enables him to see different people, to work with other artists, and to see life from a different angle.

"Travel inspires me. I really thrive on it," he says. "It's never a waste of time, even if I have a lay-over somewhere, because I find interesting subject matter to sketch everywhere. Sometimes when I get cranky, Fran will go out and get me a plane ticket and say, 'Get lost!' I'll give Ramon Kelley or another friend a call and we'll go off to paint somewhere. Ramon and I have made several such excursions to Mexico and elsewhere.

"One time, a number of years ago, Ramon called to see what I was up to. I confessed that I was feeling 'down' and then jokingly added that I was looking out the window and considering jumping out!"

"Why?"

"'I guess I'm sick of this rain, I said.'"

"Why don't you get on a plane and come down? We'll go to Taos," Kelley asked.

"Well, I'd never been to Taos, although I'd heard a lot about it and had always wanted to go to see for myself. I didn't need to be asked twice! I left immediately and we had a wonderful time. It was all new and fresh to me."

They explored and admired the organic masses of the much-painted Ranchos de Taos church, the centuries-old Pueblo, the Taos

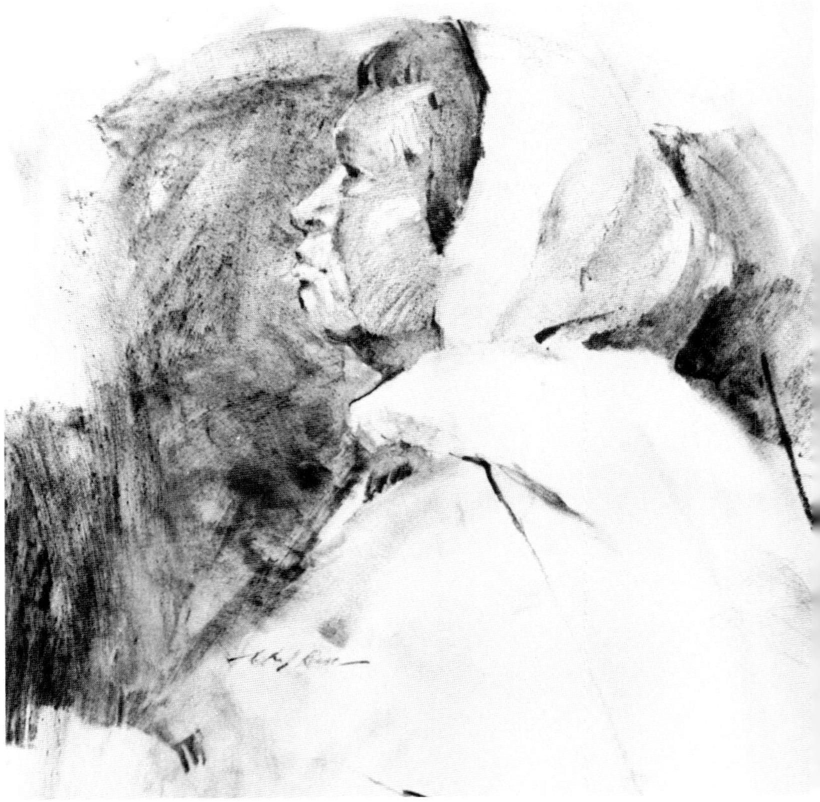

Indians, and the high-desert landscape with its earthy browns and soft, blue-green plantlife, sage brush, chamisa, and tumbleweeds. As always, gnarled piñons dotted the foothills of the western slope of the Sangre de Cristos, while crusty-trunked cottonwoods accented the Taos plaza as well as the rancheros on the outskirts of town. The houses of the Pueblo, America's first apartment dwellings, were two and three stories high, made of sunburnt adobe with heavy irregular vigas (roof beams) which protruded through the walls and sometimes served as hangers for strings of red chilies. Bright blue doors, like rectangular jewels set into slurried mud, emphasized the entrance ways. Beehive ovens (hornos) sat in many of the communal front yards, graced by the gurgling Taos Creek. In all these the two rejoiced.

"We painted and painted. And, like so many artists, I thought I had discovered the Taos Pueblo and the Taos Indians all by myself!" Reese chuckled. It was the point of no return. He became totally immersed and enamored with the joys of painting what he pleased, without inhibitions of concern for its saleability.

When he began the Taos paintings, he was certain that they would not sell because they were too regional. "I just knew I would wind up eating them; but I didn't care. I was eating most of the others anyway. These were paintings I really enjoyed doing, and it would be a pleasure to have them around. Surprisingly, that *whole* batch sold!" (Mrs. Greathouse purchased *Taos Indian* for the Frye Art Museum collection from this group.)

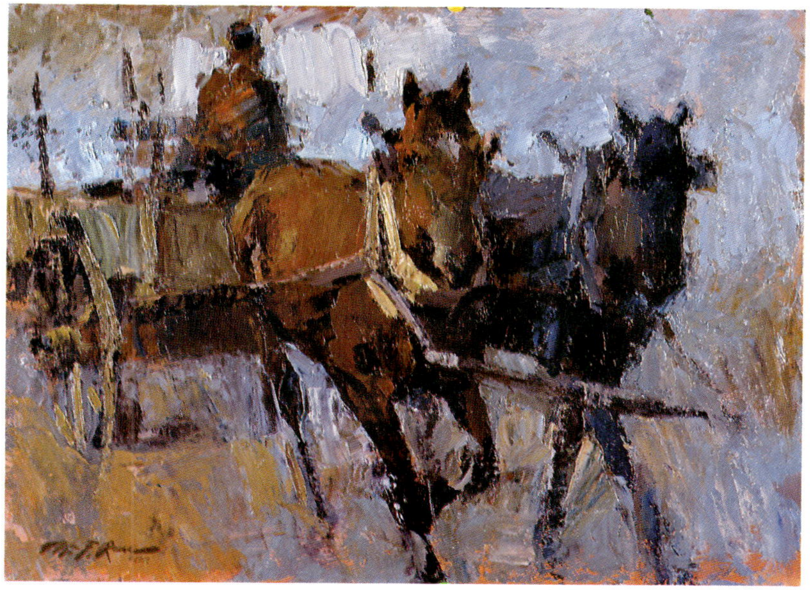

*Taos Horses*
Oil, 12x16″
Private Collection

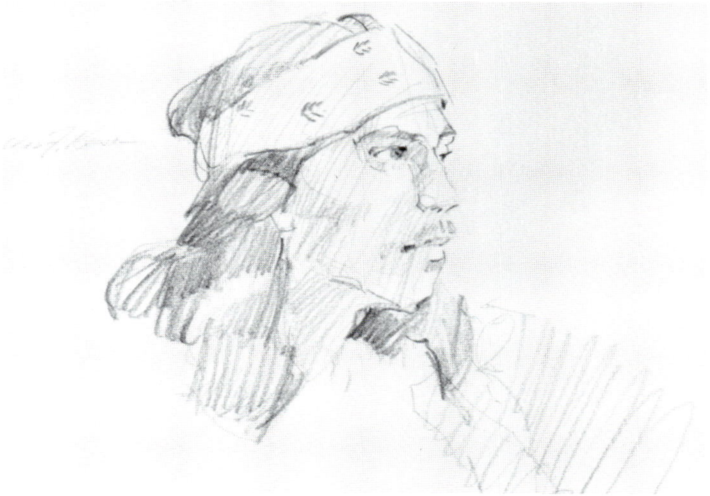

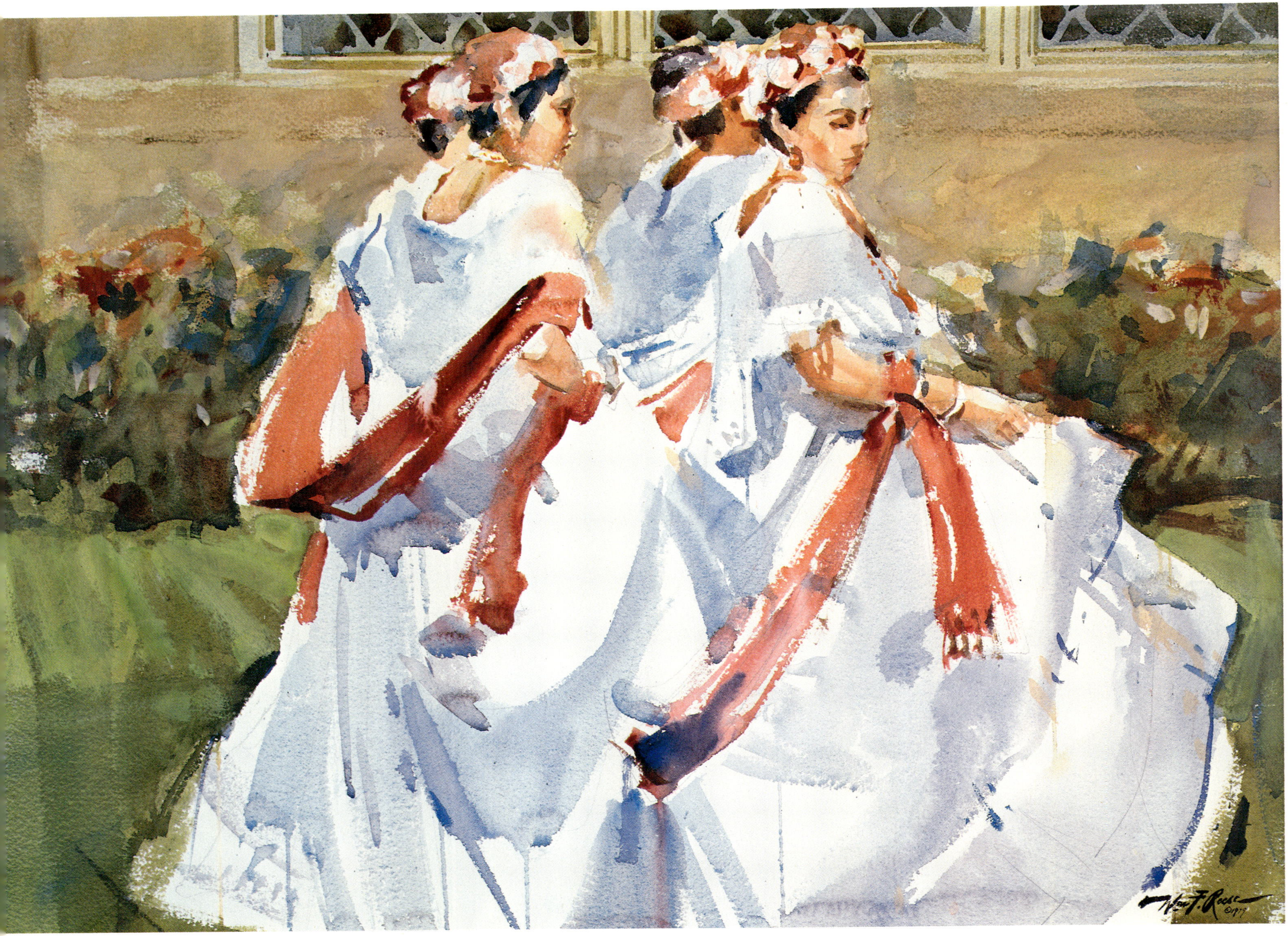

*White Lace*
Watercolor, 21x29″
Private Collection

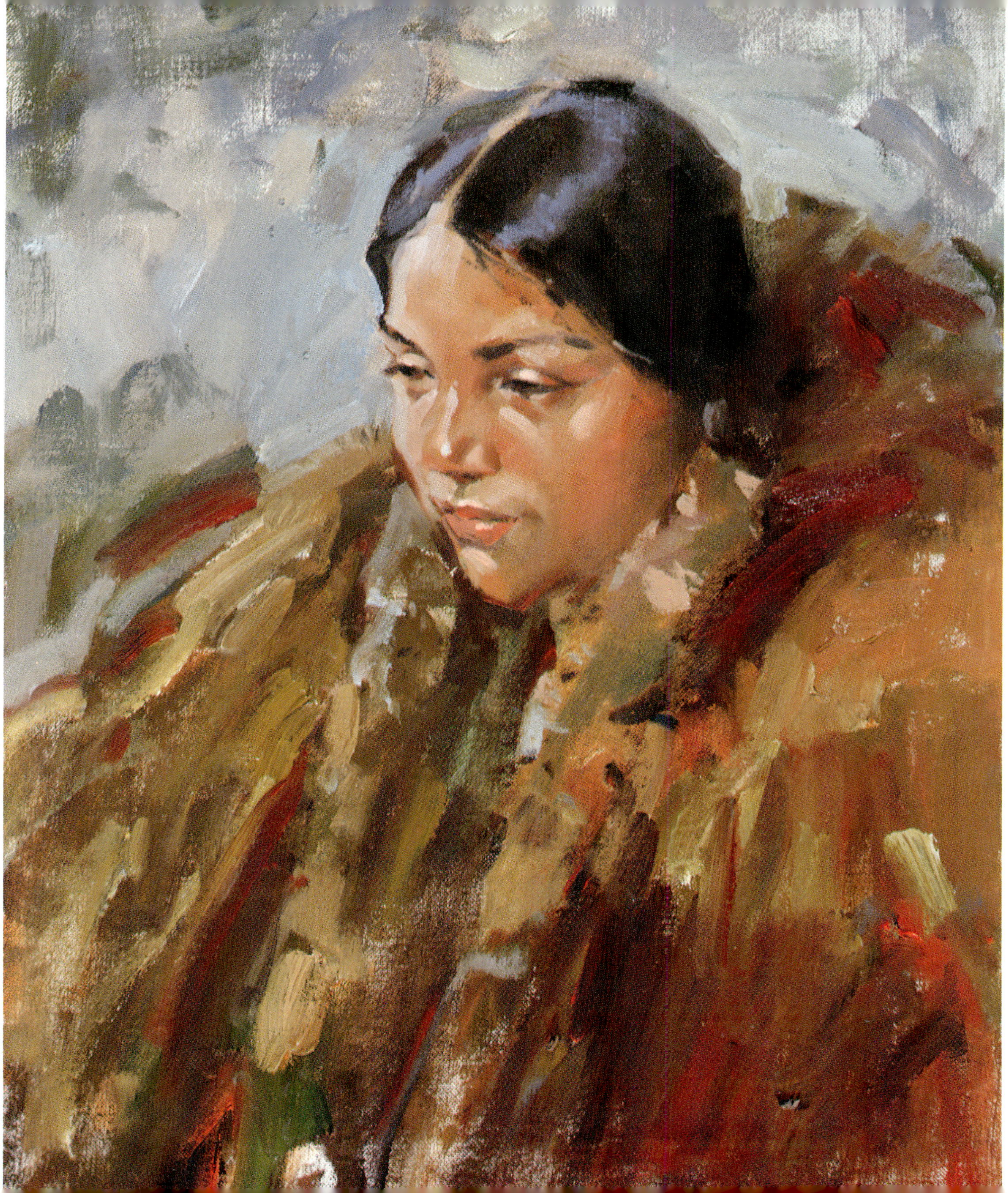

*Yellow Sunflower*
Oil, 16x12″
Collection of Mr. & Mrs.
J. Paul Mathias

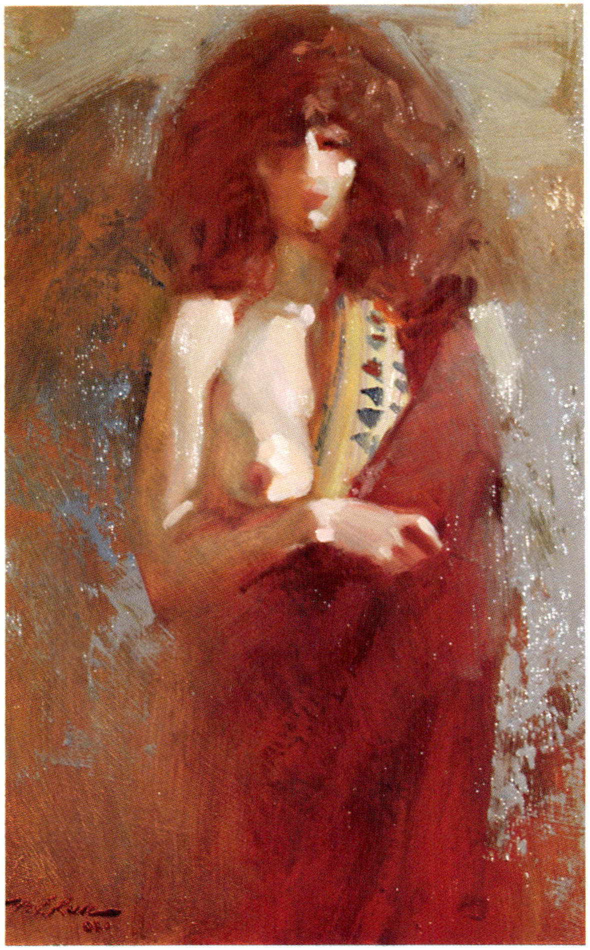

*Red Robe*
Oil, 12x8″
Collection of Gwendolyn Worthy McKay

Henri's comment "Your only hope of satisfying others is in satisfying yourself[12] was forcefully true once again.

Reminiscing about his career, Reese said that Taos was a major turning point. His subject matter, style, and technique changed, as did his sales. He talked about his early work and his fascination for "esfumato," a smoky quality given to paintings, from which the subject emerges without any hard edges. (It was a technique credited to Leonardo da Vinci, who used it in many of his paintings, including *Mona Lisa* and the *Virgin and Sainte Anne.*)

"It's a wonderful technique or style, but I used it to the extreme and in the wrong way," Reese reflected. "I purposefully looked for subjects that would fit my hazy style; and everything I painted was shrouded with an indistinct, misty veneer. As I look back at them, they were shallow, contrived. But, I suppose that is only natural; I was learning the techniques of painting. To compound the problem, I had received some recognition in working this way and it's hard to give up something that is liked by others and sells. Luckily, I didn't sell so many that I was completely caught up with it."

In the pre-Taos period, too, he said that he tried to please everyone but himself and even allowed himself to be influenced by his friends' paintings and their ideas, by subject matter that sold well: barns, boats, and more barns. If he saw that boats were selling, he painted a series of boat paintings whether he liked the idea or not.

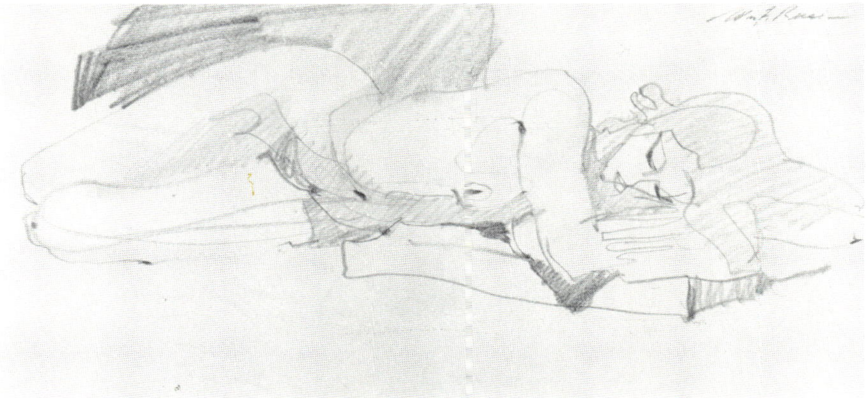

His friend Fred Oldfield, a painter, talked with empathy about those years. "For example, we set up exhibit booths in shopping malls to sell our wares. Once set up, we sat back and waited for the crowds. I had reached a point where people recognized my work and I would sell out in a few hours, while Bill didn't sell a thing — barns, boats, or anything else. He stood there very patiently, hour after hour, knowing full well he was probably the better artist. Sometimes he grumbled, 'They will buy any kind of garbage.' "[13]

Reese would return to his studio and try over and over to paint the type of paintings and subjects which he had seen being snatched up by the visitors to the mall, but his heart simply wasn't in it. It seemed that no matter what he painted, nothing sold. Oldfield said that Reese soon stopped "barnstorming" with the outdoor shows and set his sights on higher goals. He decided that if he was going to be the collector of everything he painted, he might as well paint what *he* liked, in the way it needed to be done. This decision wasn't something that happened overnight; it had been festering and building with more and more intensity toward a climax that was finally manifested through the Taos experience.

"My life and work haven't been the same since," he said with a twinkle in his eye. "I finally allowed my feelings to guide me, to select the subject to be painted, and then I allowed that subject to dictate the technique."

Excellence in paintings is a quality Reese always strives for. He feels it is an obligation not only to himself, but to the viewers and to the eventual owner of the paintings. "He just can't *stand* not to paint well,"[14] says Oldfield. Reese claims that sometimes the merit of a painting remains an unknown during its creation. He is too close to it emotionally. Not until the painting is finished and has sat in the studio awhile, is he able to detach himself sufficiently for a more objective look — like that of an "outsider."

While the initial idea is always to produce the best possible work, it is not a conscious thought as the artist paints. Many intangibles — spirit, emotions, body chemistry, innate talent, good (and bad) training — enter the complex channels of his intent and are compounded by external influences and materials.

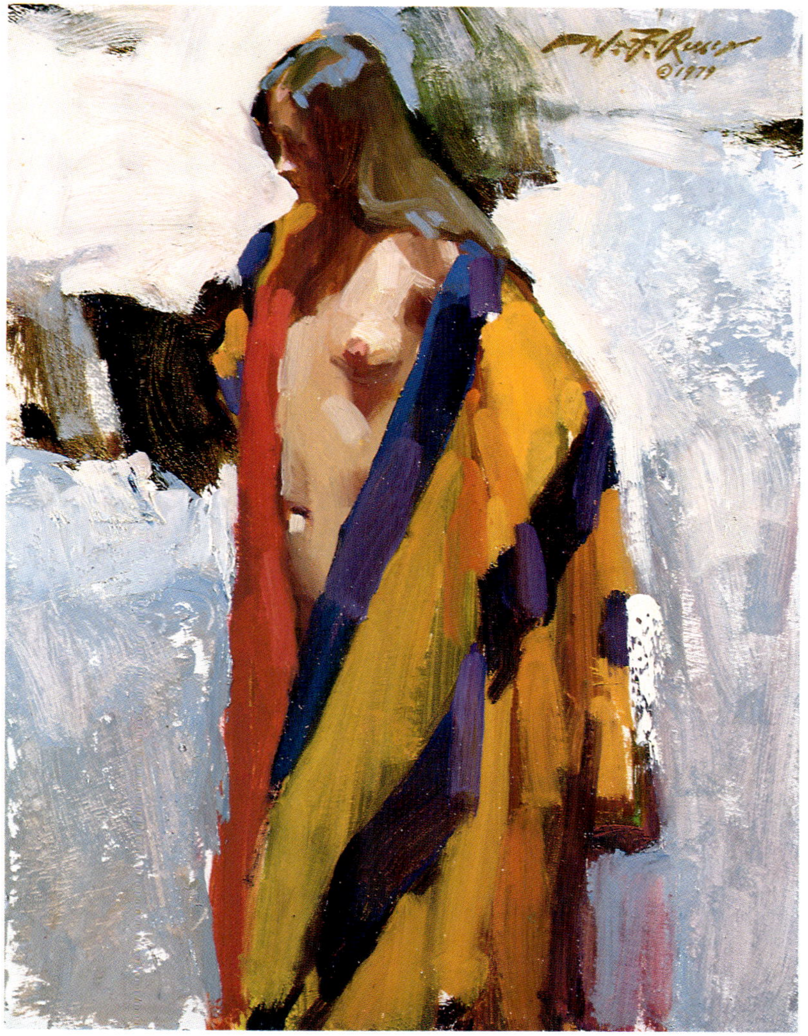

*Purple and Gold*
Oil, 12x9″
Private Collection

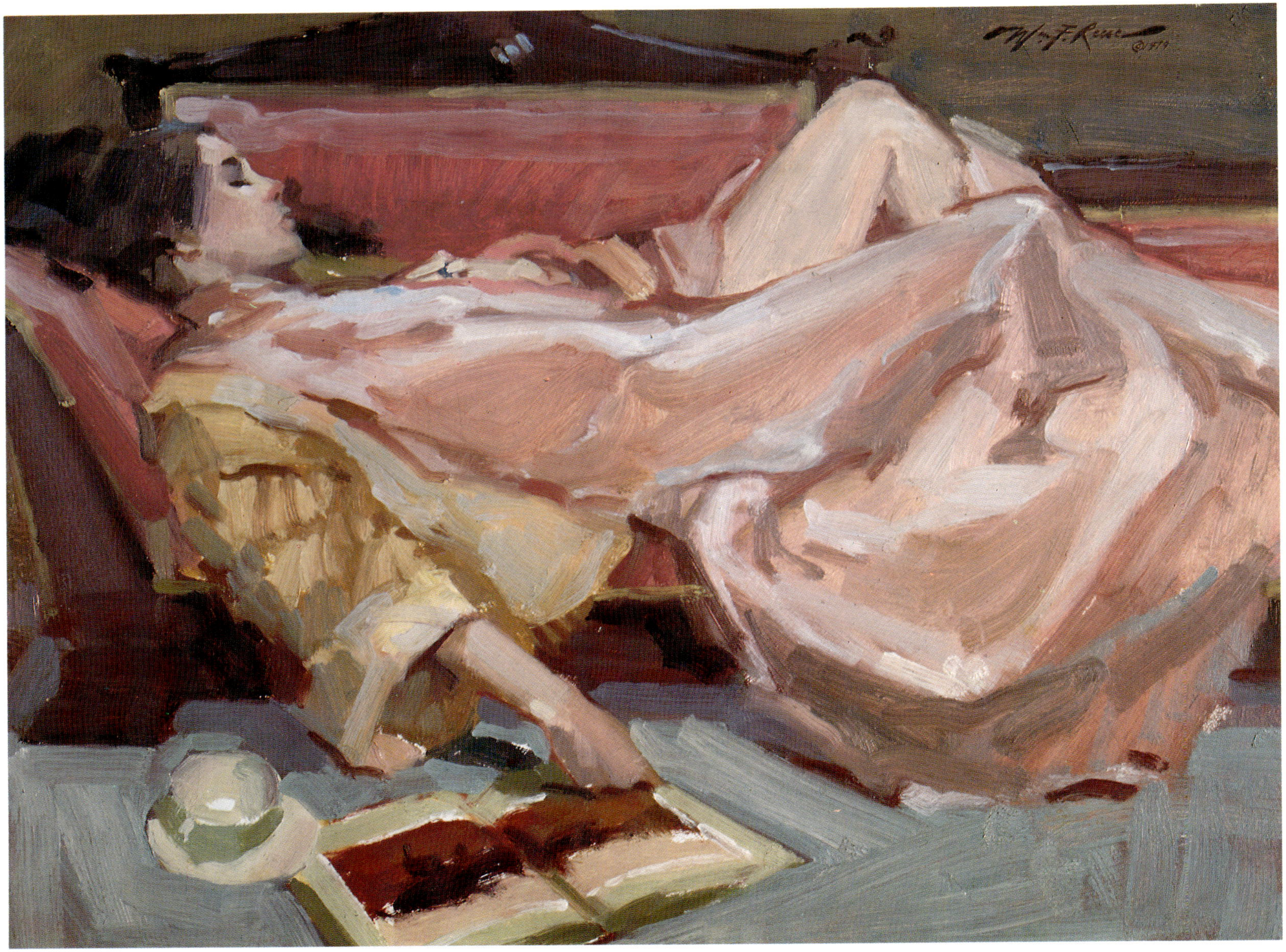

*Afternoon Nap*
Oil, 12x16″
Collection of Joyce Wampler

"If for some reason the paintings don't come up to snuff, I get rid of them. I burn them. Once in awhile I keep them temporarily for study, but I never paint over them. They aren't of good physical quality at that point and they won't hold up."

In discussing color, Reese said it takes many years of practice to learn to see color — practice in painting from life. "The eye, as well as the mind, must actually be exercised to see color. Many colors and values cannot be read properly except when you look away from them. The eye makes constant and rapid adjustments while you look at something; shadows will gradually appear lighter as your eyes adjust. A warm grey, for example, may appear neutral as you look at it for awhile. For this reason you must constantly relate one area to another. Compare similar areas to similar areas, reds to reds, greens to greens, lights to lights, darks to darks, and so on. Then paint the *difference*. Study one while looking at another. Paint out of the corner of your eye."[15]

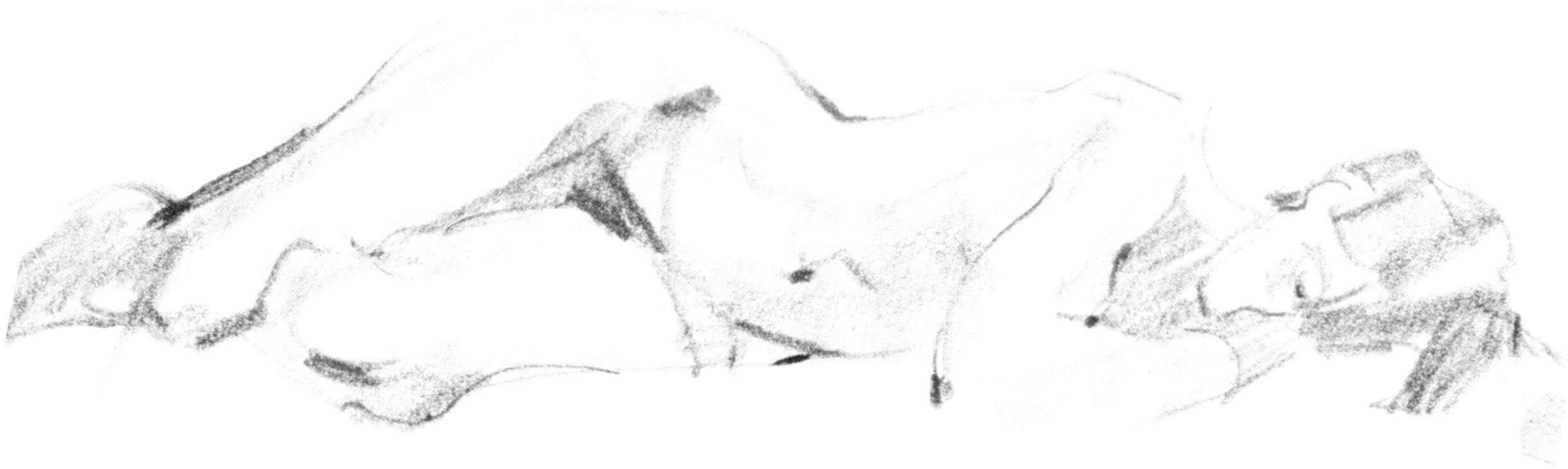

Pure colors are related. It is possible to mix one with the other without getting muddy; however over-mixing is a guarantee of mud. One should not be too concerned with an exact color match, as light conditions are variable and subject to change, thereby changing the color. Complex color charts and geometric proportion systems have been devised and studied by numerous individuals through the decades. Perhaps their greatest beneficiaries have been the non-objective painters, experimenters whose curiosity leads them to analyze, dissect, and divide color, and to juxtapose squares or concentric circles of varying proportions of tints and shades.

For a painter like Reese, who uses direct, spontaneous color, such intellectualizing is meaningless. Much of the time he is not even aware of the identity of the color he is using, only of the value or temperature as it relates to others on the canvas — he works from middle values in both directions — from middle to dark and from middle to light. His friend Harley Brown says, "Bill's sense of color is intuitive. He will often push a choice hue to extreme limits. Whatever rules there are are wide open to intepretation by him. This comes with great knowledge and security — knowing what is right and coming to conclusions. And we can't categorize Bill's work — each time we observe it, it is a new adventure, just as it was a new adventure for him to pull it off."[16]

*"I prefer failure to a safe monotony."*
*— Ye Moiseyenko*

If pressed for an answer about his painting style, Reese would say it is "mainly impressionistic." He is an American painter, painting impressions of scenes, people, and objects of America. Eminent portraitist and a founding member of the National Academy of Western Art, Bettina Steinke gleefully recalled her first acquaintance with Reese's work and their subsequent friendship. "Bill is a free spirit! It's evident in his work and in his attitude toward his work and his life. When I first saw his paintings, I was impressed with the *painterly* qualities — the color, the stroke, the texture — it was evident that he knew how to put his ideas down in a few strokes, to achieve the essence in a painterly way. I could see the potential for growth, and over the years that has proven out. He still continues to grow, while others bottom-out at a certain point. He works hard. He studies. He reads and experiments constantly, never content with the status quo.

He is not a copier, but works from life. And, there aren't many people who buy a ranch just for the sake of art, just to paint from!"[17]

Reese is a rapid painter. This trait is no doubt a carry-over from the sign shop days; however, while it was an attribute, it was also a concern which troubled him deeply. He felt guilty about finishing a painting in a matter of hours or even days. At first he thought this was not proper, perhaps the paintings were lacking in merit, not worthy of consideration because they hadn't been labored over or re-worked enough. Stories of extensive labors and time spans related to epic and historic works reinforced his guilt and plagued him, until he read Henri's statement: "Work with great speed. Have your energies alert, up, and active. Finish as quickly as you can, there is no virtue in delaying."[18] Subsequently he learned that many artists, including Hals, Degas, and Sorolla, had worked rapidly and succinctly.

"I'm not interested in superfluous detail," Reese said, "so there isn't any reason to spend days and months on a painting. I try to interpret only what strikes me about the subject — I 'borrow' from the subject, doing it with a minimum number of strokes — I try to make one stroke do as much as possible. Rather than painting or rendering the various parts, I put down symbols which the viewers can interpret or work out in their own way."

For example, in painting a tree, he uses a few directional strokes, judiciously placed, to show the *symbol* of the tree. The viewer can see by those few strokes that it is a blustery day; he can imagine the temperature and think about the feel of the wind stinging his face, or about hanging onto his hat, or about the fun he had flying a kite on such a day. The strokes in themselves carry a message. They can be horizontal and placid, diagonal and dynamic, vertical and uplifting, or rich, fluent, thin, miserly, repetitious, or abundant to reflect specific meaning.

"In painting a metal chain, a dotted line becomes the symbol which makes the viewer think of a chain," he says; "or, with sea gulls, for instance, it isn't necessary to draw a bird in flight — just flashes of light, sometimes shapes about the size of birds' wings scratched into the paper, become symbols that give you the *impression* of birds flying. Here again, the *feeling* is conveyed rather than the photo

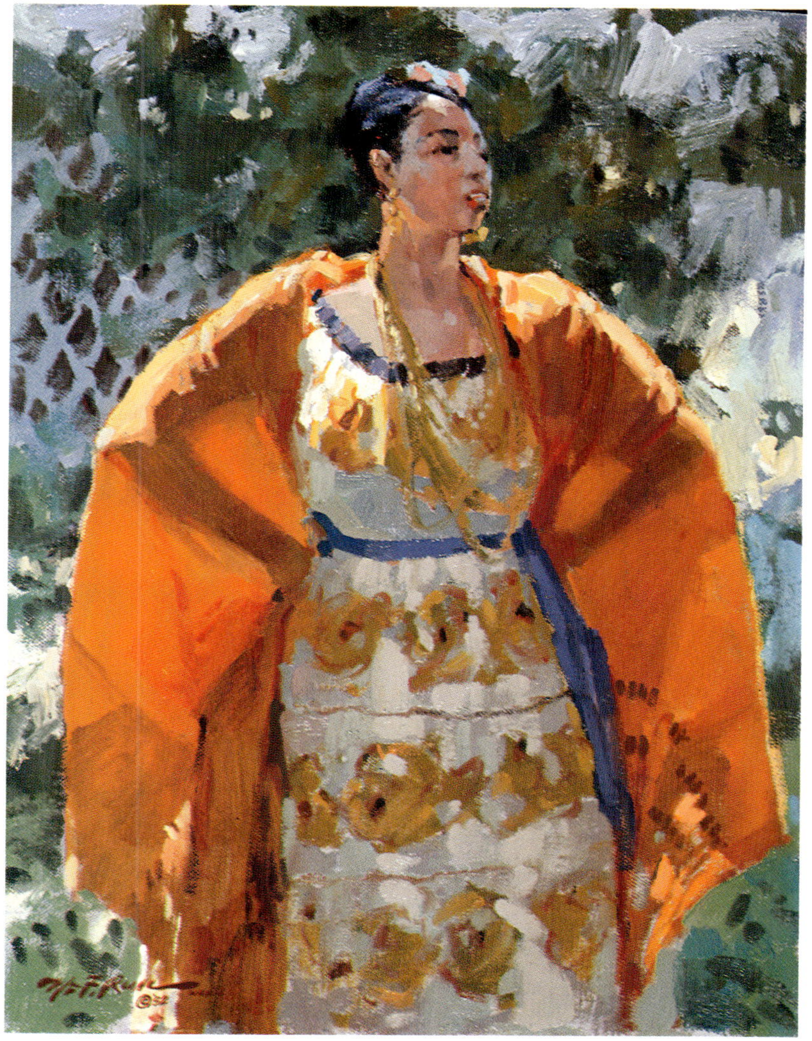

*Orange Rebozo*
Oil, 16x12″
Collection of Dodson's
Gallery, Oklahoma City

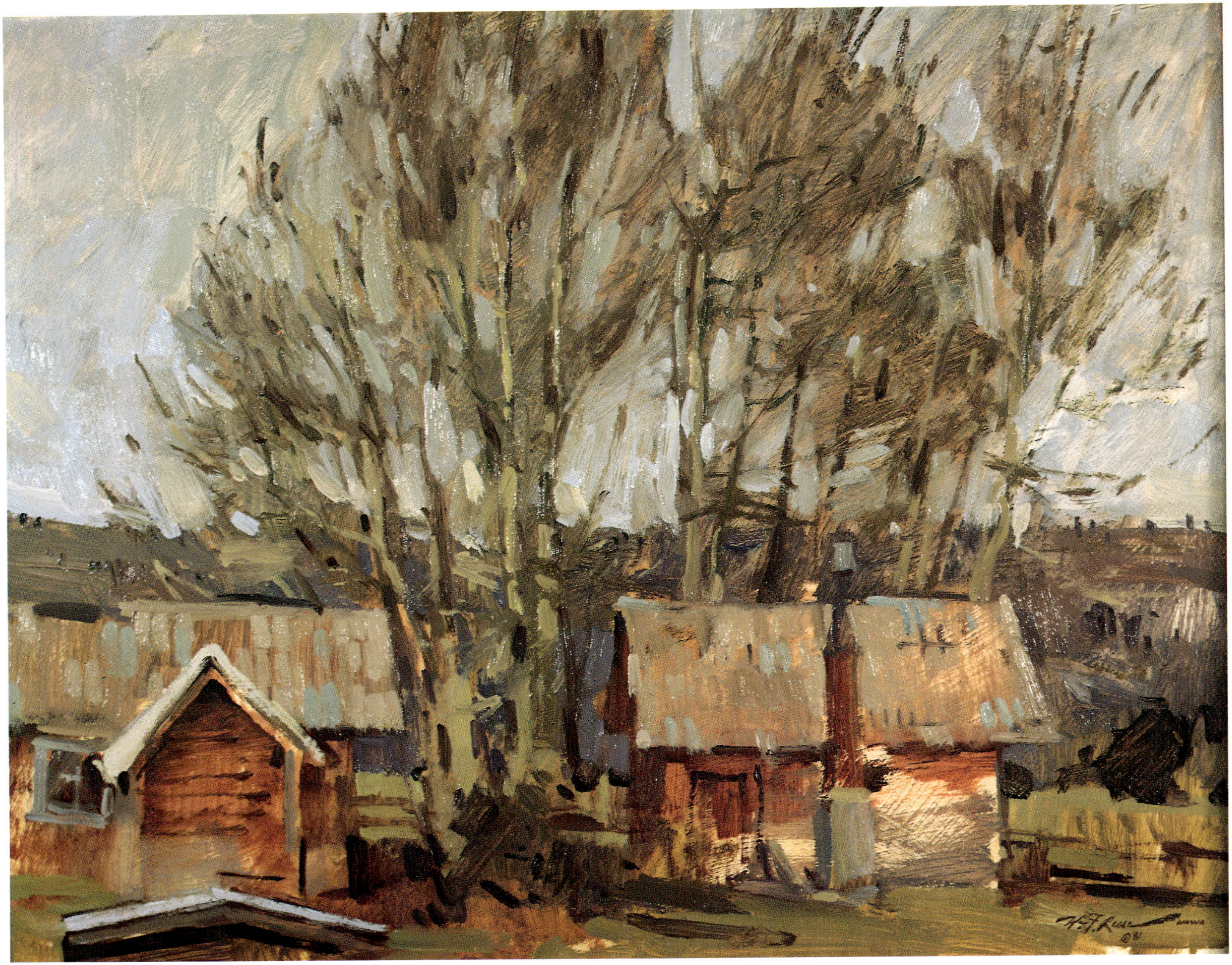

image of the objects themselves.

"The soft, velvety feel of a thick winter coat on a horse, especially one that spends its winter outside, compared with the shiny sleek look of a short summer coat, is shown with the symbols of the quality of light. The first is absorbent and matte, while the second is reflective and has much more contrast and edge — all are achieved with a few, well-placed strokes of the brush.

"My feeling about detail is that if you show a lot of it, all you are doing is telling the viewer what he already knows instead of showing him a new way of seeing things or giving him insights that perhaps he didn't have before. I prefer to suggest and imply as much of the detail as possible and to allow the viewer to finish it.

"This seems to fit my personality best and the direct way in which it requires me to work, wet-on-wet, *alla prima*." *Alla prima* is a one-phase operation. The painting is usually finished while it is wet. It allows spontaneity, freshness, and sketchiness. When used transparently it is kindred to watercolor in that the white surfaces of the ground appear and disappear. The imprimatura shows up through the overpaint at the artist's discretion. Titian, Velasquez, Goya, Hals, Degas, even the Van Eycks and other Flemish painters used a form of *alla prima*. Titian was middle-aged by the time he "discovered the charm conveyed by brushstrokes."[19] This was an extreme contrast to the styles or schools of painting in which the strokes were purposefully smooth, invisible. However, it was Frans Hals whose slashing strokes made all the other painters' works "mild by comparison."[20]

For the French Impressionists also, *alla prima*, of their own fashion (opaque and impasto rather than glazes), was the best method — through necessity they had to work fast in order to capture the effects of rapidly changing light and shade. All the final effects had to be registered at once. There was not time for underpainting — not time to build a foundation on which to construct solutions for a final work. The first strokes were the last strokes.

*"Detail is like seasoning on a meal, a little seasoning will heighten a dish, but you can't make a meal of it."*

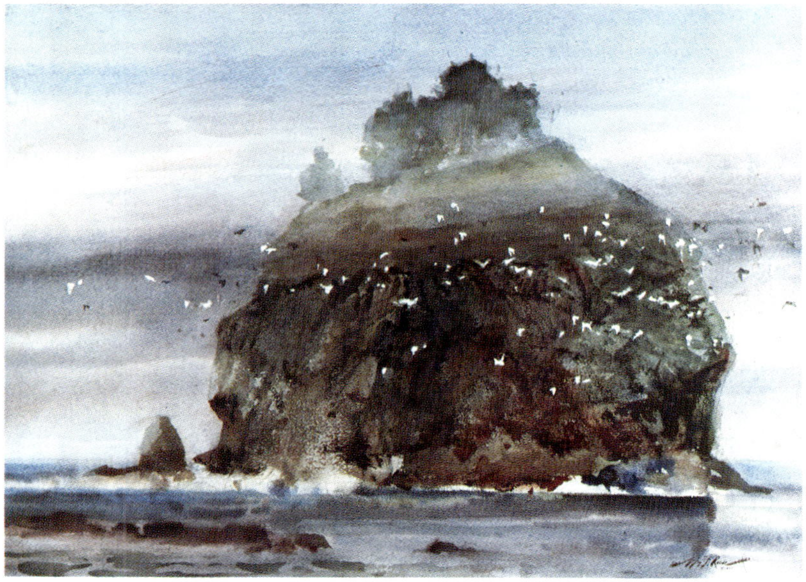

*Spring in the Foothills*
Oil, 16x20″
Collection of
Mr. & Mrs. J.E. Rawls

*Music on the Wing*
Watercolor, 21½x29½″
Collection of
Leslei Dinnison

If, for some reason, Reese does not finish the painting while it is wet, he allows it to dry long enough so that it *feels* dry to the touch, at which point he reworks the whole surface again, wet-on-wet.

"There are times when I just don't know what to do with a painting, how to finish it. So I let it sit around until I've worked out a solution. By then it is drier than normal, and I use retouch varnish on the entire surface to bring back the color, to give it the wet look of fresh paint. Otherwise the shininess of the new paint will be a distraction, too much contrast against the matte look of the drier, older paint.

"I use a painting medium if I need a more fluid pigment. When the completed painting is totally dry, I cover the surface with damar final picture varnish."

Using a simple palette of eight oil colors, Reese paints mainly on fine Belgian linen canvas with a medium tooth, or on smooth, untempered Masonite panels. One support is flexible while the other is rigid; one is more suitable in certain situations than the other, although there are no specific rules beyond size restrictions, weight, and personal feeling. The pressed panels are generally more suitable for outdoor use because they provide a more stable surface — no flutter in the wind — no light penetration as through stretched canvas, which can be distracting to work on. (Masonite, which contains no binders, is an "entirely reliable material, and under average American conditions, is superior to wood as a support for easel paintings,"[21] according to Ralph Mayer's *Handbook for Artists.*) The pressed support has other advantages over wood panels, in that it is not as limited to size since its dimensions are not restricted to the radius of the tree, it is lighter in weight, and warping can be controlled.

Reese's more extensive watercolor palette, approximately fifteen colors, was chosen for the medium's special characteristics — the choice of more pigments cuts down the possibilities of overmixing. The same possibility exists with oils, but it is especially true with watercolor — the fewer the color mixtures, the clearer the color. Although Reese is a virtuoso colorist, it is simply more expedient to lessen the mixing.

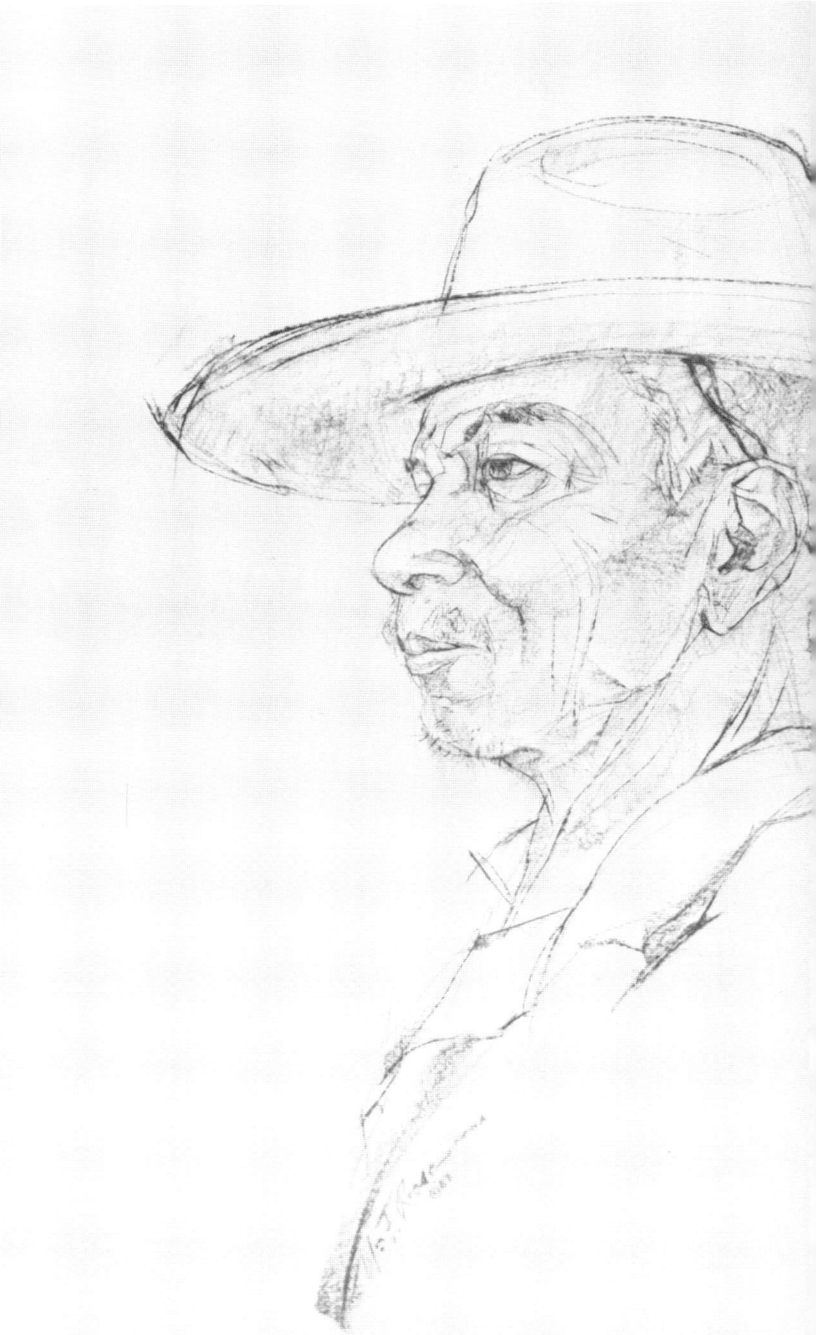

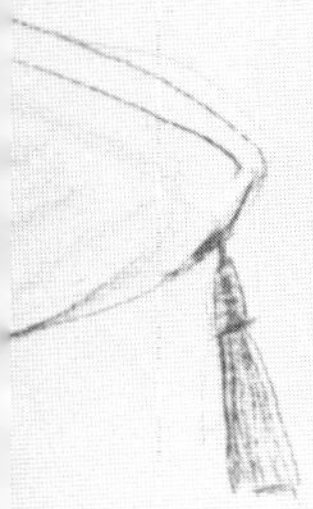

He often alternates between painting with oils and painting with watercolors, saying they complement and strengthen each other. The oils have become more painterly and solid through the use of watercolor, while the switching back and forth helps him to maintain the element of surprise. With watercolors, he works from light to dark values, letting the happy accidents occur as they may; whereas to attain special effects with oils, one must manipulate them — make the special effects happen.

The following is a list of the major tools, equipment, and supplies in Reese's studios. It does not include the large array of props nor all the other tools required for peripheral things — crating, for example.

## *Palettes, Brushes, and Equipment*

*OILS*
Cadmium yellow deep
Cadmium orange
Cadmium red light
Cadmium red deep
Alizarin crimson
Ultramarine blue
Cobalt blue
Cerulean blue
Viridian green
Cadmium yellow pale
Yellow ochre
Titanium white

*BRUSHES FOR OILS*
All white bristle, mostly filberts, some flats and brights.

*SUPPORTS FOR OILS*
Belgian linen canvas or untempered Masonite

*GROUNDS*
White lead
Gesso

*PASTELS*
Full-range

*WATERCOLORS**
Yellow ochre
Raw sienna
Cadmium yellow light
Thalo green
Cerulean blue
Cobalt blue
Thalo blue
Ultramarine blue
Alizarin crimson
Cadmium scarlet
Cadmium orange
Gamboge
Burnt sienna
Raw umber
Burnt umber

*The watercolor palette is the more extensive of the two, thereby cutting down the number of colors to be mixed and enabling the use of clearer, more intense color and diminishing the possibilities for muddying.

*BRUSHES FOR WATERCOLORS*
Mostly sable, some bristle, and "anything that's handy."

*SUPPORT FOR WATERCOLORS*
d'Arches hot press, Fabriano cold press watercolor paper

*EASELS*
French easel for outdoor painting.
Large, adjustable studio easel for oils.
Adjustable, tilting, drafting table for watercolor studio.
Reese-designed paint box and easel for outdoors

Reese-designed paint kit with palette for the lap

*MISCELLANEOUS*
6B Graphite sticks for drawing
2B Pencils for drawing
Retouch varnish
Oil painting medium
Damar Final Picture Varnish
Poppy seed oil (for wintertime, to ease sluggish pigments)

The artist's working environment, whether it be a corner of a room, a spare bedroom, or a separate studio building, Reese feels should be a comfortable, compatible space, aside from the obvious equipment and good lighting. Beyond the physical surrounds, a psychological momentum or motivation must be built up, layered with elusive, unassignable ideas to make it a fit place for creativity. Reese talked of moving from one studio to another, saying it took him "six months before I felt comfortable enough to start a painting in the new place. We put all the familiar trappings in it, but it still felt empty. It was like a clean slate, devoid of ideas, nothing floating around yet, whereas the old studio had had time to absorb the development of all kinds of ideas, thoughts, and conversations and had a mellowed ambience about it. I remember, too, the effect of the wall color in another studio . . . it was so emotionally upsetting that I had to paint the walls before I could do anything creative; so one can be emotionally bombarded with the absence, as well as the presence, of things."

*"For one to be creative it's not necessary to invent the wheel every time — the artist needs only a new look at an old idea."*

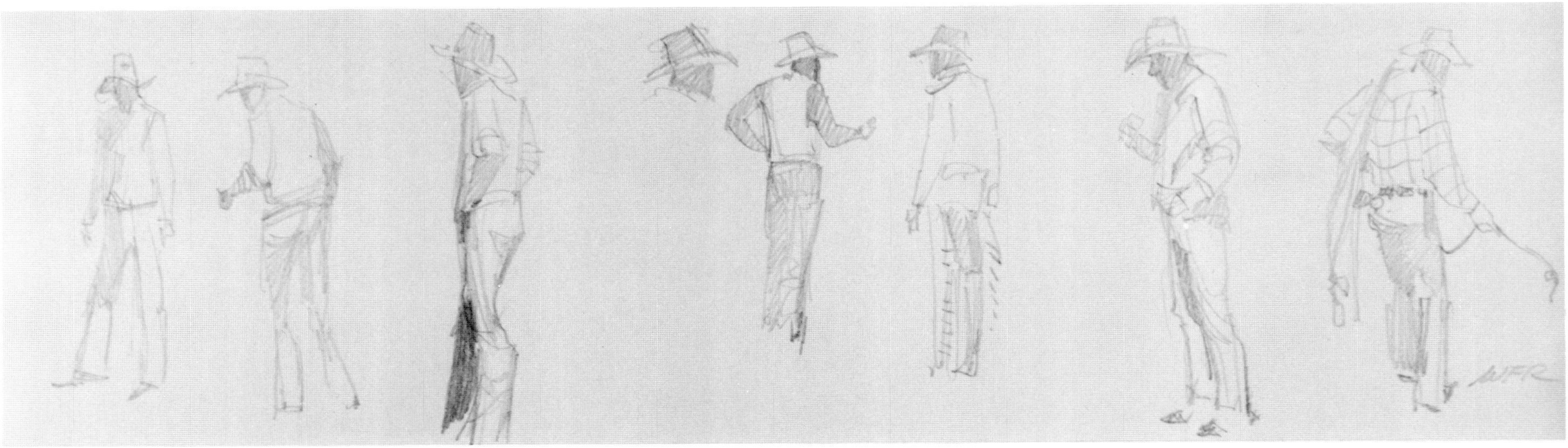

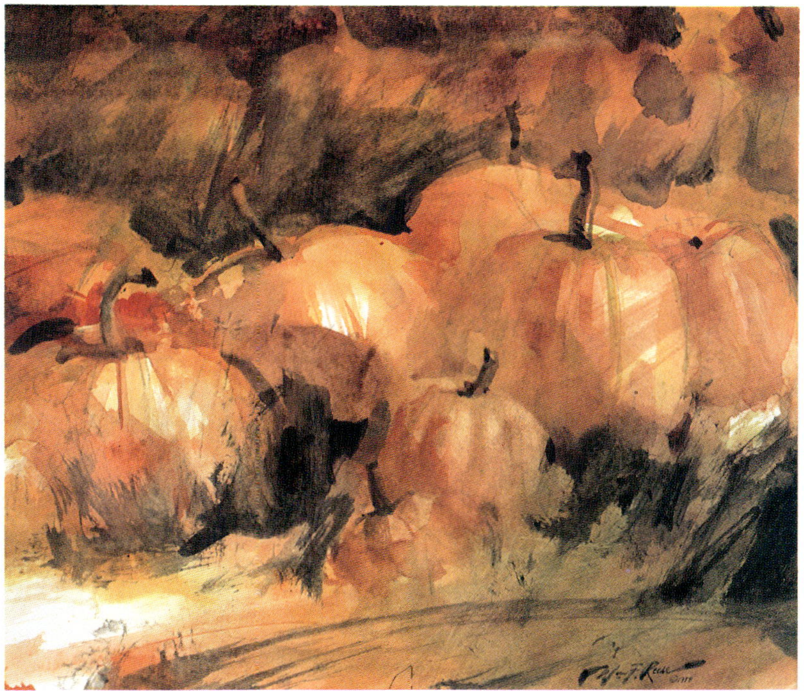

*Witch Apples*
Oil, $10\frac{1}{2}$x11″
Collection of
Cheryl Shilling

Controversy over the camera's role in fine art is as old as the camera itself. Many artists use it as a help-mate, a recorder of information; others use it as a replacement for drawing, a crutch — a support which becomes so habit-forming that they can never dispose of it.

"Too many people rely on the camera because they are lacking in drawing ability, and they haven't done enough life-study to know when the camera is wrong. The camera does not tell the truth. The distortions are considerable, the color temperature and values are wrong, and the proportions are incorrect. The unknowing painter compounds these mistakes. The final work is photographic in every detail. Every hair is in place but it is 'out of drawing'; and the work doesn't have a ring of truth to it even though it *looks just like* the photograph! Besides, all it takes to paint every hair on a horse, is time — and a small brush.

"The sad part is that these artists have bent to the will of the collectors, most of whom are just starting to collect and like photographic work because it is all they understand at the beginning. I can't help but wonder why they don't have their own slides blown up to 16x20″ or whatever size they want. It wouldn't cost them tens of thousands of dollars for paintings that aren't even good photographs.

"I've wondered, too, why it doesn't occur to them to question how a 23-year old artist paints so photographically, while a 60-year old doesn't want to. There are no child prodigies in the art business. The skills required to create are practiced over and over and can be learned, but it takes a lifetime to learn to paint loosely.

"The camera is a great, functional tool, especially for commercial art — billboards, for example — and in fine art, if used with discretion; it is indispensable for capturing moments, movements, insights, and objects which perhaps otherwise couldn't be recorded because things happen too fast. I use it a lot. But, if you simply interpret the camera's images, all you are doing is painting 'billboards,' which is not a 'put-down' of billboards — we are talking about two entirely different types of art.

"I think there is a license that goes with the use of the camera in fine art, and the license should be *earned* — painting from *life* first."

On a somewhat parallel note, Reese is a great believer in studying and copying the Old Masters — but again, only as a learning tool. Such practice enables one to learn about drawing, composition, and the application of paint.

"You will better understand the solutions to their paintings, the positioning of certain objects or colors within a composition — why a spot of red was placed at the edge of a canvas, for example. Perhaps you have an idea as to why it was put there, but not until you actually paint and reach that point in painting do you fully realize the importance of that little spot. You will instinctively sense the need for it.

"I still copy an Old Master's painting once in awhile just for the fun of doing it or when I am looking for a solution. It's almost as if I can communicate with a particular artist from the past and use him as a teacher. But again, this is only a means to 'singing my own song.' Each person must be the inventor, the imaginer, the author of his own material. Copying is for information only, to build on what you know — an addition to your own basic talent.

"I believe talent is God-given, a gift not to be wasted. Use your gift. Perfect it."

*"Good drawing must be edited and simplified to the mere essence."*

Aside from painting nearly every day, Reese has an on-going self-education program in his collection of books and works by other artists. "I figured that if I surround myself with good books and good drawings, I would get used to those and would judge my own work against what I see around me and in my books. If I learned to judge my work against the Old Masters, I'd have a better gauge of where I am on the scale and what I need to work at. I am less likely to be misguided in their company than if I judged my work against itself or the work of contemporaries. It was Henri who said, 'If in your drawings you habitually disregard proportions you become accustomed to the sight of distortion and lose critical ability. A person living in squalor eventually gets used to it.' "[22]

Reese's heroes in art include Maliavin, Serov, and Levitan, of the Russian "Wanderers" group, and Fechin, Sorolla, Zorn, Sargent, Whistler, Henri, Homer, and Dunn. He made a special trip to Europe to see certain of the Old Masters first-hand — the works of Sorolla, for one, whose *luminismo*, high-key color and sunlight, rhythm and

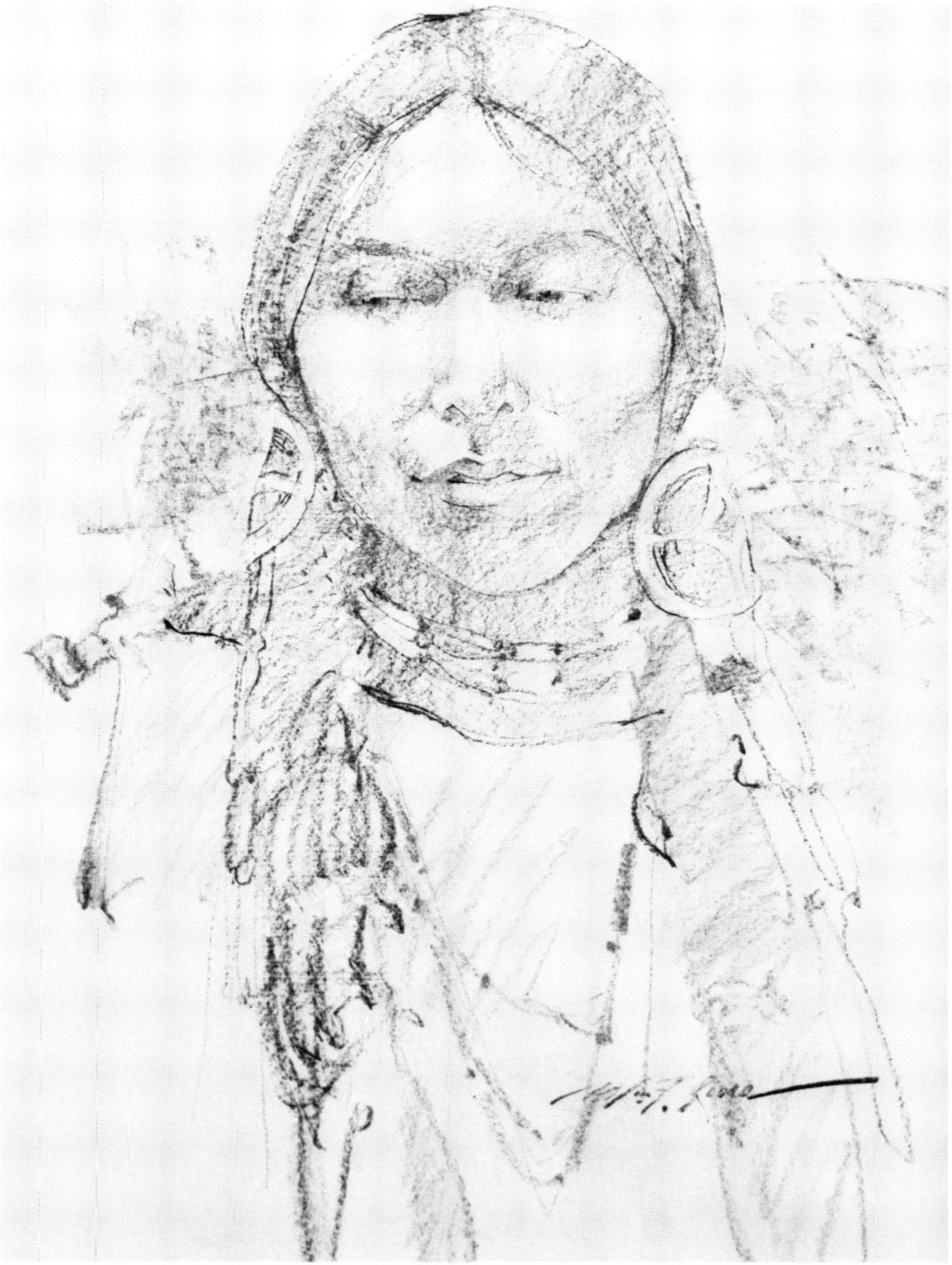

undulation in shade, and contemporary compositions made a large impact on Reese. Evidence of this is seen in his bright, luminous colors and values in *Orange Rebozo, Chiapanecas, Ronald Alley,* and other outdoor scenes.

When asked what he would consider a finishing school for artists, such as the French Academy in Rome during the mid-1800's, he replied: "BOOKS — ART BOOKS. My grandmother gave me the first one when I was a child. I bought the second one, Andrew Loomis' book on *Figure Drawing,* when I was in my late teens; and I've been collecting art books ever since. They are valuable teachers. Da Vinci's notes, for example, are as valid today as they were five-hundred years ago."

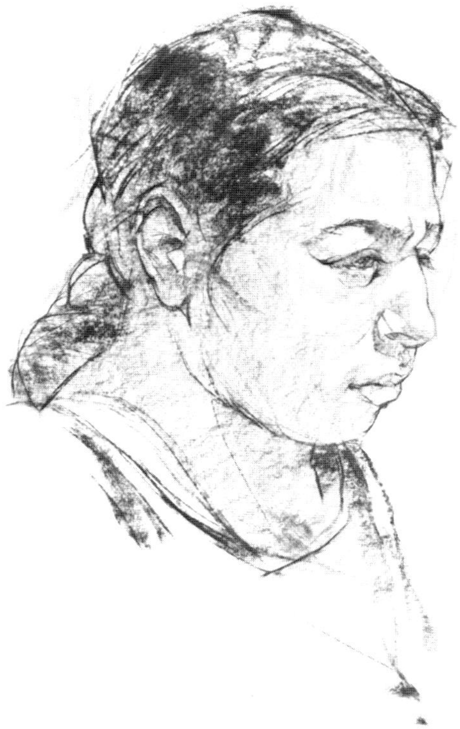

## *Drawing*

*Drawing is the artist's most direct and spontaneous expression, a species of writing; it reveals, better than does painting, his true personality — a study of even the swiftest sketch discloses the mind and nature of its author.*[23]

While painting is an extension of drawing, just as running is an extension of walking, the importance of drawing cannot be over-emphasized. "Without good drawing skills, the artist will have extreme difficulty trying to express himself. This difficulty will manifest itself not only in the obvious but also in the production of muddy color, timidity, and weak composition. Drawing errors account, many times, for the chalky, over-worked passages that plague us all. And, the only way to learn drawing is to draw. There are no short cuts. Then instead of worrying about what you are drawing or about getting a likeness, just draw what the thing is doing and it will begin to look like the thing itself."

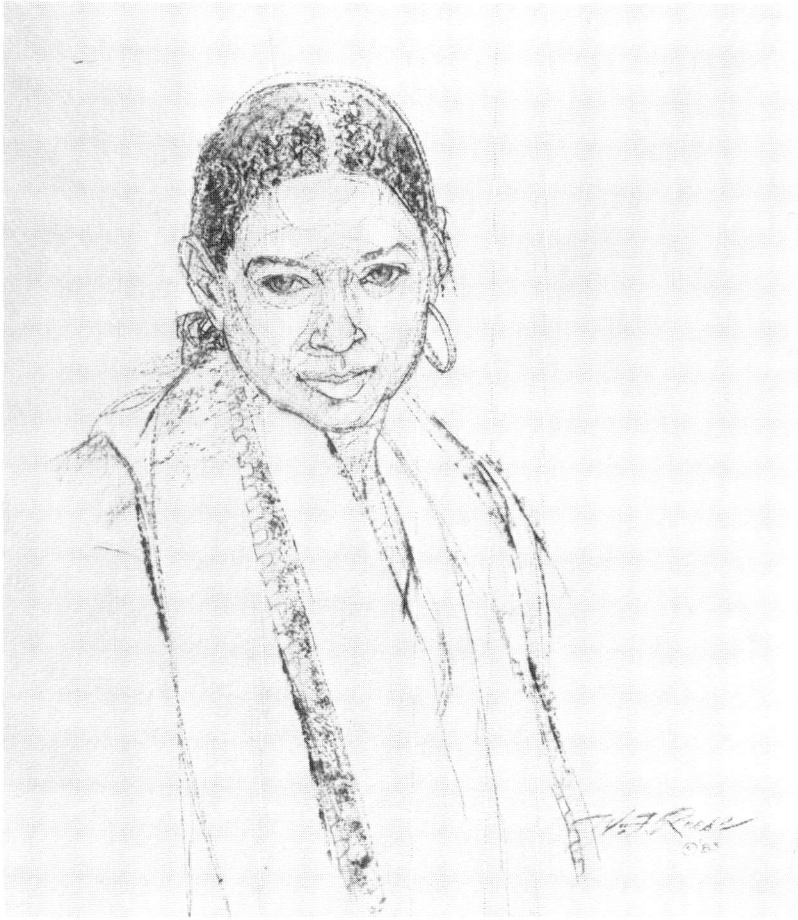

Reese uses a traditional depiction of form. His initial exploratory line meanders lightly over the paper to determine the proportion, axes, and action — in almost a playful manner — free, yet always controlled. These explorations are followed by direct delineations which vary from subtle strokes to bold ones to break a movement or to change direction. Planes and shadows are indicated with quick strokes of different values to show direction of form. Each is expressed with a spontaneity, not self-conscious or deliberate, resulting naturally from the act of drawing.

Graphite sticks, conté crayons, drawing pencils, brushes, and pens, along with a variety of papers in neutral pH quality, are his most widely used tools and materials for drawing. These he uses vertically, horizontally, or in whatever manner will best produce the desired effect. The more developed drawings have added values or modeling (lights and darks) to enrich forms, to suggest additional moods or characteristics, surface textures, and patterns, or to draw attention to particular areas of the composition.

Drawings can be made in an endless variety of media, with almost any kind of tools, from brushes to pens, nails on slate, even twigs dipped in clay slip. Lack of materials is a poor excuse for not drawing. Reese said that people always think of a dozen reasons why they can't draw, but an artist will "come up with a thousand reasons why he must!" Chuck Lawton told about improvising for the sake of creative work when he and Bill once traveled to Medicine Valley on business. While there, Bill saw something he just had to sketch.

"He had a small watercolor kit and a pad of paper, but nothing rigid or stable on which to lay it or prop it up, so he used my back as an easel,"[24] Lawton chuckled.

Reese does caution that when professionalism, durability, and performance are at stake, the artist must respect the chemistry and compatibility of materials and use the best available to him. And then, as if in summation of his creative process, he said, "Painting and drawing to me are one and the same. While painting, I am *drawing* with pigment — while drawing, I am *painting* with charcoal."

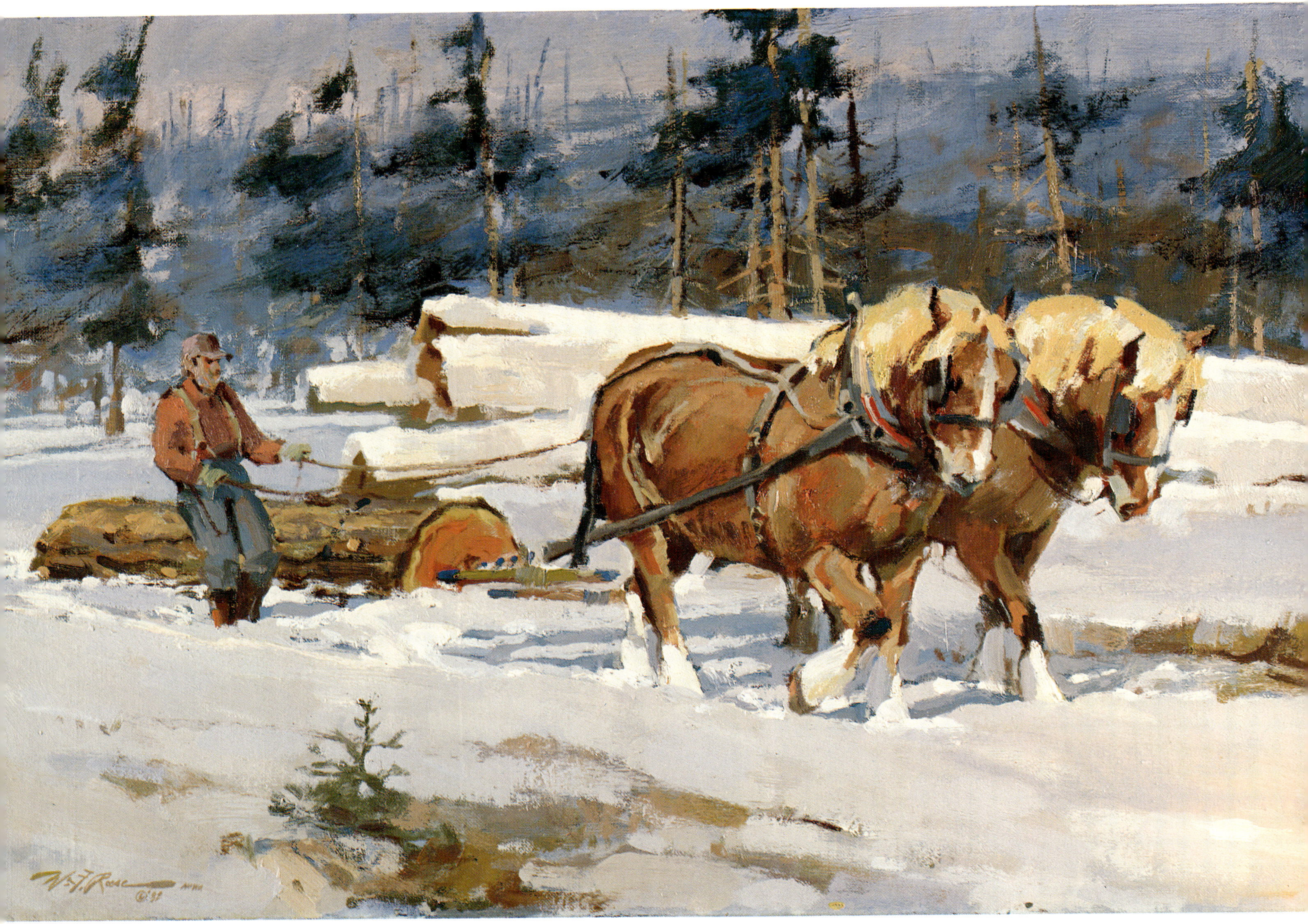

*Winter Loggers*
Oil, 16x24″
Collection of
Mr. & Mrs. W. Robert Moore

# Demonstrations

*"To paint snow convincingly, I need to be standing in it."*

# *Demonstrations*
*(see page 115 for materials list)*

"You have to grab the information as it comes by.... Position yourself at a comfortable distance from the subject and angle your easel so that you look over and beyond it to the subject rather than having to turn your head each time you want to look at it.

"Warm up before you start a painting. It's like calisthenics to an athlete. Examine your subject first, then make quick sketches or blind gesture drawings to learn more about it — what the attitude is, where the dark and light patterns are — and as you continue making sketches you develop a hand-eye coordination and your shorthand gets shorter: the drawings become more complete with fewer lines. You begin to find different, overlapping planes and more interesting shadows. Once you get the drawing started right, it is taken care of and you won't have to be overly concerned about it as you paint."

Reese's 5x7″ oil studies serve as warmups for him, although they most often end up as fine paintings in themselves. With a cigar box brought home from the Philippines, a quiver of brushes, and a small wood case sectioned to hold a dozen gessoed panels, he is equipped for a day of painting — or until he decides to work on a larger scale. The cigar box holds four tubes of color, a tube of white, paint thinner, cheesecloth, a small tin for washing brushes, a palette, and one gessoed panel in the easel-lid. This amazingly small gear enables him to work from his lap, perched on a rock or in his van or almost anywhere, with the whole spectrum of colors at his fingertips.

On this particular day he chose to paint among the melange of birds at Moss Bay, a well-used public park northeast of Seattle. The sun was playing hide and seek with the clouds, brightly coloring and lighting objects one minute and then disappearing to create semi-shadowless monotones. After zeroing in on the white ducks as they shuffled around with the mallards, pigeons, geese, and other shore birds, Reese began his initial sketches with fluid movements in thinned oil pigment. His experience, practice, and observations enabled him to understand the forms and their subtleties — how the

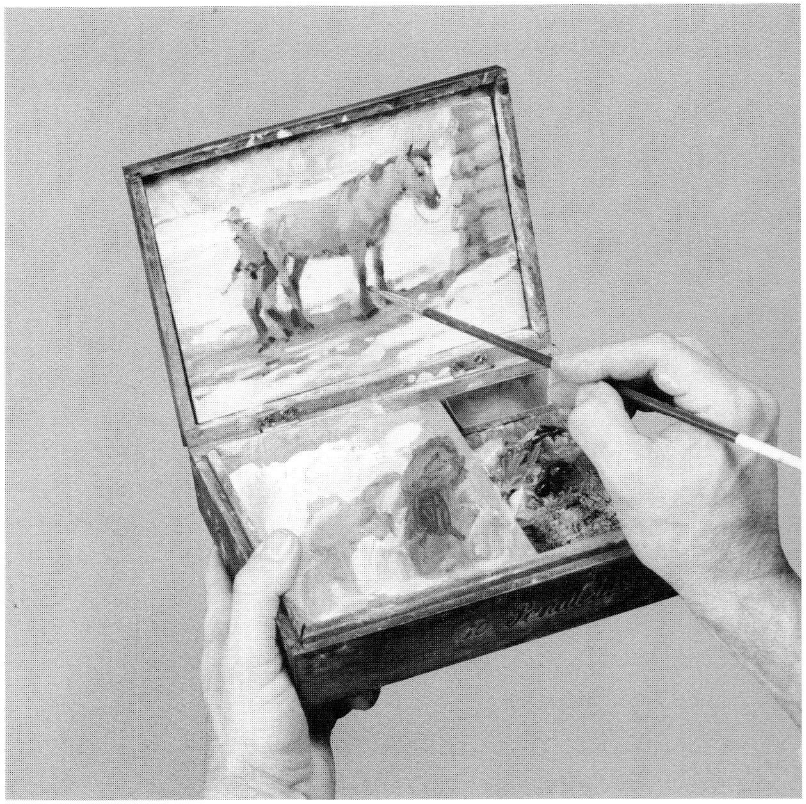

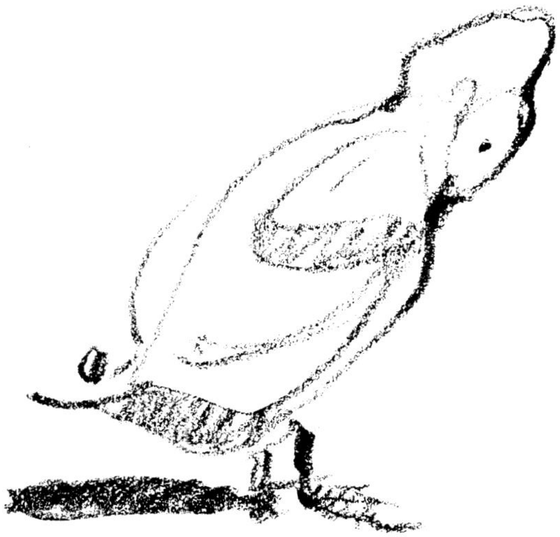

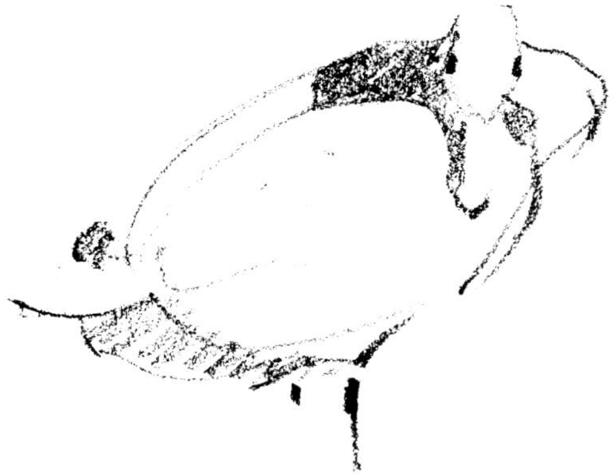

"Cigar box studio"

birds frequently slept balanced on one leg, heads precariously tilted back; or how they eased downward until their bellies hugged the ground, dough-like, with heads craned back, beaks tucked into the wing feathers. A sudden noise or the appearance of a dog will send them flying, leaving a cloud of dust as their wings beat the pulverized earth on take-off. The artist must be patient and practiced enough to be able to capture their fleeting attitudes and poses, to work on a pose and then let it rest, or to work from memory until the birds return and assume similar positions again.

"You have to glance up at the subject every once in awhile and take what you need — a piece from one, a piece from another — the work necessarily becomes a composite. Also, the steps in painting are in a different order when you paint outside because everything is changing all the time; and that's good because you are forced to make decisions in a hurry, to capture the spontaneity of the moment." (Sometimes the variables are too much and the final canvas has to be painted in the studio — this is where the studies and other fact-finders come in handy.)

After three warmup studies Reese switched to his field-box easel and a larger panel on which he began *the* painting of the day, making composites of ducks, sketching loosely with thinned pigment to block-in the forms (1a.) — this is the linear organization of the composition. Next, he began to graphically sculpt or lay-in the masses, the large general patterns of light and dark: cerulean tints on the shadow side of the ducks, yellow-white wavy reflections on the water alternated with green reflections (2a.)

"You have to think how the water moves because its surface has form, too," Reese explained as he worked in one area of the composition and then in another, building, developing the whole painting rather than concentrating on the finish of a single element. He indicated the bills and feet in a muted orange, quickly swished his brush in a wash can of thinner and dried it on a paper towel before mixing a greyish-blue which he scrubbed in-between and over various portions of the greens in the water. A darker blue under the ducks and in a few strokes around the reflections to define them, a bit of tannish-pink on the ducks' wings but not yet painting them fully so that some

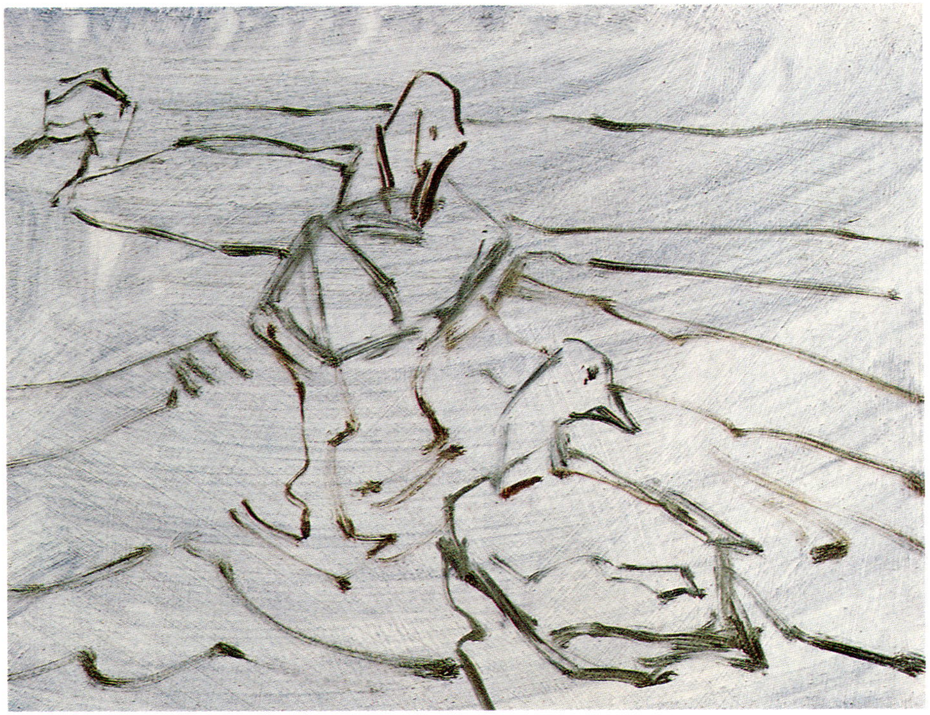

1a.

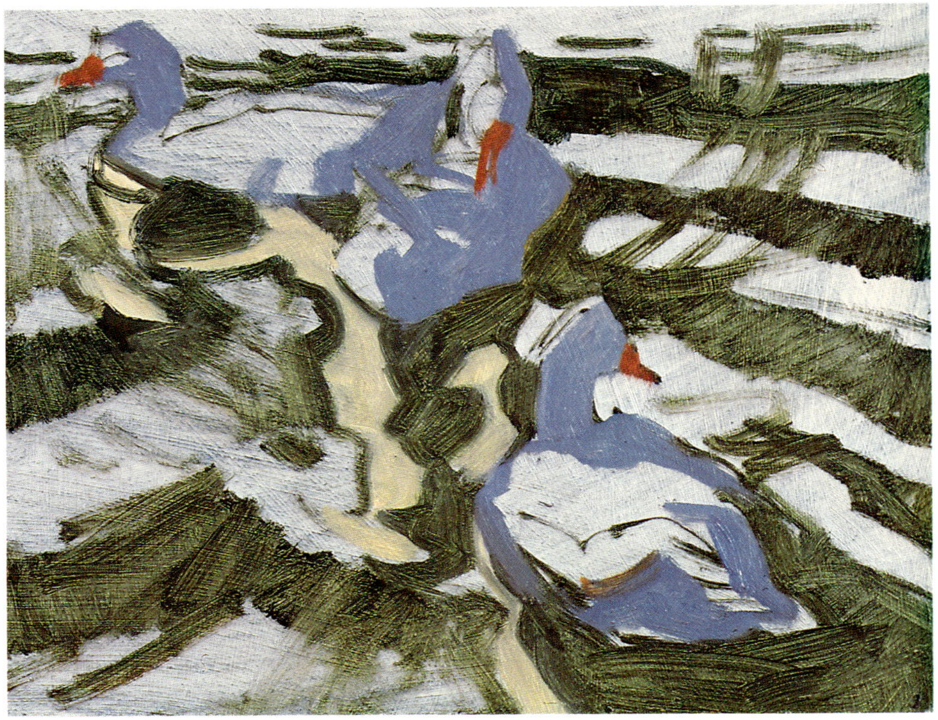

2a.

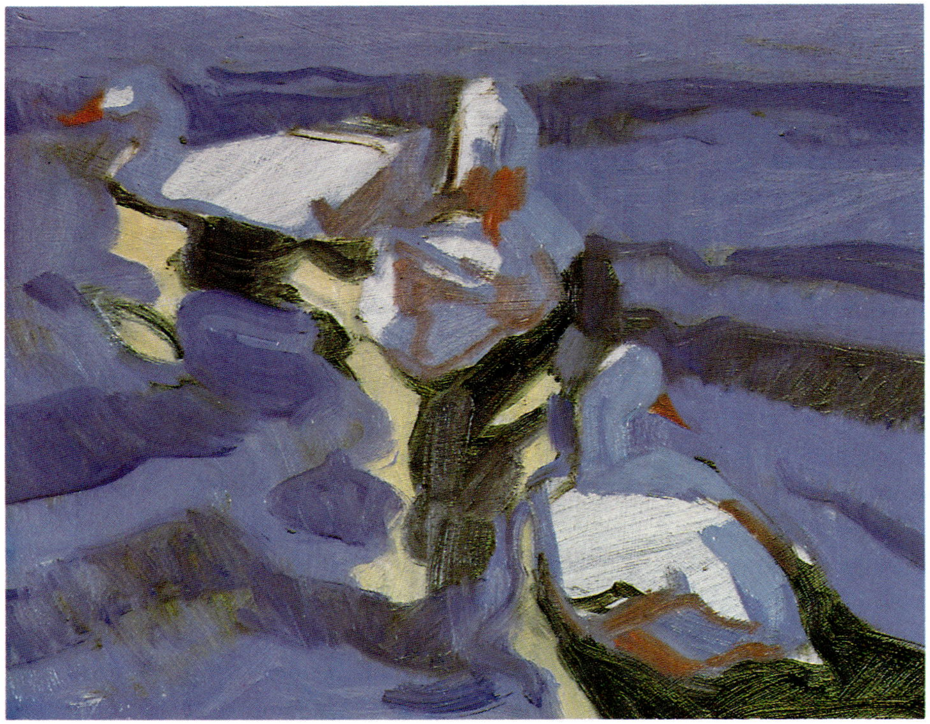

3a.

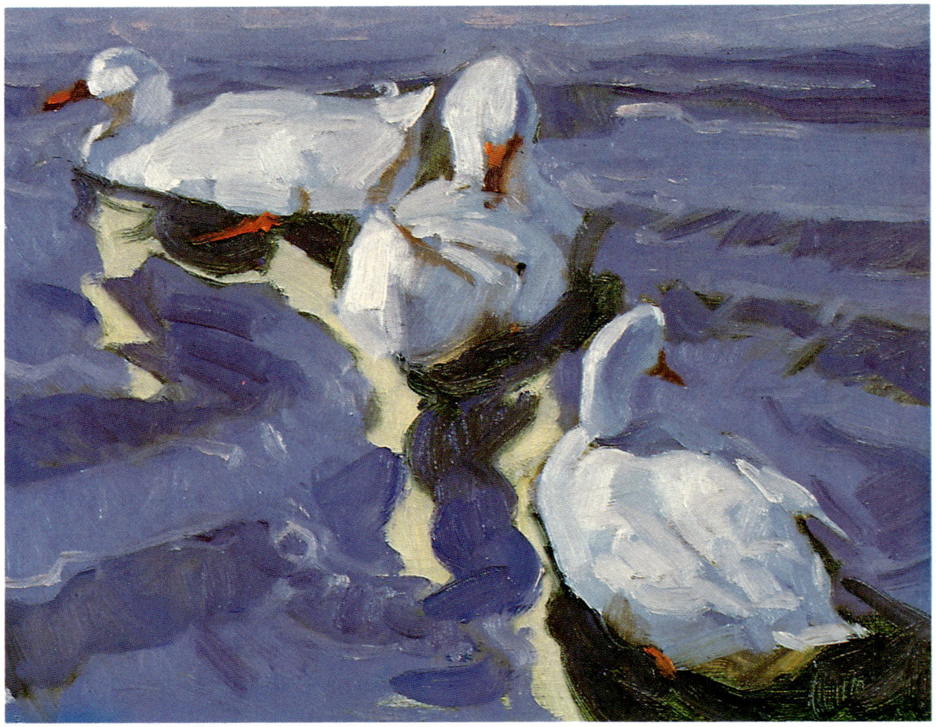

4a.

*Four Steps in Painting Ducks*
Oil, 16x20″

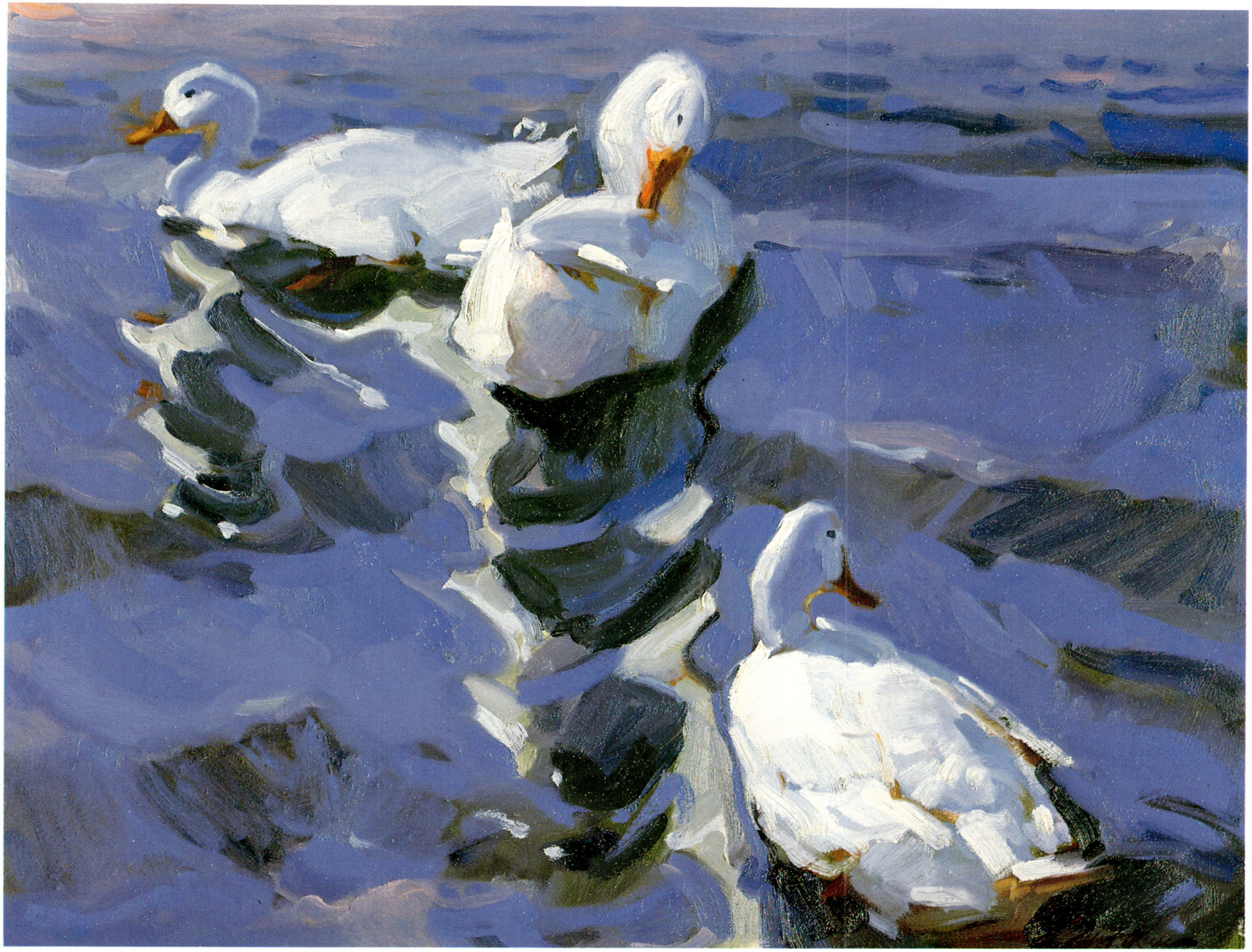

5a.

*Finished Painting of Ducks*
Oil, 16x20″

of the light tone of the panel is still visible . . . "as close to white as I need to get right now. Later, I will add lighter values but their intensity or key will depend on what develops elsewhere — everything I do with the ducks from this point must be in context, the colors must relate to each other and be close in value. When I have a subject that is extremely light in value, I work from light to dark; but that is not an absolute. Frequently I work from the mid-values or half-tones in both directions, taking the main color and keying everything else to it."

He scrubbed orange to the back-undersides and adjacent water to suggest a webbed foot below the surface, pinkish-white on the tail to depict the translucence of filtering sunlight; more cerulean on the top duck's underside, a touch of darker blue to the top of its head and one cheek, orange under the chin and neck, and a swift stroke of orange to the tail — first on one duck and then, to different degrees, on the other two. (4a.)

As he applied pink-tinted strokes on the water, he commented, "Now I have all the half-tones under control — no real darks, no light lights — I will stay within the half-tones for awhile adjusting them as I go; but I can forget about the anatomy of the ducks for a bit and become involved in the poetry and movement of the painting." He added a pinkish horizontal plane along the full width of the top of the panel and then used intermittent and varietal strokes with a loaded brush as if he were playing a musical instrument: a few notes, a crescendo of blues, an allegro of pinks interspersed with a breve of deeper pinks to complete his symphony.

"It's important to keep the color fresh. Too much opaqueness or muddiness occurs from over-mixing; the luminous quality is lost when the eyes themselves cannot mix the color. Muddiness is not a color but a state of confusion; therefore one should strive for simplicity in mixing and pay close attention to the control of edges.

"I will push the darks a little more at this point." He added orange-browns on the bills for more definition, darker browns to the bodies, blue-purples to the water, and then a dash of bright cadmium orange on the bill of the middle duck — the process is a continuous back and forth movement — a constant comparison of one area to another, an evolution in color. Next came the darkest darks, more browns to the

*"I would rather see a poorly drawn piece that exhibits great emotion than a perfectly rendered work with no soul."*

right rear of the lower and middle birds and to the watery trails to emphasize the short dark shadows of the water's reflections. He slashed a pink horizontal stroke that connects the neck of the upper duck to the panel's left edge, which immediately gave it distance. He added white-green dashes to the lightest reflections to make them less prominent, a stroke of cobalt blue mixture to the upper right edge, and pale, white-blue calligraphy to various other areas of the water. Finally, he added the whitest whites and then touched each duck with a deep red-and-viridian mixture to give them eyes and thus expression, remarking that it is important to think about what the ducks are doing so that the shape of the eyes conforms to their movements or activites.

"Also, throughout the painting I have tried to keep the strokes loose and alive to impart some of the feeling of ducks in motion, preening or just swimming; and you really have to think in terms of form, of the surface of the water and of integrating the ducks with the water instead of making silhouettes of them. The direction of each stroke can depict form, movement, attitude, and so on, while the high-key values give importance to the ducks in the composition."

In the finished painting (5a.), edges soften and disappear on the subjects, allowing the viewer's eye to move in and out over the edge or be halted by crisper edges made harder by heightened or more contrasting values. This interplay of thick and thin, hard and soft, dark and light, and curved strokes commingling with long swaths of pigment creates a rich, dynamic, tapestry of colors and textures that are vital and alive, yet always with a close value relationship that makes it a unified work — and bespeaks an excellence in drawing.

*Trees in Landscape* (5b.) presented a semi-moving challenge created by the wind in the trees, the build-up and disintegration of the clouds, and the changes in light and shadow. Step 1b. again shows the linear organization of space on a blue-toned panel. Step 2b. shows thinned pigments depicting a dominant sky, pale yellow-white at the horizon, which melds gradually from tints of cerulean to cobalt blues at the top; a yellow ochre strip represents the foreground. Step 3b. shows loosely blocked-in trees which presage their importance in the final composition. They are painted in related half-tones along

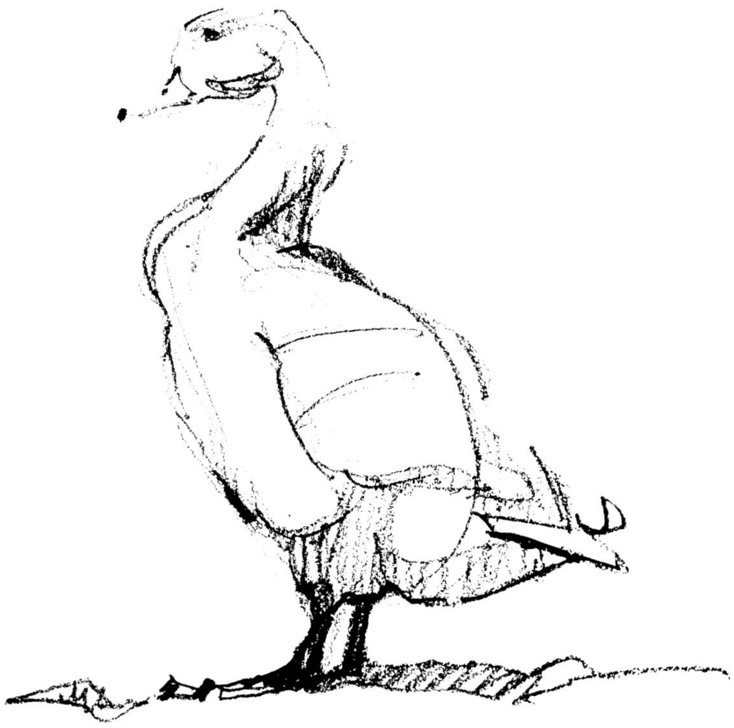

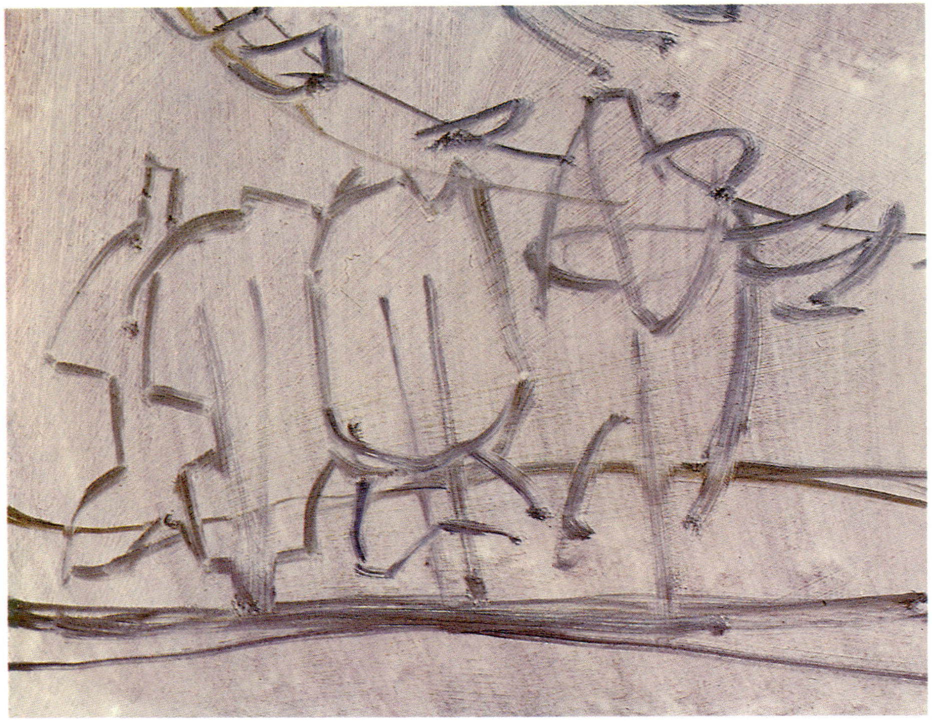

1b.

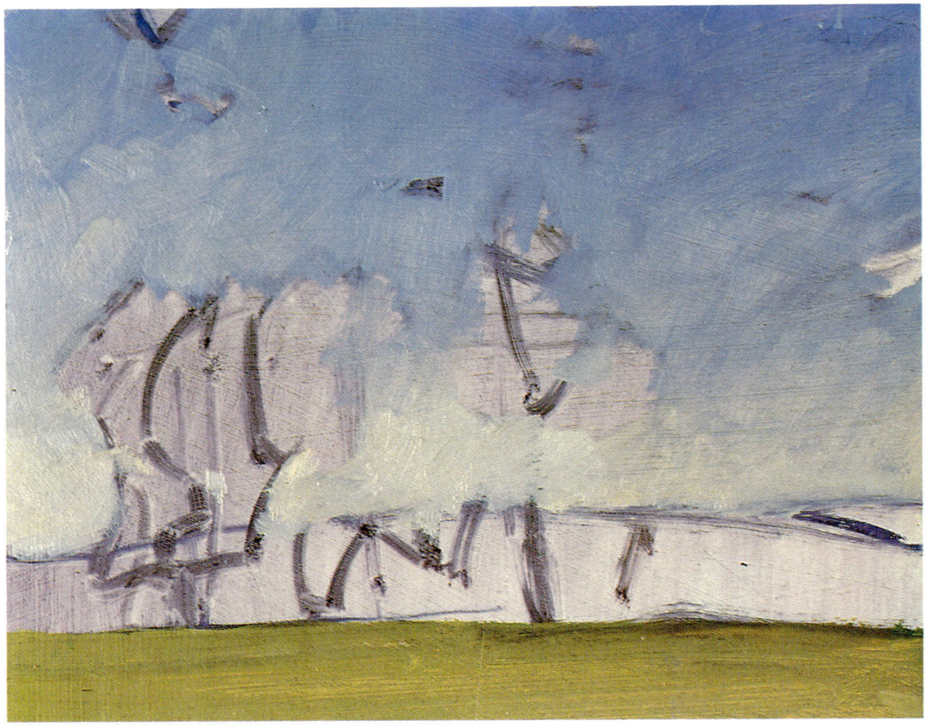

2b.

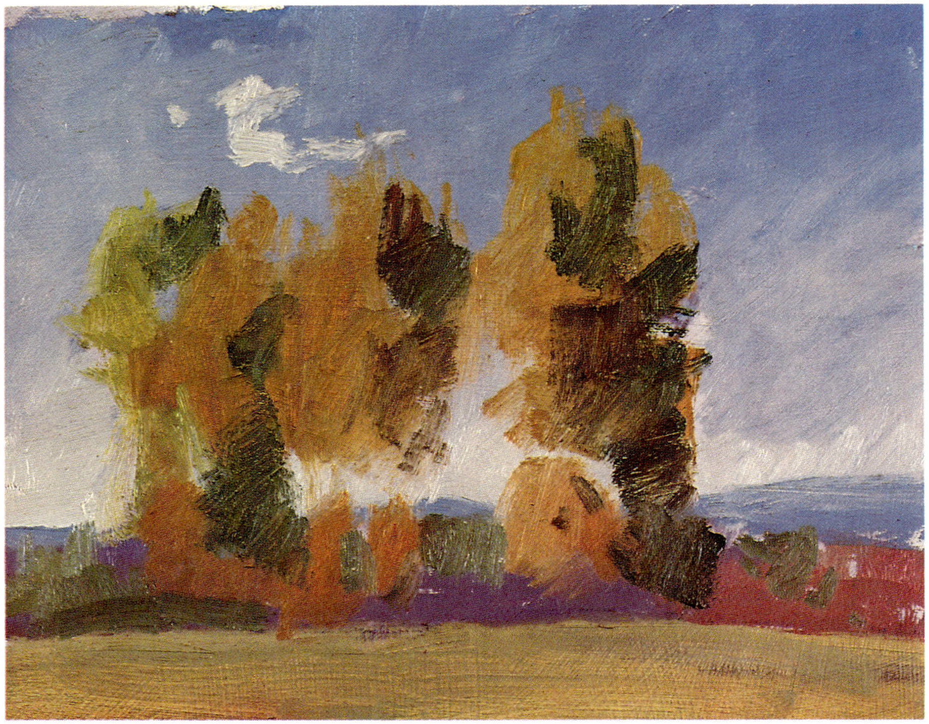

3b.

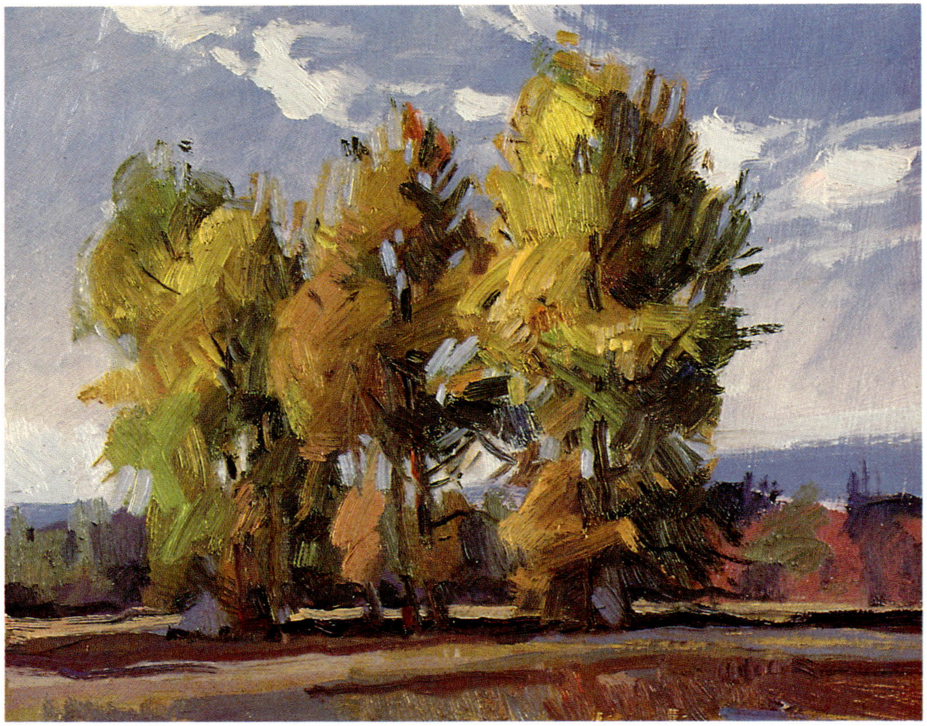

4b.

*Four Steps in Painting a Landscape*
Oil, 16x20″

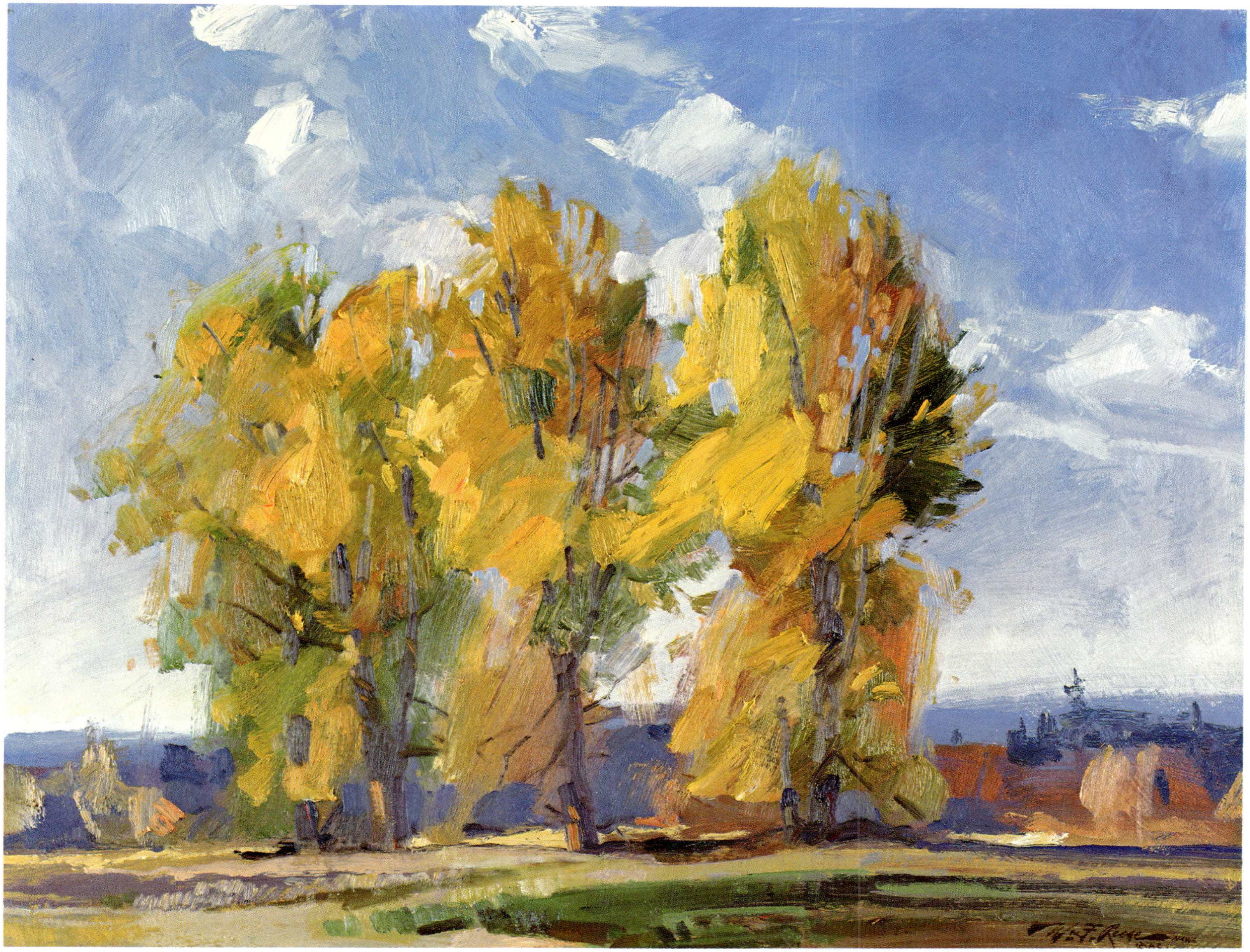

5b.

*Finished Painting of Landscape*
Oil, 16x20″

with the main shadows and the forms of the middle ground.

"Get the whole painting moving at once. Don't isolate the parts — they're related to the whole. Overstate colors at first. Think in terms of spots of light, spots of dark. Lay-in the shadows when the sun is shining and the contrasts are the greatest; then if the sun goes behind a cloud or it is a grey day, concentrate on the anatomy. Trace the light or color to the source, the thing it hit last; for example, when the sun hits the earth, that light is then reflected to the underside of the clouds, making the shadows on the clouds warm. The influence of the sky and light affects everything. Remember that the sky does not stop at the horizon but goes all the way to your feet, and that light bounces back up from the ground. Also, light does not stop at a shadow's edge but is diminished or diffused in a variety of ways.

(4b.) "After you have built-up your painting in thin washes, load your brush from tip to ferrule and then drag it lightly, letting the paint do the painting rather than the bristles. By a "loaded brush" I do not necessarily mean thick paint, but a *full* brush — one filled with pigment that has been thinned with a vehicle such as turpentine or oil. Even in doing an impasto painting, if you make your initial statement with thick paint, you'll reach your limit right at the beginning — too much impasto too soon.

"Concern yourself with the *in-line*, the three-dimensional quality of the objects, the parts that come toward you and then recede, before you work on the outline. Let the edges soften and disappear; let the outline be defined by overlapping planes."

Glimpses of sky through the trees in the finished painting are of more intense color than the sky that surrounds the trees in order for them to "read right;" and the directions of the strokes are important elements, the symbols which convey the movement and dynamic quality of the trees. Reese finished by saying, "Try to see things in simpler terms, simple shapes — make symbols for things. For example, when you paint grass, paint the shapes of the shadows and planes, not the blades — the shapes, the strokes, or the colors might all become the symbols which represent things."

*"Where simplicity prevails angels hail."*
*— Valentin Serov*

# Artist's Notes

*"Art for art's sake artists should be responsible to nothing but art, with beauty their only master."*
*— James McNeill Whistler*

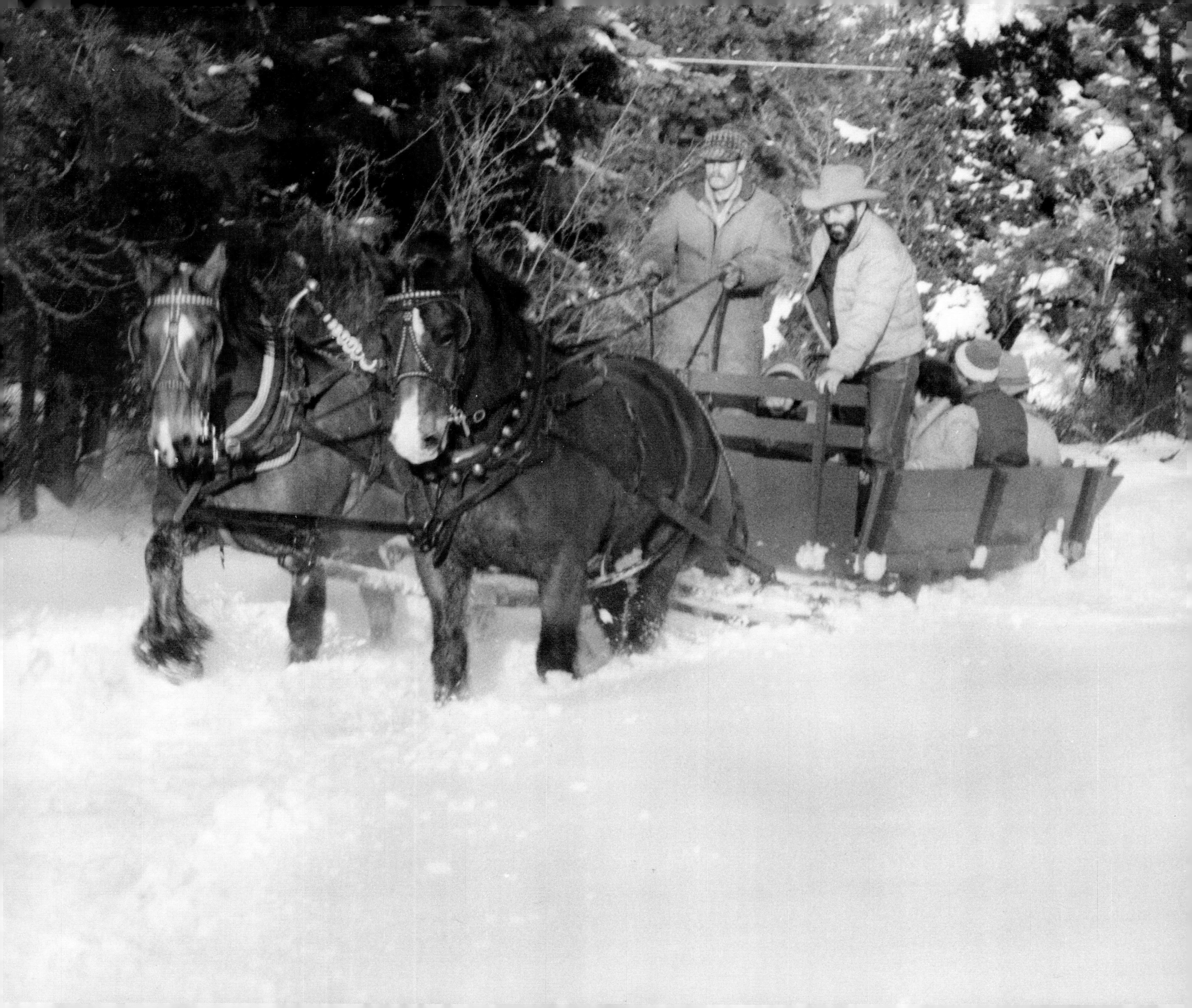

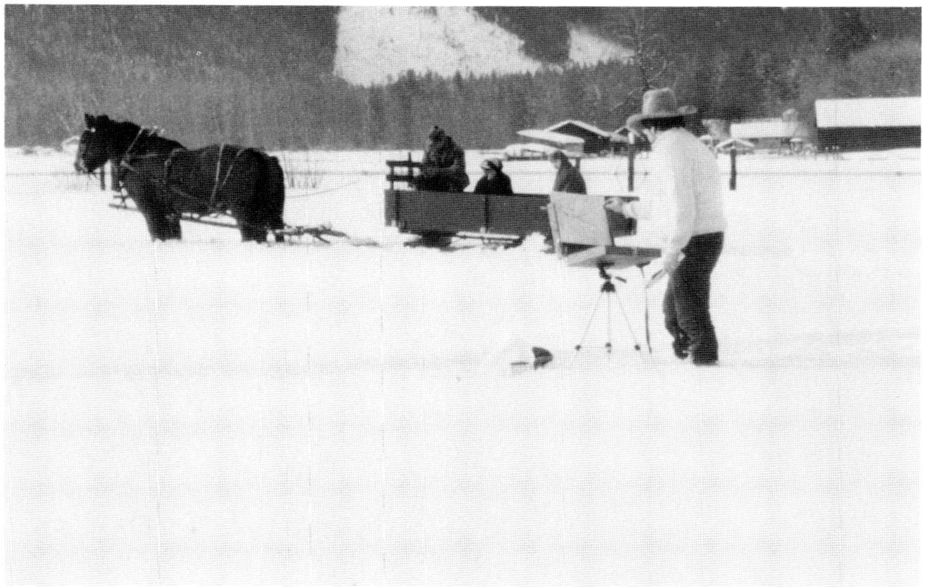

*"I'm far more interested in ART than subject."*

# *Artist's Notes*

I don't see myself as a story teller, historian, or reporter. I'm not always certain actually what it is I'm trying to do except that I feel more closely related to musicians and poets — at least in the sense that I'm trying to deal with moods, emotions, and other visual and emotional stimuli. A painting or sculpture is an orchestration of color, mass, texture, motion, mood, and nearly everything else you can think of. Poetry on a flat surface — I believe these were the words of Robert Henri.

For some reason there seems to be very little said about the emotion and poetry required to make a painting a work of art. All books are centered around the *mechanics* of painting and drawing. Not that painting and drawing skills are not important, but what about the emotion which makes them art? Shouldn't even the most amateur of painters be considering this even if only in the back of their minds? I think this regard for the expression or interpretation of feeling in one's work cannot start too early.

The subject is secondary — I am far more interested in the essence, the art, than in the subject and will sacrifice any part of it for the sake of the elements of art — and this can be done without losing the integrity of the subject. The creation of a piece of art is and must be an emotional experience, and that is why an artist should paint only that which is dear to him; it is difficult to be emotional about something he knows nothing about. The subjects I choose are selfishly chosen — I paint only what interests me or has some meaning to me — things that inspire in me ways to interpret color, movement, texture, and mood. Poetry is the goal.

*SUPERFLUOUS DETAIL.* I will sacrific superfluous detail always for the sake of the whole. Detail is like seasoning on your meal, a little seasoning will heighten a dish, but you can't make a meal of it. Short of being a medium for exhibiting one's patience, I can see no great value in the excessive use of detail which we see so much of today. All this method requires is incredible patience, steady hands, and the mastery of tiny brushes.

There are bigger and more important things to work for in a piece of art; why spend days and weeks explaining to people what they already know? Many paintings are done with such incredible accuracy both in regard to research and literal content that the very life and reason for painting are all but beaten out of it. Accuracy of statement should be expected, but it should not become the *reason* for the painting.

I've always enjoyed the *emotional* response from the viewer, much more than the microscopic inspection in which the response is: "My God, you can see every hair!" Highly detailed work seems to amaze many; yet strangely enough, many times even though every hair is drawn with great accuracy, the arms and legs are coming from the wrong part of the body. The human eye cannot clearly see the individual hairs and the mass at the same time; and laymen naïvely overlook such errors because they are so dazzled by the detail.

It's so easy to just reproduce nature on canvas, stroke for stroke, hair for hair; but it is much more difficult to *represent* her. If I could symbolically diagram rhythm, attitude, feeling, vibration, and so on — by showing those symbols, I believe I could better represent nature not just on the canvas but in the mind of the viewer. Edvard Munch, for one, used symbols to show moods and expressions, as in *The Scream* — wavy, repetitious lines and garish colors surround the screamer — these as well as the crazed expression on the subject's face elicit strong responses from the viewer; one can hear and feel the scream, its vibrations and piercing sounds, and sense the terror.

It is not my intent to paint mirror images of objects or make a census count of the trees in the forest; instead, I want to awaken the imagination of the viewer through the power of suggestion — implying detail while painting the *essence* of the subject, not the subject itself. I believe the viewer should be allowed to participate. After all, the creation of a piece should be enjoyed not only by the artist, but by others as well.

Many artists feel that if their photographic reference material is sufficient they can effectively paint anything. Unfortunately they fool only those who know less about the subject than they do. The artist needs to be emotionally involved or at least have empathy for the subject to be effective in his work — he must be able to recall the smells and sounds, feel the chill in the air, in order to convey these things with conviction; as strange as it may seem, to paint snow convincingly I need to be standing in it, to be cold, fighting the glare of the sun. The camera is an indispensable tool but never a replacement or substitute for drawing skills, which must be practiced to be kept.

Painting is more than rendering, it is a way of transferring a thought too big or personal to be put into words. It should express feeling and not be a showcase for technique or mechanical ability or virtuosity.

*MOTIVES AND INTEGRITY IN PAINTING.* Why do we paint? Purpose or motive is important to our basic thoughts of creativity. Do we paint for money? Love of subject? Reaction to such things as mood, design, texture, movement? Or, to see how clever we are in interpreting a line, how precisely we can draw, or how photographically we can render — or is it something much bigger like the need for self-expression? Whatever the motive is, it will be apparent.

Money is indeed a necessary evil. It is as important to the artist as it is to anyone else, but no matter how important it must never be considered while painting. Like oil and water, money and aesthetics won't mix. Do your painting well and the money will follow. Your

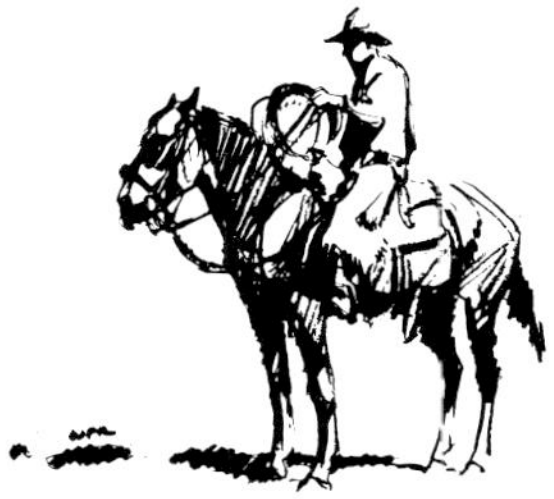

motives will show and you will be known by them.

If the reason for painting is for self-expression, then why don't more artists start expressing themselves instead of trying to be a bigger and better camera?

I have trouble expressing myself verbally and in writing — and I think this may be true of other artists; but as artists we can express our feelings through the medium of paint. Therefore, it seems reasonable, if not absolutely necessary, to develop those feelings and to keep a clear path for self-expression right from the beginning instead of placing those needs on the back burner while we work for years and years on the mechanics of painting. Drawing, values, color, and design must be worked on with great diligence, but we must not forget *why* we paint in the first place. It is the fire that keeps us warm, not the stove. The stove, no matter how fancy, expensive, or beautiful, is only as warm as the flame inside. For this reason a painting has to be deeper than the cosmetology of the detail, the brush stroke, and the subject.

An artist can be read through his art. The very basic personality traits of the artist are laid open for everyone to see. His deepest and most private thoughts and feelings are shown in his art. When I view and study a quantity of someone's work, I often get strong feelings and impressions of the artist's character; this has proven itself many times during the past few years as I've met painters from various parts of the country. Because we had both seen much of each other's work, the time it took to get personally acquainted was shortened drastically. So if an artist can read this much consciously, then I'm sure the viewer might be able to sense some of it, at least subconsciously. If this is true, the motive for painting becomes very important. This motive must be much more than monetary — to be effective it must come from deep within you. Your work must be full of conviction.

The word *integrity* has great meaning in the world of art. When I look at a piece of art and that certain essence of the moment is captured by the artist and it has that ring of truth, plain and unvarnished, this to me is most inspiring.

Fine art that will last requires absolute integrity — you must make a statement all your own; consequently it is not always monetarily rewarding. As a fine artist you must accept art alone as your reward, many times the *only* reward. All this sounds negative, I know, but I believe it is necessary as an ingredient to maintain the proper attitude to create fine art. On the brighter side I feel that however original and individual an artist may become, he remains a human being and a member of a species that includes many more individuals just like him. It is here that you will find your following, and the more you satisfy yourself the more you will satisfy that following. Actually, human beings the world over usually react pretty much the same to the same basic emotions — this means to me at least that the more integrity and sincerity put into a work of art the deeper the public response.

I feel that the truth, no matter how small, can be larger than life itself.

*INTERPRET YOUR OWN IDEAS.* Since man started creating art, he has searched for beauty. Not that beauty is always the only reason to create. It is not. In recent years beauty has become a corny idea in many of our so-called elite circles; but I believe it will endure this with little difficulty. Beauty may take many forms; the canons have changed constantly throughout time as they still do today, from culture to culture and individual to individual. It is this fact that should be remembered and applied. In other words, the true artist paints *his* idea of beauty, not that of his neighbor or patron.

The artist, being a dreamer basically, is one of the few people in this world who has the unique ability to create for himself his very own world, to make things just as he would like them.

*ART AS COMMUNICATION.* In a world where communication has become highly important, in fact

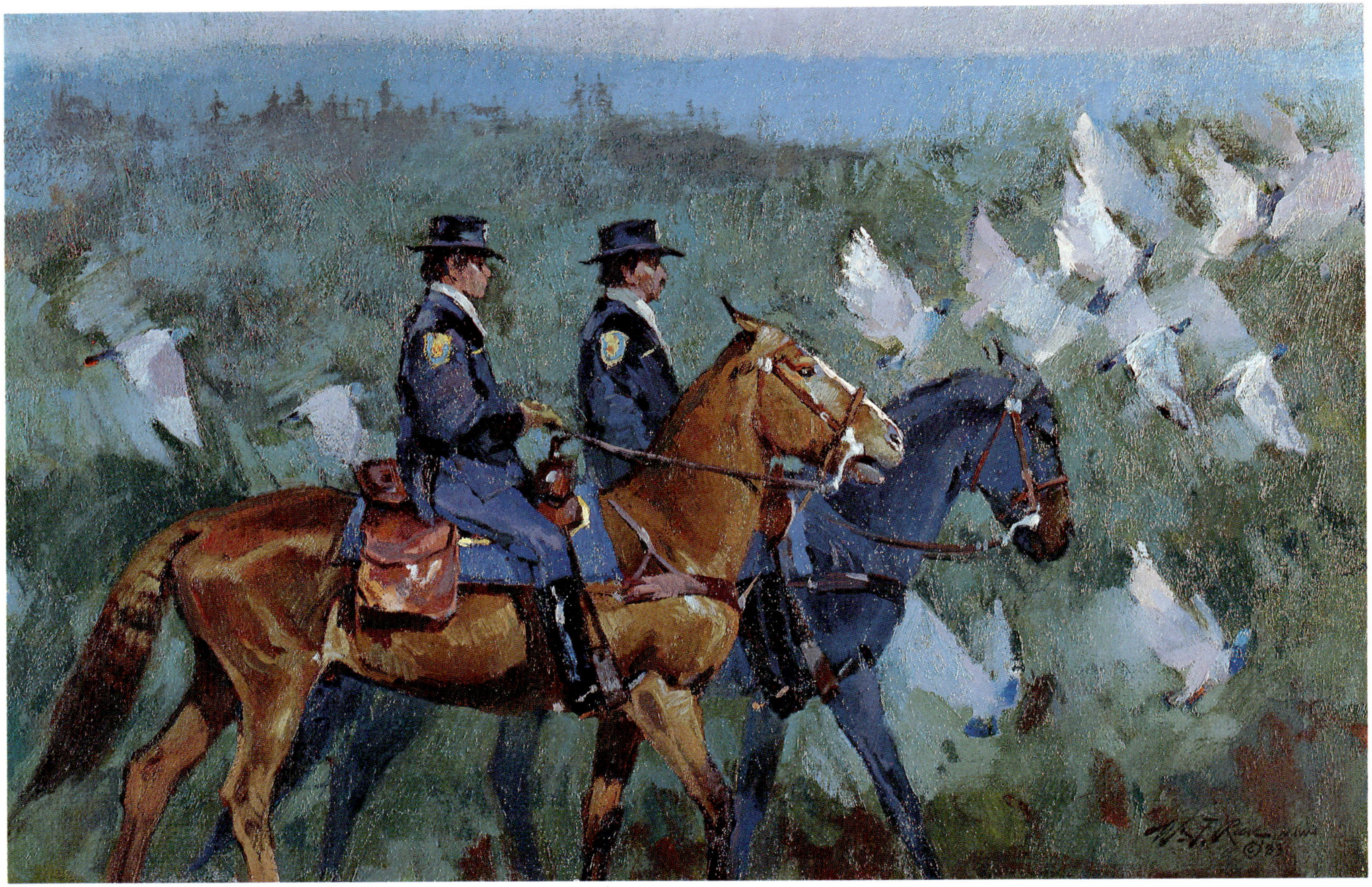

*Seattle Horse Patrol*
Oil, 16x24″

imperative, art that communicates is considered trite. Art that seems meaningless to most who view it and reeks with irrelevance is for some reason given the gold-engraved label of *High Art.*

Art, to my way of thinking, involves the sharing of an experience. I do not necessarily believe that art is for the masses, but it should not exclude the masses either. Not everyone is interested in art, but anyone who is should not need a Ph.D. to understand it. I wonder at times about the artist who develops an earth-shattering idea and then paints it in such a way that only he and his psychiatrist can understand it, even though the critics quite often seem to pretend to. It is true, to understand a discipline, that viewers, listeners, or any audience must do some homework for themselves. We need to know how to read in order to fully enjoy prose or poetry, just as we must know something of art to be able to enjoy and appreciate it. However, the artist must also meet his viewers half way. Too many modernists have discovered the cure-all for a bad painting: they blame the intellectual incapacity of the viewer if the painting doesn't work. When one speaks in tongues, can he really expect anyone to understand him, much less place the blame on the listener?

*EARLY YEARS, ENCOURAGEMENT AND INFLUENCES.* When I was in high school, even though I was fortunate to know already what career I wanted, I didn't have the vaguest idea what it was exactly that an artist did. The small town I was raised in didn't have museums, galleries, or anything even resembling them. My exposure to art was limited, to say the least, and my experience with art, if you can call it that, was only through an inborn drive or desire to create. I have a clear memory back to four years of age (although there are times when my wife doubts if it's clear much past last week). I wanted to be an artist then, and I haven't given up hope yet. I don't know what happened before that to give me this interest; all I know is that I've always had an urge to create images.

During the fifties our country was just coming out of the Korean War, World War II, and the Great Depression before that, all too well remembered by my elders who, I'm sure, must have thought that there were many things more important than art to consume a young man's time and energy. The decision to pursue a degree in fine art was met with little approval, except from my parents, who, I'm proud to say, told me if that's what I wanted "then go for it."

Timing probably had a great deal to do with it, a word of encouragement at the right time, a word of disapproval at the right time. Actually there is just enough rebel in me that a well-timed note of discouragement probably did more to push me than anything else, that and the constant approval I received from my parents and from my wife. Actually I have always felt I was blessed with ignorance because by the time I realized one couldn't make a living at art, at twenty five, I was already doing it.

*"The art of the painter is so closely bound to his inner self that it forms an integral part of his personality."* — *Igor Grabar*

*"Only that which one has oneself lived through can be the stuff of true art."* — *Ye Moiseyenko*

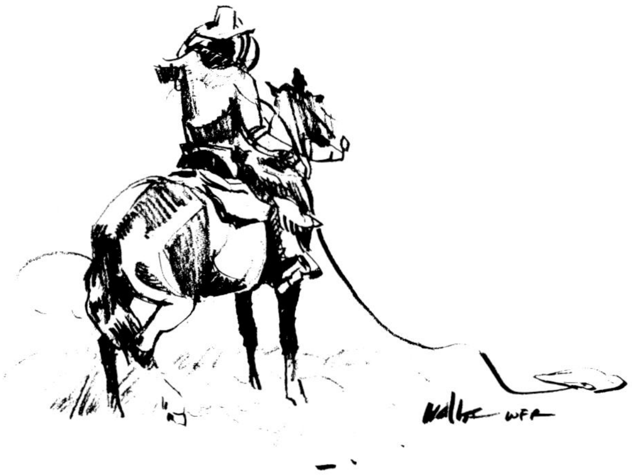

*PAINT WHAT YOU KNOW.* Many artists living in the western half of the country today were born and raised in and around the cattle industry, so it's not surprising to me that this is a dominant theme. We are painting that which we know. Ayn Rand's definition of art, "Art is the re-creation of one's view of life," pretty well explains my interest in western subjects as well as the landscapes and people that dominate my work.

When I was a youngster, cattle and horses held a fascination for me and were some of my earliest and most accessible models. Not only was I raised around cattle, but through the stories my father loved to tell I relived the cattle business during the first part of the century throughout the Dakotas. My father was born and raised in Fort Pierre, South Dakota, and he often told of working cattle in the Badlands and the plains in that part of the country. Even though I paint all kinds of subjects, I have a special feeling, an affinity, for cowboys and horses, and I paint them as often as possible.

*PHILOSOPHIES ABOUT PAINTING — HOW IS NOT AS IMPORTANT AS WHY.* Painting is to art what carpentry is to architecture. Painting is no more art than sculpture, dancing, or writing. What is it that makes something art? Emotion, excitement, drama, poetry. Fine craftsmanship should be expected in a work of art, but it should not be glorified — the poetry and soul are what we should celebrate. All the technique in the world does not make a work of art; however without technical ability there is no artistry. There must be a balance — a work of art is not an accident.

It seems most art instruction is centered around technique, laws, and rules. Everything to do with *how,* and nothing of *why.* I am convinced that *why* a piece was created is at least as important as *how.* I have always believed in excellence and do not favor weak drawing, color, or design; but in judging for myself a piece of art I look for emotion and expression. I take good craftsmanship for granted. After all, it was the emotion and expression that it was painted for. Painting must be more than an exercise in technique.

*Where Shadows Embrace the Light*
Oil, 12x16″

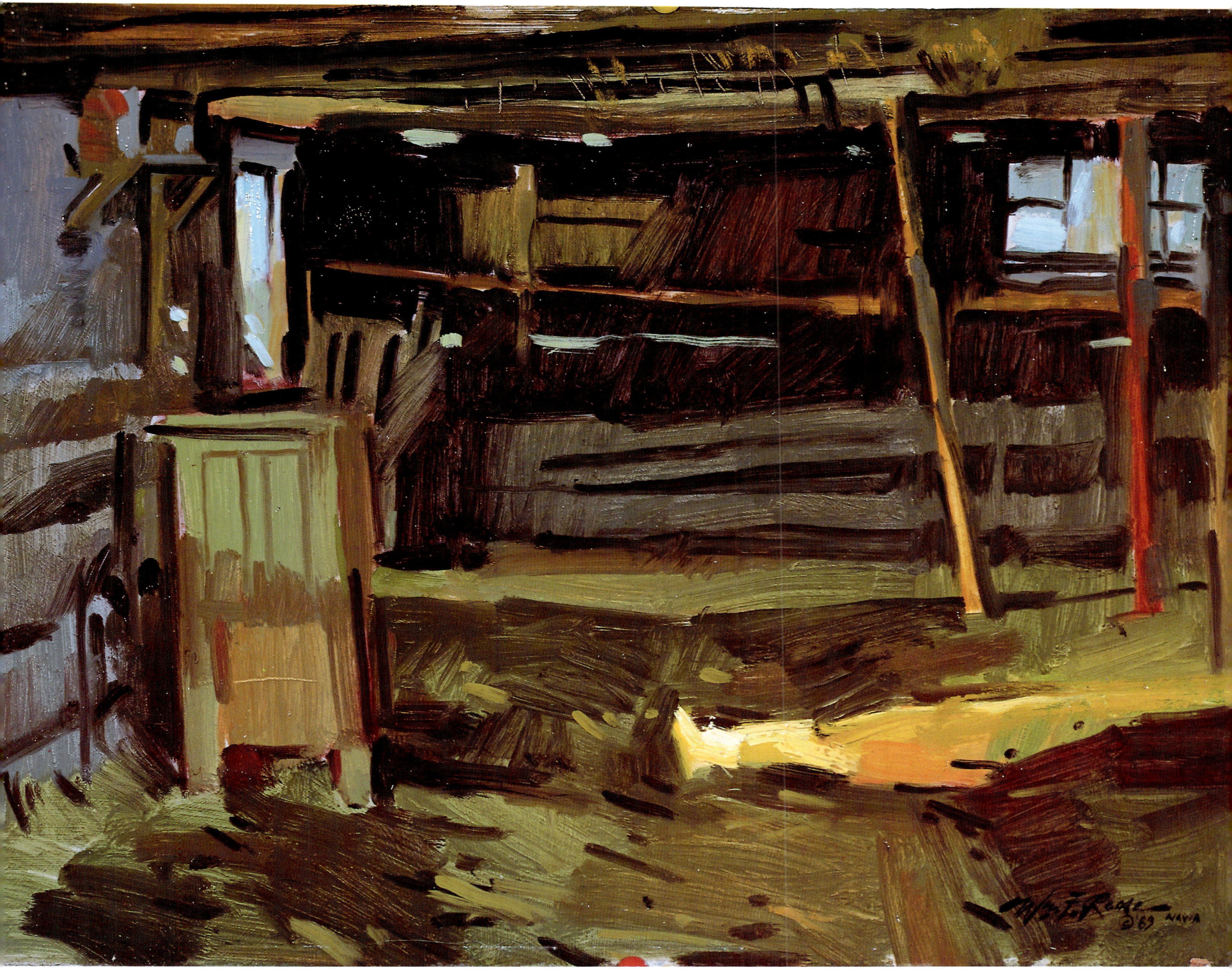
NAVA

A painter must be in tune with his painting: listen to it and it will tell you what to do. All intellectualizing must be done before you begin the painting; all logic considered before you pick up the brush. You must call on the sum of all your senses, react to what is happening on the canvas, and make painting decisions without thinking, that is, on the subconscious level. When a musician is called upon for a concert performance, this is no time to learn to play the piano. If you make a mistake, play through it. No one wants to hear you practice. The same with painting — no one wants to watch your suffering.

A painting or any work of art must be exciting at all stages of development, much like the blooming of a rose: if a rose were to bloom one petal at a time it would be grotesque. A painting finished one area at a time loses this excitement and also becomes grostesque. The relationship and balance of one part to another are essential. The composition of a painting is no different than that of a musical score — no note is either good or bad, flat or sharp, until compared one to the other; likewise with color, value, or any passage in a painting. Again, as Henri said, "Painting is just poetry on a flat surface."

The energy level developed by the artist must be transferred to the canvas in the form of intense excitement in order that this energy level be maintained within the artist — a very sensitive balance.

*SEEING COLOR.* To learn to see color takes many years of practice, and the best practice is painting from life. Sir Kenneth Clark, the noted art historian, said "The naked body is a starting point for a work of art embodying the highest reaches of human emotion and intelligence." This cannot be stressed enough. The study — working direct from life — is better than all the theory in the world; the eye as well as the mind is exercised to see. Not until there is sufficient practice or exercise, is there good drawing and color. More and more I believe it's not how well one paints that makes the difference, but how well one *sees.*

Many colors or values cannot be read easily except when you look away from them and read them out of the corner of your eye. The eye makes constant and rapid adjustments as you look into an area: a warm grey may appear neutral after staring at it for a time, a shadow will soon appear lighter, and the light areas will appear darker. For this reason you must relate one area to another and paint the *difference.* Compare hues to similar hues and like values to like values: reds to reds, greens to greens, lights to lights, and darks to darks. Find all your reds and rank them for value, temperature, and intensity, and paint the difference. Do not try to match color. Study one while looking at another — paint out of the corner of your eye!

It is a great help to me to consider the souce of light for color — not only the primary source, but all the incidental ones as well. By this I mean that if the primary source is the sun, the color temperature is warm. Shadows are cool because of the influence of the sky; however, where the influence of the sky is less, the shadow areas will appear slightly warmer as in the interior of a barn or room with only a small amount of exterior or natural light filtering in.

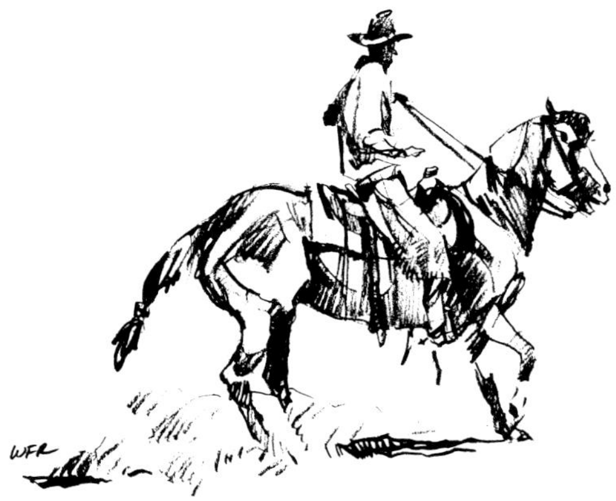

I've found that when I'm struggling for control of the drawing, composition, and color, it is impossible to get involved in the aesthetics of the work. This illustrates the importance of thumbnail sketches, color studies, and drawings in which many of the problems are solved. With these solutions behind me, the painting can be more of a poetic and aesthetic involvement. Many times after starting a painting from life (which supplies the necessary information), I will finish it from memory, often re-painting it entirely. This enables me to concentrate totally on the aesthetics and the statement I wish to make.

Painting is a lot like trying to fly — great when it works, hell when it doesn't — and there is no hell like the one you go through when a painting decides not to work; but I suppose that is what makes it worthwhile when it does. There are times when it seems as though everything I've ever learned, every discipline I've ever practiced, suddenly escapes me.

*IS IT DRAWING? IS IT PAINTING?* Drawing and painting. Which is drawing? Which is painting? What's the difference! To me, painting and drawing are one and the same. While painting I am drawing, while drawing I am painting. It was either Degas or daVinci who defined drawing as "understanding the form" — I would amend this to say, "Drawing is understanding form and *movement*."

A beginner should be aware that without good drawing skills, an artist will have extreme difficulty trying to express himself. His difficulty will manifest itself not only in the obvious, but also in muddy color, timidity, weak compositions, and busy paintings. Drawing errors account many times for the chalky over-worked passages that plague us all. Drawing must be practiced on a regular basis, with discipline and purpose — from life — and requires more than just showing how correct one can be: it is more important not to be incorrect. Edit the work. Leave only the essentials and make sure that the information which is left is not the wrong information.

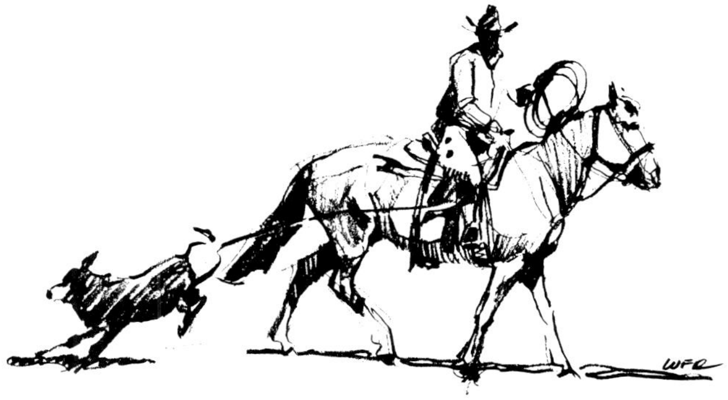


Good drawing skills are much like honesty or proper manners — they should be taken for granted and noticed only when missing. Drawing should be practiced so much that one doesn't have to think about it when painting. It should be a reflex. It is not too much to expect good drawing in a work of art; it *should* be expected.

As important as drawing, color, and composition are to me, I think I would still rather see a poorly drawn piece that exhibits great emotion than a perfectly rendered work with no soul. Even though the drawing is accurate and precisely done, if it does not have energy and feeling, all you have is a blueprint. As a good friend of mine so often says, "It must have blood." This is what makes children's art so great — they are completely honest about what they want to say. Their art is not good because it is primitive, but because it is honest. Small children have not yet become affected by techniques and by what other people think — at least until they go to school. They put into their art only that which is germane to what they are trying to say. They do an incredible job of editing, leaving only the essentials — everything is always read in the order of intended importance.

I'm sure that if the importance of honesty in art is someday recognized and some attempt is made to preserve this quality, while we go on to teach the mechanics, the results will take the form of great works of art.

*NEW APPROACHES TO OLD IDEAS.* For one to be creative it's not necessary to invent the wheel everytime — he needs only a new look at an old idea. Sometimes we try so hard as artists to be original that we become ridiculous and irrelevant.

Much is written today about the choice of subject matter. I don't believe that the quality that makes art *art* ever really balanced on the choice of subject matter; this choice has a great deal to do with how well you'll sell, certainly, but nothing to do with whether or not it's good art. There is no bad or overworked subject — only poor, tired, and overworked approaches to the subject. Take the corniest idea, paint it with a fresh eye and with emotion and conviction, and you will make a piece of art.

In many ways my paintings are an improvisation. I've been told that I might be a fair painter if I could only stay within the lines. Well maybe, but that's no fun.

Wm F. Reese

*Chiapanecas*
Pastel, 30x40″
Private Collection

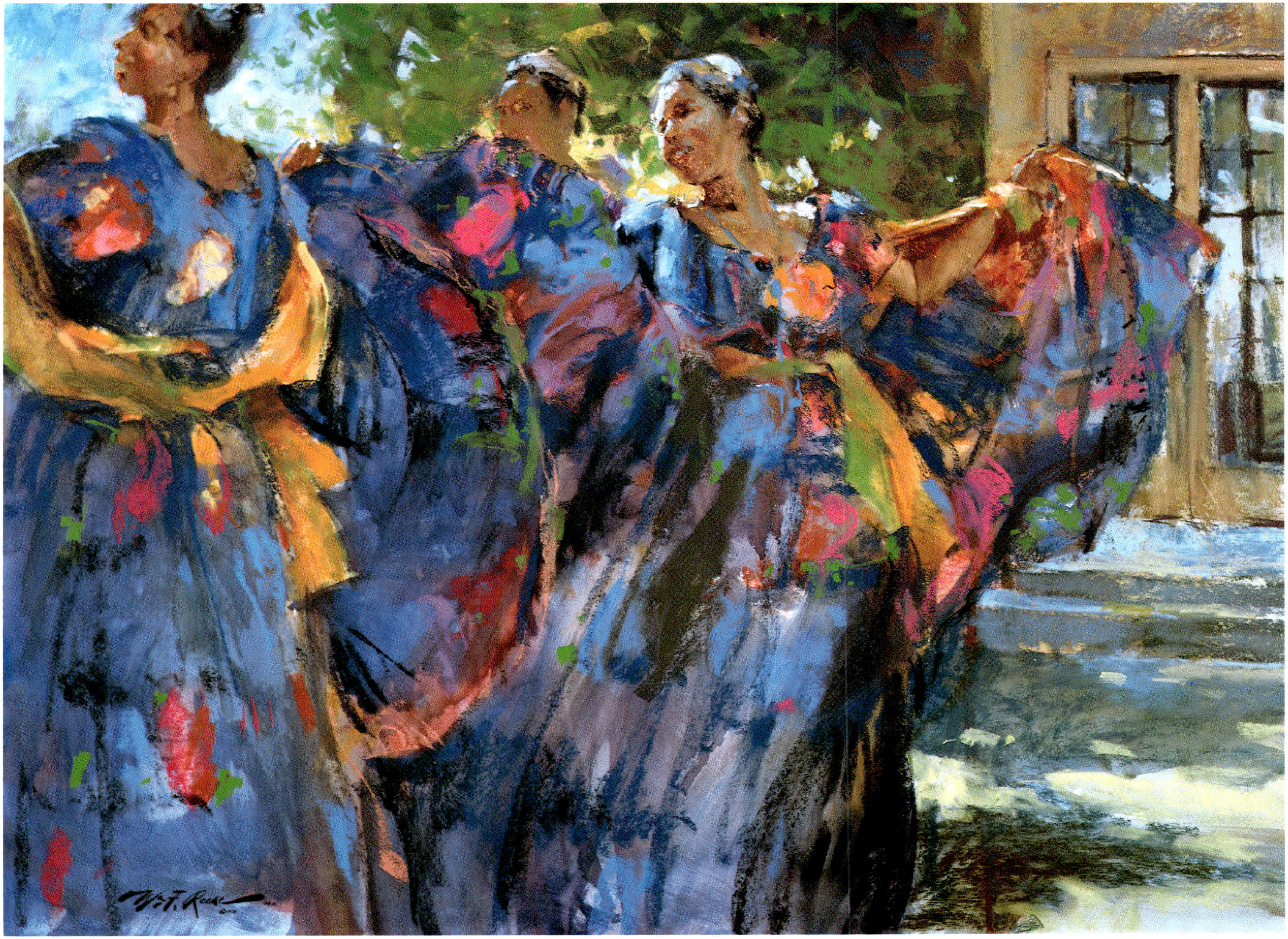

# CHRONOLOGY, AWARDS, AND MAJOR EXHIBITIONS

## *Major Life Events:*

1938 Born in Pierre, South Dakota, July 10
1956-58 Attended Washington State University
1959 Married Fran
1959-61 Moved to Eugene, Oregon
1961-66 Moved to Los Angeles
1964 Son Dean is born
1964-66 Attended Art Center, night school
1966 Moved back to Washington
1966 Daughter Shelly is born
1970 Had ruptured appendix-peritonitis
1971 Quit sign business
1980 Father dies
1981 Bought farm
1982 Held first art workshop at farm

## *Major Travel:*

1978 Mexico with Ramon Kelley, Joe Bohler, John Encinias, and John Axton
1978 Spain, France, and Holland
1979 Mexico with Ramon Kelley, Lowell Smith, and Tim Stortz
1980 Mexico with Ramon Kelley, Lowell Smith, Tim Stortz, and Ernie Gallegos
1981 China

## *Awards:*

1967 Childe Hassam Award, West Coast Oil Show, Frye Art Museum, Seattle
1975 Leon Augustine Lhermitte Award, Frye Art Museum
1975 Golden Award, Rocky Mountain National Watercolor Exhibition, Golden, Colorado
1975 Western States Art Show, Second and Third Awards
1976 Business Community Award, Rocky Mountain National
1976 Best of Show, Museum of Native American Culture, Spokane, Washington
1976 Grand Galleria Award, Northwest Watercolor Society Exhibition
1977 Honorable Mention, Oklahoma Watercolor Exhibition, Oklahoma City, Oklahoma
1977 Leon Augustine Lhermitte Award, Frye Art Museum
1977 House of Heydenryke Award, National Arts Club, 78th Annual Watercolor Exhibition, New York City
1978 Best of Show, Museum of the Great Plains, Ninth Annual Watercolor Exhibition of Painting and Sculpture
1978 Honorable Mention, Oklahoma Watercolor Exhibition
1978 House of Heydenryke Award, Pastel Society of America, National Arts Club, New York
1978 A.I.C.A. Exhibition, Gold medal, watercolor
1978 A.I.C.A. Exhibition, Silver medal, oil
1978 A.I.C.A. Exhibition, Silver medal, drawing
1979 Art Association Award, Northwest Watercolor Society, Seattle
1979 A.I.C.A. Exhibition, Nominated for Best of Show, watercolor
1980 Best of Show, Puget Sound Area Exhibition, Frye Art Museum
1980 Kenneth R. Fisher Award, Northwest Watercolor Society Exhibition
1981 Award of Merit, Northwest Rendezvous Group, Helena, Montana
1982 Eugene Boudin Award, Best of Show, Frye Art Museum
1982 Art Galleries Award, Northwest Watercolor Society
1983 Award of Merit, Northwest Rendezvous Group

## *Major Exhibitions:*

1972 Frye Art Museum, Seattle, Two-man show: William F. Reese and Harry Bonath
1973 Maxwell Galleries Ltd., San Francisco, Art of the West Exhibit
1976 Linda McAdoo Gallery, Scottsdale, Arizona
1977 Frye Art Museum, One-man show, William F. Reese
1978 Louise Matzke Gallery, Seattle, Two-man show William F. Reese and Perry Acker
1978 Images Gallery, Minneapolis, One-man show, William F. Reese
1979 Gallery Mack Northwest, Seattle, One-man show, William F. Reese
1980 Gallery Mack Northwest, Two-man show, William F. Reese and Tex Wounded Face
1981 Frye Art Museum, Four-man show, William F. Reese, Ramon Kelley, Lowell Ellsworth Smith and Tim Stortz
1981 Driscoll Exhibition, Peking, China
1982 Wichita Gallery of Fine Art, One-man show, William F. Reese

## *Membership in Professional Associations (Elected Fellow):*

National Academy of Western Art
Northwest Rendezvous Group
Northwest Watercolor Society
Pastel Society of America
Puget Sound Group of Northwest Painters
Society of Animal Artists
Whiskey Painters of America

# NOTES

[1]Robert Henri, *The Art Spirit,* compiled by Margery A. Ryerson (New York: J.B. Lippincott Co., 1960), p. 212.

[2]Henry Miller, *The Paintings of Henry Miller, Paint As You Like and Die Happy,* Edited by Noel Young (Santa Barbara: Capra Press, 1960; reprint ed., San Francisco: Chronicle Books, 1982), p. 65.

[3]Harold Craig, personal letter.

[4]Venita Van Caspel, *The New Money Dynamics* (Reston, Virginia: Reston Publishing Co., 1978), p. 426.

[5]Sara Dobberteen, "National Academy of Western Art," *Persimmon Hill,* Vol. VII, No. 4 (Oklahoma City: National Cowboy Hall of Fame and Western Heritage Center), p. 41.

[6]Judith Gamble, *Artists of America* (Denver: Rotary Club, 1982), Introduction by Grant Wilkins, p. 5.

[7]Miller, *The Paintings of Henry Miller,* p. 62.

[8]Mary N. Balcomb, "William F. Reese, The Art of Painting," *Southwest Art,* (October, 1982): p. 107.

[9]Stan Galli, personal letter.

[10]Tony Angell, personal letter.

[11]Mary N. Balcomb, "William F. Reese: Form Follows Function," *American Artist,* Vol. 42, Issue 437 (December, 1978), p. 46.

[12]Henri, *The Art Spirit,* p. 175.

[13]Fred Oldfield, personal letter.

[14]Ibid.

[15]Balcomb, "William F. Reese: Form Follows Function," p. 47.

[16]Harley Brown, personal letter.

[17]Bettina Steinke, telephone interview, July 11, 1983.

[18]Henri, *The Art Spirit,* p. 26.

[19]Frederic Taubes, *Painting Methods* (New York: Viking Press, 1963), p. 118.

[20]Ibid., p. 118.

[21]Ralph Mayer, *The Artist's Handbook of Materials and Techniques,* Third Edition (New York: The Viking Press, 1970), pp. 265-266.

[22]Henri, *The Art Spirit,* p. 89.

[23]Maurice Serullaz, *Drawings of the Masters, French Impressionists,* selected and edited by Ira Moskowitz (New York: Shorewood Publishers, Inc., 1962), p. 13.

[24]Chuck Lawton, personal letter.

# SELECTED BIBLIOGRAPHY

## Books


ARNOLD, EVE. *In China.* New York: Alfred A. Knopf, 1980.

BALCOMB, MARY N. *Nicolai Fechin.* Arizona: Northland Press, 1975.

CLARK, SIR KENNETH. *The Nude.* New York: Double Day Anchor Books, 1956.

COPPLESTONE, TREWIN and MYERS, BERNARD S., gen. ed. *Art Treasures in Spain.* New York: McGraw-Hill, 1969.

DUNLAP, IAN. *Degas.* New York: Harper and Row, 1979.

EISLER, COLIN T., ed. *Drawings of the Masters, Flemish and Dutch Drawings.* New York: Shorewood Publishers, Inc., 1963.

EMERSON, RALPH WALDO. *Essays.* New York: Thomas Y. Crowell, ____ .

EMERSON, RALPH WALDO. *Self Reliance.* New York: Roycroft Shop, 1902.

GOLDWATER, ROBERT and TREVES, MARCO, *ed. Artists on Art, From the XIV to the XX Centuries.* New York: Pantheon Books, 1972.

HENRI, ROBERT. *The Art Spirit.* Compiled by Margery A. Ryerson. New York: J.B. Lippincott Co., 1960.

HERBERT, ROBERT L., ed. *Modern Artists on Art.* New Jersey: Prentice-Hall, Inc., 1964.

HOMER, WILLIAM INNES, *Robert Henri and His Circle.* New York: Cornell University Press, 1969.

KELLEY, RAMON and NELSON, MARY CARROLL. *Ramon Kelley Paints Portraits and Figures.* New York: Watson-Guptill, 1977.

LINN, CHARLES F. *The Golden Mean, Mathematics and the Fine Arts.* New York: Doubleday and Co., 1974.

LISLE, LAURIE. *Portrait of an Artist, A Biography of Georgia O'Keeffe.* New York: Washington Square Press, 1980.

MAYER, RALPH. *The Artist's Handbook.* New York: Viking Press, 1970.

MENDELOWITZ, DANIEL M. *A Guide to Drawing.* New York: Holt, Rinehart, and Winston, 1976.

MILLER, HENRY. *The Paintings of Henry Miller, Paint As You Please and Die Happy.* Edited by Noel Young. California: Capra Press, 1960, and Chronicle Books, 1982.

NIN, ANAÏS. *The Diary of Anaïs Nin.* 6 vol., Edited by Gunther Stuhlmann. New York: Harcourt, Brace, Jovanovich, 1977.

ORMOND, RICHARD. *Sargent. Paintings, Drawings, and Watercolors.* London: Phaidon Press Ltd., 1970.

RICHARDSON, E.P. *A Short History of Painting in America.* New York: Thomas Y. Crowell Co., 1956.

RUMES, DAGOBERT D. and SCHRIKEL, HARRY GO., eds. *Encyclopedia of the Arts.* New York: Philosophical Library, 1946.

SERULLAZ, MAURICE. *Drawings of the Masters, French Impressionists.* Edited by Ira Moskowitz. New York: Shorewood Publishers, 1962.

SIMON, HENRY W. *What is a Teacher?* New York: Collier Books, 1964.

SLOAN, JOHN. *Gist of Art.* New York: Dover Publications, 1977.

TAUBES, FREDERIC. *Painting Methods, A Guide to Traditional and Modern.* New York: Viking Press, 1963.

TAUBES, FREDERIC. *The Technique of Portrait Painting.* New York: Watson-Guptill, 1968.

THOREAU, HENRY DAVID. *Walden.* New York: Libra Inc., 1960.

TRAPIER, ELIZABETH DU GERE, contributor, "Paintings." *The Hispanic Society of America Handbook.* New York: The Hispanic Society of America, 1938.

WOLF, ADOLF HUNGRY. *Good Medicine.* British Columbia: Good Medicine Books, 1971.

# SELECTED BIBLIOGRAPHY


## Articles in Museum and Gallery Catalogues which Include William F. Reese

________________. *National Academy of Western Art.* Oklahoma City, Oklahoma: National Cowboy Hall of Fame and Western Heritage Center, 1978-83.

________________. *The Puget Sound Group of Northwest Painters — The First Fifty Years, 1928-1978.* Seattle: The Puget Sound Group of Northwest Painters Inc., 1979.

GAMBLE, JUDITH. *Artists of America.* Denver Colorado: Rotary Club Foundation, 1981-83.

MOLLRING, TED. *The Artists of Trailside Galleries.* Scottsdale, Arizona: Trailside Galleries, 1979-80, 1980-81, 1981-82, 1982-83.

NELSON, MARY CARROLL, ed. *American Western Art in Peking.* Denver, Colorado: Driscoll Gallery, 1981.

PALADIN, VIVIAN A. *Western Rendezvous of Art. Helena, Montana: Helena Arts Council, 1981-1983.*

## Published Prints

REESE, WILLIAM F. "Winter White, Ptarmigans." Austin, Texas: Golden West Publishing, 1982.

REESE, WILLIAM F. "Seattle Horse Patrol." Seattle: Save Our Steeds, 1983.

## Calendars and Catalogue Cover Illustrations

REESE, WILLIAM F. "Winter White, Ptarmigans." Seattle: Eddie Bauer Inc., 1981.

REESE, WILLIAM F. "Music on the Wing." New York: New York Life Insurance Company, 1980.

REESE, WILLIAM F. "Blossom by Blossom Spring Begins." New York: New York Life Insurance Company, 1981.

## Video Films

RODKEY, BOB, director. "William F. Reese: Painting with Emotion." *Creative Craft Arts,* Video #8004. Oklahoma City, Oklahoma: KTVY Inc., Metropolitan Library Systems, June 9, 1980.

## Articles on William F. Reese in Journals and Magazines

ANDREWS, LAUREL. "The Visual Poetry of William F. Reese." *Art West,* Vol. III, Issue I, 1979, pp. 32-39.

BALCOMB, MARY N. "William F. Reese: Form Follows Function." *American Artist,* December, 1978, pp. 46-51, 77-80.

BALCOMB, MARY N. "On Tour in Seattle," *American Artist,* April, 1981, pp.70-72, 101.

BALCOMB, MARY N. "William F. Reese, The Art of Painting." *Southwest Art,* October, 1982, pp. 100-107.

HARVEY, BETTY. "Bill Reese: Art is a Process of Self-education," *Artists of the Rockies and the Golden West,* Vol. III, Issue 4, Fall 1976, pp. 30-33.

HEARN, ED. "Bill Reese: He Uses Paint Like He Invented It." *View Northwest, June, 1974, pp. 20-27.*

JACQUES CATTRELL PRESS, ed. *Who's Who In American Art.* New York: R.R. Bowker Co., 1976, 1978, 1980, 1982.

KETCHAM, KATHY. "View on People, Bill Reese." *View of Puget Sound,* Volume 1, No. 2, October, 1978, pp. 54-55.

SCHADE, LILA. "William F. Reese." *Southland Artist,* Volume II, No. 10, October, 1965, pp. 24-25.

TAYLOR, ELOISE. "Prized Reacquaintance with William Reese." *Art West,* Volume VII, Issue 1, November-December, 1983, pp. 52-61

## Unpublished Materials

Taped recordings:

GREATHOUSE, MRS. WALSER. Frye Art Museum, Seattle, Washington, 27 April 1983.

PERHACS, KATHERINE AND LES. Port Ludlow, Washington, 1 March 1983.

REESE, FRANCES AND WILLIAM F. Bellevue, Washington, 4, 11, and 20 January 1983, and 5 March 1983.

## Telephone Interviews

STEINKE, BETTINA. Telephone interview (to Santa Fe, New Mexico) 11 July 1983.

## Letters

ANGELL, TONY, Seattle, Washington.
BONGART, SERGEI, Santa Monica, California.
BROWN, HARLEY, Calgary, Alberta, Canada.
BROWN, REYNOLD, Los Angeles, California.
CAVANAUGH, ROBERT M., Kalispell, Montana.
CRAIG, HAROLD, Tacoma, Washington.
CRAIN, PATRICIA M., Plano, Texas.
DOYLE, JO ANNE, Bellevue, Washington.
FILLERUP, MEL, Cody, Wyoming.
GALLI, STAN, San Francisco, California.
GISH, DEL, Medicine Lake, Washington.
GREATHOUSE, MRS. WALSER, Seattle, Washington.
HURLEY, WILSON, Albuquerque, New Mexico.
LAWTON, CHUCK, Richland, Washington.
LEE, CHARLENE and BRILL, Bellevue, Washington.
LORD, LOIS, Kent, Washington.
LYNN, GENE, Bellevue, Washington.
McKAY, BRIAN and GWEN, Redmond, Washington.
METCALF, ALDEN, Bellevue, Washington.
MILOTTE, ALFRED and ELMA, Sumner, Washington.
OLDFIELD, FRED, Federal Way, Washington.
POWELL, LLOYD W., Bend, Oregon.
RHODES, JOE S., St. Louis, Missouri.
SALKIN, JOANNE, Bellevue, Washington.
SCHOENBERG, WILFRED P., Spokane, Washington.
SCHWIERING, CONRAD, Jackson, Wyoming.
SHEPARD, CATHERINE, Corpus Christi, Texas.
SMITH, LOWELL ELLSWORTH, Hudson, Ohio.
SMITH, TUCKER, Clancy, Montana.

## Interviews

(in Cle Elum, Washington, July 25-30, 1983)

BENNETT, MARGARET
BITELLI, ALESSANDRA
COOK, IRENE
DE CLERCQ, KATHLEEN
GREGORY, DELLA
MARRON, JOAN
MC FARLAND, LOIS
OBERG, GLENN
RICKS, DON
RINGEN, JOHN
SEVERSON, KAY
TUCK, GENEVIEVE
VAN HEES, JOSANN STENSBY
WYMAN, BOBBI

## Interviews

(in Bellevue, Washington)

MANOWSKI, BONNIE REESE. 19 March 1983.
REESE, DEAN. 7 April 1983.
REESE, DON. 5 March 1983.
REESE, FRANCES. 12 January 1983.
REESE, MARGARET. 12 January 1983.
REESE, ROBERT. 19 March 1983.
REESE, SHELLY. 19 March 1983.
REESE, TOM. 5 March 1983.

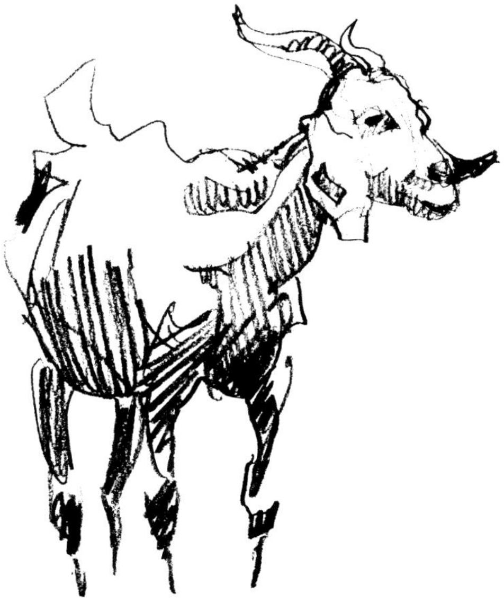

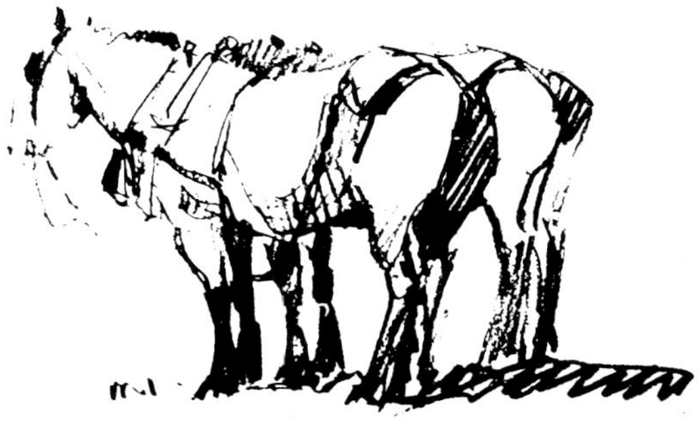

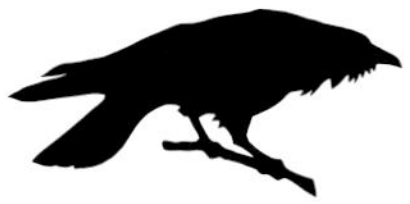

Design and Production: *Amie Cole Balcomb,* Seattle
Printing: *Paragon Press,* Salt Lake City
Color Director: *Gene Fan,* Paragon Press
Binding: *Hiller Industries,* Salt Lake City
Typesetting: *Thomas & Kennedy,* Seattle
Typeface: *ITC Garamond Book*
Text Paper: S. D. Warren's *Cameo Gloss 100lb. Book*
Calligraphy: *Anne Timlick*
Photography: *Mike Walmsley.* All color transparencies for paintings and black and white photographs except as indicated below:

*William F. Reese,* pp. 1, 6, 7, 137.
*Amie C. Balcomb,* pp. 4, 5.
*Thomas Nygard,* p. 39.
*Bill Abbey, p. 60.*
*Renee Tewell,* p. 69.
*Cheryl Rossi,* p. 73.

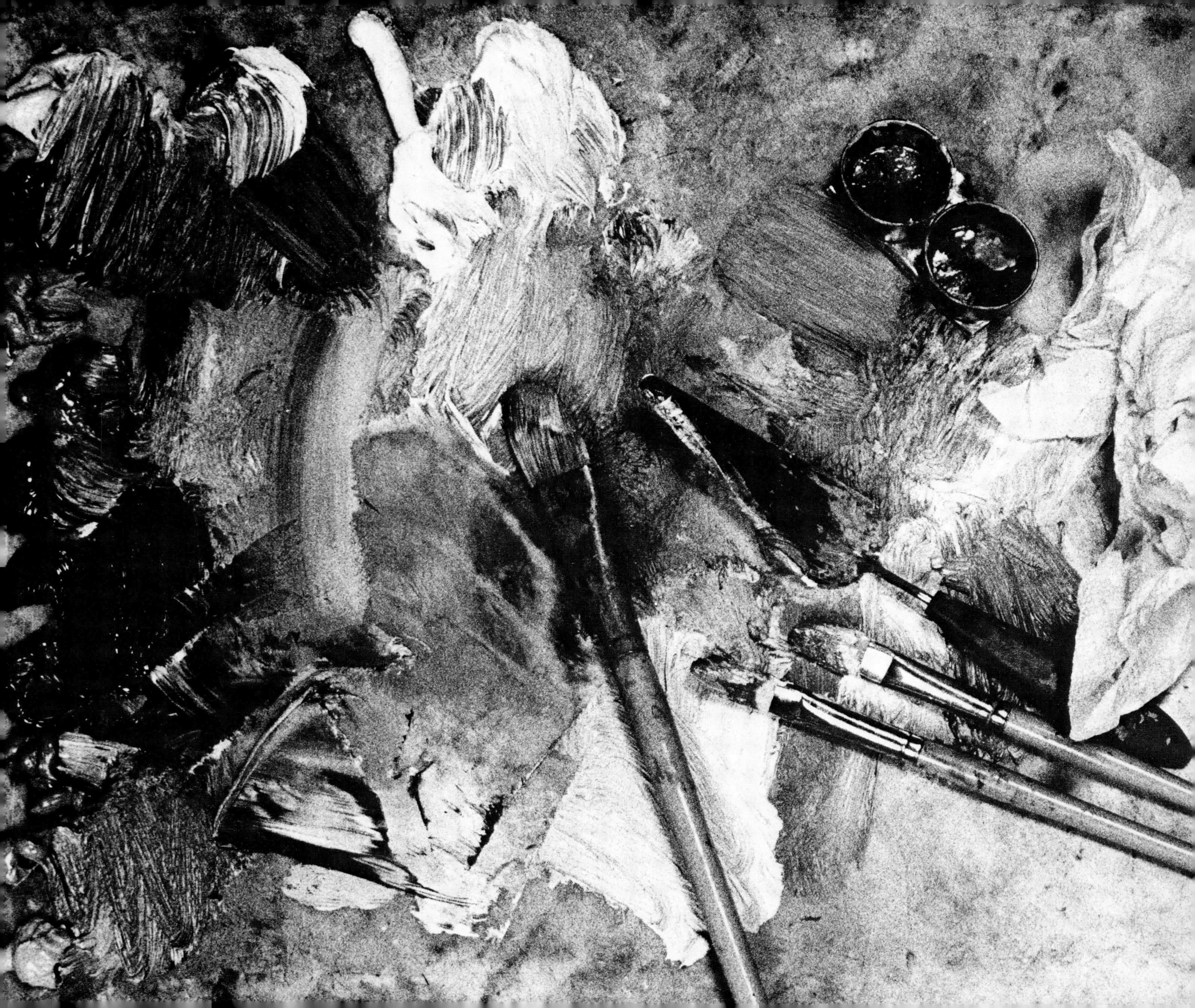